PUSH PAST IT!

A Positive Approach to Challenging Classroom Behaviors

by Angela Searcy, EdD

Gryphon House

www.gryphonhouse.com

LIBRARY OF CONGRESS CATALOGING-IN-PUBLICATION DATA

Names: Searcy, Angela, author.
Title: Push past it! : a positive approach to challenging classroom behaviors
   / by Angela Searcy.
Description: Lewisville, NC : Gryphon House, Inc., [2019] | Includes
   bibliographical references and index.
Identifiers: LCCN 2019000877 | ISBN 9780876598153 (pbk.)
Subjects: LCSH: Behavior modification. | Behavioral assessment. | Problem
   children--Behavior modification. | Classroom management.
Classification: LCC LB1060.2 .S38 2019 | DDC 371.39/3--dc23
LC record available at https://lccn.loc.gov/2019000877

Reprinted June 2024

BULK PURCHASE

Gryphon House books are available for special premiums and sales promotions as well as for fund-raising use. Special editions or book excerpts also can be created to specifications. For details, call 800.638.0928.

DISCLAIMER

Gryphon House, Inc., cannot be held responsible for damage, mishap, or injury incurred during the use of or because of activities in this book. Appropriate and reasonable caution and adult super-vision of children involved in activities and corresponding to the age and capability of each child involved are recommended at all times. Do not leave children unattended at any time. Observe safety and caution at all times.

Acknowledgements

Success never occurs in isolation, and I want to express my deepest appreciation for my husband, Reginald B. Searcy Jr. Thank you for supporting me at every stage of my career. I am forever grateful for your love and patience. Without your unwavering encouragement and spiritual support, this book never would have been possible.

Dedication

This book is dedicated to my parents, Freeman Nelson Jr. and Mathrell Nelson, who personified perseverance, set an example of excellence, and equipped me with the ability to achieve my goals regardless of the obstacles.

It is with genuine gratitude that I also dedicate this work to my husband, Reginald, whose own tenacity, encouragement, and patience carried me through each step of this journey, and to our four children, Daniel, Maya, Lena, and Zaria. I hope this inspires you to achieve your own dreams.

Lastly, I dedicate this book to the teachers and children of the world.

Table of Contents

Introduction

The first time I touched something wet in my classroom, was not sure where it came from, and was not particularly grossed out by it, I knew I had found my dream job! I was born to be a teacher.

Teaching is a long, bumpy journey filled with potholes and detours. When children demonstrate challenging behaviors, the road seems longer, the bumps feel bigger, and the potholes and detours appear impassable. But with a good navigation system, there is a way out. This guide can support you in understanding why a child might hit, punch, kick, bite, curse at you, and, occasionally, lick stuff.

You are probably reading this book because you have finally realized that your most challenging student will always have perfect attendance, be the first to arrive in the morning and the last to leave in the evening, and—wait for it—have younger siblings! To help you get through the rest of the school year without losing your sanity and to help you prepare for that new-and-improved version of your most challenging student, I am sharing my challenging-behavior navigation system: PUSH PAST It (hence the title of this book).

This system and this book are the result of almost thirty years of experience in education, which includes teaching at all grade levels, providing assessment and treatment as a therapist for all age levels, and consulting with schools and families across the United States in diverse settings. In the same way popular rap artists earn street credibility, I also have earned (and am still earning) my own level of credibility as a parent by raising four children with my husband, Reginald.

To help you make PUSH PAST It work for you, I also present facts and research about challenging behaviors. As a former teacher, I realize that I lost half of you when I mentioned the word *research*. As educators, we often tune out at the very mention of research because it is often conducted by people who have little to no experience in the classroom; is written in dense, dry academic language aimed at researchers rather than at teachers; and studies people who do not reflect the children in our classrooms. I am all for teachers developing evidence-based practice. However, at the end of the day, it is a teacher, not a scientist, who will consider the implications of relevant research and apply them in the classroom. Furthermore, I understand that research can be confusing, even misleading. I want to believe the study I saw on Healthbeat claiming that a glass of red wine is better for you than three hours of exercise at the gym, but I am just not sure whether that claim is valid.

Keeping these ideas in mind, this book seeks to make research both understandable and useful for you. I base my conclusions on numerous studies from diverse locations. I also focus on applied research, which is not research for research's sake; it is research focused on finding solutions that can be directly applied to real-life practice. Most of the research I highlight does not look at what takes place in labs. It looks at what happens in actual classrooms, just like yours. I encourage you look up my references and read even more details about the research I present.

Oh, and I have a warning—this reading might be more entertaining when accompanied by a glass of red wine, but it will not replace three hours of exercise at your local gym.

My Own Serious Challenge

Even though I cannot see every aspect of what you see as an early childhood educator, I know what you are going through. I am in real classrooms daily and have been for almost three decades. I have used the ideas in this book to eliminate challenging behaviors—hitting, biting, tantrums, throwing furniture, swearing, spitting, and so on—in some of the worst situations. Here, for example, is one of the most extreme situations I have ever faced.

Let's step back in time to 2010, when I was a consultant for an early childhood program on the West Side of Chicago. During the dog days of summer, I received an email about a student in this program, whom I'll call Harry, who not only was aggressive and noncompliant but also touched students' private areas inappropriately and urinated on them. When I walked into the classroom to observe, Harry noticed me immediately, sucked his teeth, and asked if I was there for him. I managed to stammer, "No," and was stunned when Harry told one of the teachers, who was expecting, that he was going to kill her baby. The teacher cried that day.

Family members of the other children had called the child-abuse and neglect hotline, and the program had received a visit from the department of children and family services the day before. One parent, whose child had been urinated on repeatedly, said, "Let that kid pee on my child one more time, and I am going to . . ." I am sure you can imagine the rest of what was said. The other children told their parents how scared they were to come to school every day. Families wanted to take their children out of the program because of Harry. It is amazing how the behaviors of one child can jeopardize an entire program.

During my visit, the administrators told me that if Harry acted out one more time, he would be removed from the program. Then they dropped a stack of incident reports on a desk for me to review. I knew we had a daunting task ahead, but I also knew that PUSH PAST It could help us succeed. And it did. Through careful, consistent observation of and reflection on the situation, the teachers, the administrators, and I were able to carefully craft strategies specific to Harry, his teachers, and their circumstances. We were able to help Harry learn to eliminate his challenging behaviors, stay in the program, and finish out a successful school year.

How This Book Can Help You

If you are reading this book, I realize that you are dealing with serious, often dangerous, and emotionally charged situations every day. The idea that educators, children, and family members are not equipped to deal with these challenges is the driving force behind this book. Using the frameworks from this guide, I hope you will learn effective techniques to teach young children prosocial behaviors.

This book provides a process for navigating and understanding your own situation, and it honors the fact that the best solutions are created collaboratively and take on different forms depending on the circumstances. This logical model helps you examine your own potential blind spots and unveils approaches that you otherwise might not have considered. It facilitates the self-awareness, reflection, and mindfulness needed to clarify and sharpen your own thinking in a way that will help you pick solutions that fit your situation and make you as confident in those selections as a three-year-old wearing a tutu with galoshes in the grocery store.

Interventions for challenging behaviors often aim to strengthen young children's abilities; however, because the only person you can control is yourself, this book examines ways to strengthen *your* abilities. When you know your own perspectives and feelings, you are better equipped to help that child who challenges you every day.

Behavior challenges provide opportunities to build better programs and better teachers. When adults become frustrated and remove a child from a program, they remove an opportunity not only for the child to improve but also for the adults in that program improve. I hope this book equips you with practical skills and frameworks that allow you to find your route, stay on track, and handle whatever is around the next corner.

CHAPTER 1

Current Approaches to Discipline

My journey as an educator began in 1990. I realized I had found my place in the world when I entered the Yellow Room and a three-year-old greeted me by asking what color my thoughts were. Even though I had found my calling, working with young children wasn't easy. I will never forget the day in 1996 when one of the adorable little preschoolers under my care bit a chunk out of the face of a smaller child. As the injured child was carried away on a stretcher, I was left with some very angry parents. I felt a mix of emotions: confusion, helplessness, anger, horror, shame, and embarrassment. But now, after so many years have passed, I don't mind airing my own dirty laundry. As it turned out, my situation was not unique.

Defining the Problem

Children's challenging behaviors—crying, tantrums, biting, swearing, and everything in between—may be the most frequently encountered occupational hazards in teaching young children. In a review of research from around the world, Paul Frick found that the prevalence of conduct disorder (a long-term pattern of serious behavior problems) does not vary much across continents. Furthermore, when asked about their greatest needs, early childhood professionals highlight one thing above all others: they need training on how to deal with challenging behaviors. Teachers have described challenging behavior as one of the greatest barriers that they encounter in providing quality instruction. As researchers Neal Glasgow and Cathy Hicks and June Zuckerman assert, the ability to prevent and manage aggressive behaviors is frequently what principals, supervisors, and the public focus on when assessing effective teachers.

No pressure, right?

I know the toll that this constant struggle can take. As a new teacher, I felt an enormous amount of stress as the behavior challenges in my classroom began to pile up faster than the traffic on the interstate. I worried constantly about how I was affecting future generations by my inability to either prevent these behaviors in the first place or deal with them effectively when they occurred. I couldn't escape my classroom even in my sleep! I dreamed about children eating my lesson plans or destroying materials during an important classroom observation.

I just didn't get it. Despite all my training and all my efforts, there were new shenanigans to deal with each day. What was I doing wrong? Why couldn't I get my students to behave?

During this time, I received truckloads of well-meaning and often unsolicited suggestions for dealing with challenging behaviors. Unfortunately, I discovered that all this advice can lead to gridlock and actually cause *more* problems. Do any of these scenarios sound familiar?

- My principal starts snooping around and finding stuff wrong with me instead of with the child.
- My well-meaning colleague gives me some thick book on dealing with challenging behaviors that I do not have time to read because I am too busy *actually* dealing with challenging behaviors.
- My school's mental-health consultant, Ms. Help Helpington, either regurgitates what I already know or gives me a ridiculous number of ideas. Either way, she leaves me stranded in my classroom without any support to implement her suggestions—not that I could have realistically done that anyway.
- My education coordinator sends me to a bunch of behavior workshops full of irrelevant hypothetical situations and magical unicorns—I mean, impractical solutions—that seem impossible to implement. Often these "professional-development opportunities" chip away at my self-confidence. Meanwhile, back in my classroom, the child whom I left to find more ideas to support is getting worse.

According to research, you are not doing it wrong. It is just *that* hard. A report by Allison Gulamhussein of the Center for Public Education highlights how teachers are bombarded with behavior-management ideas without being given any structures to organize those ideas or any methods to match new techniques to their teaching styles or the needs of their own classrooms. Then, when teachers try these strategies and do not get the results they want, they despondently conclude, "This stuff doesn't work."

However, there are many factors that play a part in why a strategy becomes successful. You cannot always simply copy someone else's idea and expect to get the same results. My friend, fellow consultant, and frequent copresenter Antoinette Taylor often uses the phrase "adult assembly required" to explain this concept. I love this analogy because it implies that neither children nor our ideas about children come to us fully formed. Relationships with children and strategies to support them are *built*. Biologically, children contain all the necessary parts to build strong relationships. But, similar to your IKEA dining-room set, *adult* assembly is required. Just like the road construction in Chicago, the assembly of the ideas that support children in this process can take days, weeks, months, or even years to complete. How fast this process goes depends on how good you are at putting it all together and how many parts must be assembled and understood. Later chapters will discuss how you can assemble ideas, match them to your unique needs, and "werk" them out (I will explain that spelling in chapter 8) in your classroom. But before we can explore a new approach to dealing with challenging behavior, we need to examine the approaches that many of you are likely using—and why, despite your best efforts, they are not working.

▼

There are no perfect solutions—
just solutions that you perfect over time with trial and error.

▲

Common Approaches to Discipline in Early Childhood Education and Their Drawbacks

Early in my career as a teacher, before I developed PUSH PAST It, I often put the label *challenging* on behaviors that I now know are normal, integral parts of learning and development. Because of this mindset, I didn't always take time to customize a strategy to a situation and instead went for quick fixes just to make behaviors stop. Some of my past approaches to discipline are quite common among educators. Do you recognize any of them?

REMOVING MATERIALS

Imagine yourself in my classroom back in my teaching days. Is a child eating the seashells in my discovery area? Easy! I remove the seashells! Are two children fighting over a toy? No worries! The toy automatically becomes Ms. Angela's toy, stashed out of reach on top of my cabinet with other confiscated toys. Problem solved. And thank goodness for fold-and-lock storage cabinets in my centers! When behaviors in a center become too much, I quickly push the two sections of that cabinet together, sealing its materials inside and "closing" that center.

I used these strategies often as a teacher. They provided quick ways to put a stop to challenging behaviors. But I eventually discovered that, even after I removed all problematic items and closed centers where squabbles had broken out, the children soon began fighting over something else. Furthermore, this discipline strategy did not fit with the learning objectives in my lesson plans. Looking back now, I am not sure how I thought my students were ever going to *learn* how to interact with others, *learn* to play appropriately with toys and materials, and *learn* how to cooperate and share materials if I was constantly removing opportunities to practice those skills. For example, how could the children gain experience taking turns with a doll if the doll kept ending up on top of my cabinet? How could they learn to play appropriately in the discovery center if it was never open or if I kept taking away the interesting objects?

REMOVING A CHILD FROM AN AREA

Imagine yourself in my classroom again. Is a child dousing his friends with cups of water from the sensory table? Easy! I say, "It looks like my friend does not know how to play at the sensory table," and I make him go to a different area. Is a child knocking down all his friends' blocks? I announce that it's time for that child leave the block center.

Granted, if a child is misbehaving in a center, removing him from the center typically does stop that behavior. But I found that when I removed children from areas, some children went willingly, while others put up a fight. This resistance, in turn, only escalated situations. Also, similar to the problems with removing toys or materials, removing a child from his mess or his friends removes the opportunity for him to learn how to clean up a mess or play with friends appropriately. And those are the things we really want him to learn, right?

REMOVING A CHILD FROM A GROUP

Picture my classroom again. Is a child reenacting the latest World Wrestling Entertainment event on my circle-time carpet? Easy! I give my assistant "the nod" to take that child for a "walk"—or, if he has really crossed the line, to the principal's office. After all, I am usually under a lot of pressure to make circle time a productive learning time, which is hard to do when challenging behaviors disrupt the activities. Why let this one child ruin circle time for everyone else?

I knew a teacher who used this technique so often that when I asked a child from her class what happened when children didn't listen at circle time, the child said, "They disappear." After my initial chuckle, I paused. Could I actually be ruining circle time for the rest of the children by not including everyone? When we remove a child from the group, what message are we really sending? If a child chooses to leave, that is one thing, but removing a child sends a message that that child doesn't belong. It also removes the opportunity for the child to learn how to be with a group and for the group to learn how to interact with that child. To make matters even worse, it undermines a child's relationship with his classmates and teachers each time he is removed from a classroom.

TAKING AWAY A PRIVILEGE

Let's go back to my classroom. Is a child pushing in line? That child loses his turn as line leader. Is a child having a bad day and not listening? Easy! I make him sit for two minutes during outside time—or, if he has really been acting up, I take away recess altogether or assign him a seat at lunch away from his friends. I think, "That will make him think twice before he misbehaves again!"

However, I discovered that when I used these discipline techniques, I was actually punishing myself. After losing privileges, children frequently behaved worse than before. As I gained a better understanding of child development, I began to understand that taking away a privilege does not teach children to control their emotions or impulses. *Taking away a privilege only works if a child already has the necessary self-regulation skills to demonstrate the appropriate behavior.* Young children need lots of opportunities to develop these skills. Is it really fair to punish children for not demonstrating skills that they have not yet mastered?

In fact, for a child who does not yet have these skills, taking away a privilege can actually make the situation worse in two ways. First, this punishment may remove an opportunity for the child to let off some steam and thereby improve his behavior. This is why recess is not an optional reward but an important time of the day. Second, the child may become upset over the lost privilege and continue to engage in the challenging behavior because he (still) does not know a more appropriate way to vent his feelings. For example, if Max hits another child and loses the privilege of sitting with friends at lunch, he may become angry, hit someone else, and lose the chance to sit with his friends tomorrow. This cycle of hitting and sitting alone can lead to a pattern of Max being isolated from his peers.

PUTTING A CHILD IN TIME-OUT

Let's return to my classroom one more time. Is a child hitting or pushing his friends or not cleaning up? Easy! I give him a time-out in the thinking chair to ponder what he has done and what he should do differently.

Time-out is a time-honored disciplinary technique for young children. But what educators sometimes forget is that young children are still developing self-awareness. As a result, they usually do not have the cognitive capacity to reflect on their own behavior, so they need help understanding how their behavior affects others. Thus, sitting alone in time-out is not likely to teach a child how to behave better.

(For those who are about to jump in to defend time-out, I am all for a calm, safe, or quiet space that a child goes to *voluntarily*. I am not in favor of adults *putting* children in time-out.)

Putting a child in time-out can also cause other difficulties. If you have ever been in a classroom, you know the typical response from a child who doesn't want to be moved: going as limp as a wet noodle and making himself impossible to hold or move. As a consultant, I learned that children often get hurt when they are forced to move but are not ready to. Furthermore, a child who does not want to be moved may resist by escalating his challenging behavior, potentially resulting in other children or even teachers getting hurt.

*As a professional who works with all ages, I find it interesting how we expect teenagers, for example, to **come to** adults when they have challenges, but we teach preschoolers to **go away** from adults when they have challenges.*

HOPING THE CHILD OUTGROWS THE BEHAVIOR

When faced with challenging behaviors, especially if early attempts to resolve them don't work, some adults throw up their hands. Family members often protest when their children are punished for challenging behaviors: "Seriously? My kid is only four! Boys will be boys, you know." Or they might insist, "He's only a kid. He'll grow out of it eventually."

It is true that the preschool period is closely associated with challenging behaviors. For instance, in one study, Carolyn Webster-Stratton and Mary Hammond observed four-year-old children in Head Start classrooms and found that one-third of the children exhibited problem behaviors. As a result, the teachers in this study faced some episode of challenging behavior *every six minutes*. (Welcome to preschool!) Additionally, in "Do Children in Canada Become More Aggressive as They Approach Adolescence?" Richard Tremblay and his colleagues point out that preschool is the most aggressive period in human development. According to this study, physical aggression (biting, hitting, spitting, and so on) first appears at the end of infancy, peaks in the preschool years, and then continues to decline throughout development as children gain the capacity to speak and regulate their emotions. Throughout early childhood, children make the transition away from physical aggression with varying degrees of speed and ease. In other words, the preschool period is a time in which human beings learn to regulate the use of physical aggression. And unfortunately, the only way they can master those skills is by *being* aggressive and thereby prompting the adults around them to teach them alternative ways to behave.

If positive social and emotional skills are not taught and developed during the preschool period, challenging behavior is not outgrown—just redirected. Research by Ji Hong and her colleagues shows that children with frequent, high-intensity challenging behaviors are at highest risk of continuing those behaviors during adolescence. Susan Campbell and Linda Ewing point out that hard-to-manage preschoolers are more likely to have the same challenging behaviors at age nine. Furthermore, Kenneth Dodge notes that interventions for challenging behaviors show only minimal success after age nine.

These situations can result in dire consequences for children later in life. A study by researcher John Reid shows that conduct challenges in preschool can potentially lead to more serious challenges—such as drug use, gang membership, violence, and adult incarceration—later in life. Researchers Thomas Dishion, Doran French, and Gerald Patterson point out that when antisocial behaviors emerge at young ages and children do not have opportunities to learn new skills, not only can those behaviors continue as children age, but they can also escalate. In a review of research, Paul Frick notes that children with serious conduct disorder can later experience mental-health problems that put them at risk for arrest, dropping out of school, and even poor job performance. Candice Odgers and her colleagues agree, based on a study in which they followed children in New Zealand from birth to adulthood and discovered that children with conduct disorder were more likely to experience depression, become homeless, have anxiety, become dependent on alcohol, attempt suicide, and be convicted of criminal offenses as they grew up. These are just a few examples of how children with intense and frequent challenging behaviors often move on to more serious challenges later in life.

Why Exclusion Isn't the Answer

Have you ever looked at a heap of laundry the size of your city and just considered throwing it all away and buying new clothes? That is how I was beginning to feel about the pile of problems in my classroom. I remember the relief I felt when my little troublemakers were absent and I had my classroom back! Maybe I was onto something. What would happen, I wondered, if those children just were not allowed to come back? Why not give those little rascals the gift of time? They obviously were not ready for preschool. If they had all these problems, clearly something was wrong with them. It was up to them to fix it, and they would be accepted back once their issues had been resolved. There! You're welcome! However, as I later learned, this approach does not help anyone in the long run.

DEFINING EXCLUSION

When all other options have been exhausted, teachers and administrators may feel that they have no choice but to resort to *exclusion* (also called *exclusionary discipline* or *removal*). At their most basic, these terms mean the removal of a student from an educational setting. Depending on the length and the conditions of the removal, it might be called *in-school suspension*, *out-of-school suspension*, or *expulsion*. In early childhood settings, exclusion may include many of the approaches we've already discussed in this chapter, along with others:

- Removing materials
- Removing a child from an area, group, or classroom
- Altering or discontinuing an activity or routine
- Asking or requiring the child's family members to remove him from your program, justifying this action by saying that the child and the program are "not a good match" or that the child "needs more time" before entering school

Notice that the last approach uses harmless-sounding arguments, but they actually imply that there are places where some children do not belong.

*Note that children with social or emotional disorders may need special-education services. However, special education is not a place where children go but a set of resources that adults bring into **any** setting to provide supports for children who struggle.*

Like many teachers, when I became frustrated, I resorted to this type of punishment. Additionally, we as educators often see ourselves as doing the best thing for a struggling child by deciding that our program "isn't the right setting" and "helping" the child's family members find a new arrangement for him. But as we have discussed, exclusion removes a child's opportunity to practice social skills, interferes with what educators really want to teach children, and removes the opportunity to reinforce social skills with the entire class. And that is just the start of the problem.

THE SCOPE OF EXCLUSION IN EARLY CHILDHOOD EDUCATION

Words such as *removal* often conjure images of rebellious high schoolers, but in fact, the youngest students are arguably the most likely to experience exclusionary discipline. In one study, Ann Cutler and Linda Gilkerson report that over 40 percent of the child-care programs surveyed have asked children to leave because of aggressive behavioral problems. Similarly, a report by Sarah Hoover and an article by Chalkbeat's Ann Schimke show that in a single year in Colorado, children in preschool were removed from the classroom at a rate of ten out of one thousand, while children in K–12 settings were disciplined this way at a rate of approximately three out of one thousand. Walter Gilliam of the Yale University Child Study Center, who is also the director of the Edward Zigler Center in Child Development and Social Policy, published a broader study entitled *Prekindergarteners Left Behind* that contains further alarming information: across the United States, the expulsion rate for prekindergarten children is more than three times the expulsion rate for children in grades K–12.

Yes, you read that right. Preschoolers are getting expelled more often than high schoolers.

Furthermore, as Rasheed Malik of the Center for American Progress reports, a US-wide survey shows that approximately fifty thousand preschoolers have experienced exclusionary discipline at least once, with an estimated 250 preschoolers expelled or suspended every day. Assuming a seven-hour school day, that means about thirty-five students are being removed every hour! Perhaps most worrisome of all, preschoolers are not the youngest students to experience exclusionary discipline. Researchers Marsha Gerdes and Natalie Renew point out that even toddlers have been asked to leave child-care settings because of challenging behaviors.

EXCLUSION DOES NOT TEACH THE DESIRED BEHAVIORS

If I had to stand up in a court of law and defend a case on exclusionary discipline, I wouldn't have any evidence to show how it helps to develop skills in children or their teachers. Yes, exclusion may teach children that behaviors such as hitting a classmate or swearing at a teacher have certain (often unpleasant) consequences. But it does not teach them what they *should* do instead. Children, especially preschoolers, are very young and still learning about the world, so adults have to teach them how to behave appropriately.

EXCLUSION IS UNFAIRLY APPLIED

Another key problem with exclusionary discipline is that this technique is used disproportionately with certain types of children. In particular, children of color, boys, children with disabilities, and children living in poverty are often punished this way. The outcomes for these excluded children are disturbing.

CHILDREN OF COLOR

People in the United States often use the phrase *children of color* to refer to all children who are not White. However, these children's experiences vary much more than this catchall label suggests. When it comes to discipline, certain children of color receive shockingly disproportional rates of exclusion. For example, compare these statistics from the report *2015–16 Civil Rights Data Collection: School Climate and Safety* by the US Department of Education (all percentages are rounded):

- White males make up 25 percent of students enrolled in school and, of the total number expelled, they make up 27 percent.
- Asian males make up 3 percent of those enrolled, and of those expelled, they make up 1 percent.

- As a combined group, American Indian or Alaska Native, Native Hawaiian or Other Pacific Islander, and multiracial males make up 3 percent of those enrolled. Of those expelled, they make up 4 percent of the total.
- Latino males make up 13 percent of those enrolled. They make up 16 percent of those expelled.
- Black males make up 8 percent of those enrolled. However, they make up 23 percent of those expelled.

Lest you think this issue only affects male students of color, the report also provides statistics for female students:

- White females make up 24 percent of students enrolled in school and, of the total number expelled, they make up 10 percent.
- Asian females make up 2 percent of those enrolled, and of those expelled, they make up 0.3 percent.
- As a combined group, American Indian or Alaska Native, Native Hawaiian or Other Pacific Islander, and multiracial females make up 3 percent of those enrolled. Of those expelled, they make up 2 percent of the total.
- Latina females make up 13 percent of those enrolled. They make up 6 percent of those expelled.
- Black females make up 8 percent of those enrolled. However, they make up 10 percent of those expelled.

EXPULSION IN A FICTIONAL SCHOOL DISTRICT

To make these statistics clearer, let's apply them to an imaginary school district with ten thousand students. Using the (rounded) percentages from the report, the total student enrollment would break down by race as follows:

- **American Indian or Alaska Native:** approximately 100 males and 100 females
- **Hispanic or Latino/Latina:** approximately 1300 males and 1300 females
- **Asian:** approximately 300 males and 200 females
- **Black:** approximately 800 males and 800 females
- **Native Hawaiian or Other Pacific Islander:** approximately 20 males and 20 females
- **White:** approximately 2500 males and 2400 females
- **Multiracial:** approximately 200 males and 200 females

Now let's imagine that this district has a particularly rough year and expels one thousand students. Using the applicable (and, again, rounded) percentages from the report, that smaller subgroup breaks down by race as follows:

- **American Indian or Alaska Native:** approximately 10 males and 10 females
- **Hispanic or Latino/Latina:** approximately 160 males and 60 females
- **Asian:** approximately 10 males and 3 females
- **Black:** approximately 230 males and 100 females
- **Native Hawaiian or Other Pacific Islander:** approximately 30 males and 1 female
- **White:** approximately 270 males and 100 females
- **Multiracial:** approximately 30 males and 10 females

So even though only a subset of our total fictional student body has been expelled in this example, that subset includes nearly twice as many students of color as White students.

While these statistics specifically illustrate the experiences of K–12 students, similar patterns hold true for young children. Walter Gilliam's research shows that Black preschool children are twice as likely to be expelled as Hispanic and White preschool children.

Taken together, these statistics show the alarming racial disparities that currently exist in exclusionary discipline. In particular, Black students are excluded at disproportionately higher rates than any other ethnic group. In short, race may be the most significant factor—even more than gender—to predict how much exclusionary discipline a child might experience.

Statistics like these might make you wonder whether children of different races have inherent differences in how they behave. You do not have to be racist to consider this idea. After all, the National Center for Children in Poverty suggests that Latino and Black children are more likely than White children to be living in poverty. Could poverty, not race, be the underlying issue? Professors Russell Skiba and Natasha Williams set out to answer that very question in a summary of research called *Are Black Kids Worse? Myths and Facts about Racial Differences in Behavior*. However, this report indicates that poverty alone cannot account for the disproportional rates of exclusionary discipline among children of color. Among the children studied in this research, upper-class Black children were still more likely than their upper-class White peers to experience exclusionary discipline. Furthermore, Black, White, and Latino children all engaged in similar types of challenging behavior at similar rates. The only difference that Skiba and Williams discovered was that the consequences for Black and Latino students were more severe than for White students, even for the same type of behavior.

BOYS

Along with the troubling statistics mentioned earlier, Walter Gilliam's study *Prekindergarteners Left Behind* shows that boys are kicked out of preschool at a rate 4.5 times higher than girls are. Researcher Richard Tremblay—professor of pediatrics, psychiatry, and psychology at the University of Montreal and founding director of the Research Unit on Children's Psychosocial Maladjustment—sheds some light on why this may happen. His articles "Prevention of Injury by Early Socialization of Aggressive Behavior" and "Development of Physical Aggression from Early Childhood to Adulthood" state that preschool boys exhibit slightly higher rates of physical aggression than preschool girls, and girls tend to reduce these behaviors at earlier ages than boys. Not as many girls reach the highest rates of physical aggression, and girls start transitioning to acts of verbal aggression, such as saying, "You are not my friend," at earlier ages.

This information led me to wonder about my role in this phenomenon. As a teacher, was I more comfortable dealing with verbal aggression than with physical aggression in the classroom? Did I view verbal aggression as less dangerous (and therefore less worthy of punishment by exclusion) than physical aggression? If so, I might be disproportionately excluding boys without even realizing it.

CHILDREN WITH SPECIAL NEEDS

You might be surprised to find out that exclusionary discipline also disproportionately affects children with special needs, often with harsh consequences. According to the report *2015–16 Civil Rights*

Data Collection: School Climate and Safety by the US Department of Education Office for Civil Rights, children with disabilities are disciplined at higher rates than children without disabilities. Specifically, Rasheed Malik of the Center for American Progress notes that a survey of children's health found that children with disabilities represented 75 percent of children excluded from preschool.

If you are now slouching back in your seat, shaking your head, and wondering what in the world is going on in those preschools, remember that exclusionary discipline in preschool often has different labels than it does in elementary, middle, or high school. Instead of expelling or suspending preschoolers with special needs because of challenging behaviors, educators often send these children to the office or call family members to pick them up early. In my work as a mental-health consultant, I knew one parent of a child with special needs who actually lost her job because of the number of calls she received from the child's school. As her experience shows, exclusionary discipline is problematic not just for children with special needs but also for their family members.

CHILDREN WHO LIVE IN POVERTY

Several studies have found consistent use of exclusionary discipline with low-income students. However, the amount of exclusionary discipline often correlates with additional factors. For example, Amity Noltemeyer and Caven Mcloughlin studied patterns of exclusionary discipline in more than three hundred school districts and found that schools in poverty-stricken areas use exclusionary practices more often than schools in wealthier areas. These results also show that exclusionary discipline is used at greater rates in large urban districts with high-poverty schools than in rural high-poverty areas with small numbers of students. Another study by Joe Nicholas and his colleagues demonstrates that being in poverty does not necessarily increase the risk of exclusion for nonminority students.

Even though children in poverty likely experience more adversity overall, such as community violence, than their nonimpoverished peers, Rebekah Coley and her colleagues point out challenging conduct at each end of the economic spectrum in their study of the effect of income on behavior. In another study, Ellen Brantlinger explores the idea of how income affects punishment in school and finds that both low- and high-income students believe that low-income students are unfairly targeted. Additionally, low-income students report a greater number of punishments than high-income students. Similarly, researcher Shi-Chang Wu and her colleagues show that students who are in poverty or whose fathers do not have full-time employment are more likely to experience exclusionary discipline than their classmates. Research by David Ramey further corroborates these findings. In his examination of sixty thousand schools, he demonstrates that schools with high numbers of children in poverty are less likely to use services such as behavior planning or psychological services to deal with challenging behaviors and are more likely to use suspensions, expulsions, police referrals, and arrests.

CHILDREN WITH MULTIPLE RISK FACTORS

Let's take in all this information together. Imagine a child with every single risk factor discussed in this chapter, such as an impoverished Black boy with special needs. How much exclusionary discipline do you think this child might experience in school? What might happen to him as a result?

You might be worried about this child. At the same time, you might feel confused. Shouldn't early learning experiences provide great benefits for children of color, children in poverty, and children with special needs? Yet what we have learned in this chapter paints a disturbing picture of this child's future.

In contrast, you might have thoughts such as these:

- "Where did that research take place?"
- "I am Black, and that is not my experience."
- "I know So-and-So, who has several of those risk factors, and that is not his experience."
- "That is not the experience for the children at our program."
- "Hey, I was the product of some of the discipline you describe, and I turned out fine!"

To those responses, I say, "I wish more children had experiences like the ones you describe. I am so grateful that you are out there doing wonderful work at your program, and I am so happy you turned out fine!" But data from around the globe shows that not everyone has these positive outcomes.

I get it—hearing such alarming statistics might have validated some of your long-held assumptions and shattered others. Right now, you might feel affirmed or intrigued, or you might be uneasy or skeptical. If you fall into the second category, consider the following questions:

- Even if you and everyone you know turned out fine, does that mean we should not worry about children who are struggling?
- Can you consider ideas that are outside of your own experience?
- Even if things are going well, shouldn't we stay on the path to improvement?

I honor each reader's perspective, and I realize that these ideas will take some time to digest. I only want you to consider doing something that you ask your students to do each day: listen and learn about something new.

EXCLUSION MAY SIGNAL TEACHER STRUGGLES

If a teacher quickly removes disruptive students from his classroom, many people would consider him a good teacher because he does not allow challenging behaviors to interfere with learning. Yet exclusion can actually be a sign of poor teaching quality. Mary Mitchell and Catherine Bradshaw probe this idea in a study of different approaches to discipline in thirty-seven public schools in the eastern United States. Surprisingly, Mitchell and Bradshaw conclude that teachers who frequently rely on exclusionary discipline have classrooms with less order. In other words, high rates of exclusion might signal that the teacher, not the student, needs support.

Research also demonstrates what happens to student behavior when teachers use best practices in their classrooms. Glen Dunlap and his colleagues describe how children who are in high-quality classrooms and experience high-quality interactions with their teachers are less likely to have challenging behaviors. In a summary of research, Glen Dunlap and Lee Kern show that adjusting teacher behavior during learning activities leads to positive adjustments in child behavior. Dunlap and Kern highlight study after study illustrating how student conduct improves when educators modify classroom activities to match students' interests and provide choices that allow children some control over how they learn. Interestingly, these results do not just apply to formal educational programs. Researcher Allison Fuligni and her colleagues note that whether preschool children attend traditional schools or home-based-provider settings, teachers who use mostly child-directed, free-choice activities and few teacher-directed activities have positive behavioral outcomes in their classrooms. Jane Barker and her colleagues add that more structured activities lead to less self-direction and slower development of planning, decision-making, and goal-achievement skills in children. Together, these studies call into question teacher-directed, overly structured learning and its effect on behavior.

If you think about it, you have probably seen these patterns before. Some children do great during free play but struggle during large-group time. They act out when you make demands on them but are sweet little angels when they get to do what they want.

Researcher Judith Carta and her colleagues highlight how this concept applies to children with special needs. The researchers tracked individual children across all activities in a typical preschool day and found that the probability of challenging behaviors depends on the organization of the classroom. More specifically, when students are actively engaged, there is a change in behavior. The study suggests that rather than immediately removing a child with challenging behavior, educators should first try restructuring transitions to make them active. In short, when we restructure daily events to make them engaging, we can modify child behavior.

Of course, most educators do not seek to use less-than-ideal practices. In my case, I think the stress I was under trying to complete lesson plans, making sure all classrooms had proper teacher-to-child ratios, calling parents, refereeing endless squabbles among large numbers of children, and holding my pee during a long school day all contributed to the problem and influenced my behavior as a teacher. As it turns out, my stressful experiences were not unique. In his report *Implementing Policies to Reduce the Likelihood of Preschool Expulsion*, Walter Gilliam suggests that structural elements such as large class sizes, high student-to-teacher ratios, and longer school days all correlate to higher rates of exclusionary discipline. The report also shows that when teachers have high levels of stress and no access to mental-health support staff, they tend to use higher levels of exclusionary discipline.

To sum up, removing a child does not resolve the classroom characteristics that potentially led to the challenging behavior in the first place. All of these studies show that to gain a meaningful understanding of student behavior, we also need a meaningful understanding of adult behavior and the context in which all of these behaviors occur. As with a tandem bike, you can't maneuver one component without affecting the others. For me, after so many years in the classroom, challenging behaviors are now my signal to push myself and my team to reflect on our practice, structure, and room arrangement instead of resorting to pulling out a child.

RESULTS OF EXCLUSIONARY DISCIPLINE

So far in this chapter, we have mentioned a few of the negative outcomes from exclusionary discipline, notably isolation and lost opportunities for learning. These are only the beginning of an alarming series of consequences for excluded children—and for their classmates and caregivers.

A report from the Committee for Children, which is dedicated to supporting students' social and emotional well-being across the globe, notes that removing a child, activities, or materials can put that child behind academically, which in turn can increase the chance of the child disengaging from school activities and further missing out on academic learning. This practice can even lead to the child being held back, dropping out of school completely, and experiencing decreased success in the workforce. Similarly, the report *Policy Statement on Expulsion and Suspension Policies in Early Childhood Settings* by the US Department of Health and Human Services and the US Department of Education points out that students who are suspended or expelled can experience negative views about school, grade retention, poor academic achievement, dropping out of high school, and trouble with the law at rates ten times higher than their peers.

This last item brings us to perhaps the most disturbing outcome of all. An unsettling report by Kimberlé Crenshaw, Priscilla Ocen, and Jyoti Nanda describes children being arrested for behaviors such as dropping cake and having tantrums. When such normal behaviors are met with harsh discipline, students may receive unnecessary medical and psychological interventions that can actually create problems where they did not previously exist. The phenomenon of criminalizing children at early ages has been dubbed the *preschool-to-prison pipeline* because these practices increase the likelihood of future criminal behavior by these children and create a path into the justice system for them. As if that were not enough, this cycle also distorts reality for all students and creates a negative school climate even for those not being excluded.

If you had asked me back in 1999 if I was using exclusionary discipline, I would have clutched my invisible pearls to my chest, gasped, and vehemently exclaimed, "My goodness gracious, no!" But now that I understand what exclusionary discipline tends to look like in early childhood settings, I realize that closing learning centers, confiscating toys, and helping family members "find a good fit" were all exclusionary tactics. As I searched for answers to the challenging behaviors in my classroom, my actions and statistics like the ones in this chapter began to weigh on my mind. By trying to get rid of my little troublemakers, was I actually contributing to the pipeline to prison? Yikes!

BUT WHAT ABOUT THE "GOOD KIDS"?

If you are like me, you might now be thinking, "Okay, I see why exclusion is bad, but what about the kids who follow the rules? How are they supposed to learn if I don't remove the troublemakers?" I understand where you are coming from. As a teacher, my rationale for implementing exclusionary discipline was to support the "good kids," the ones who wanted to learn without disruption from the children with challenges. I wanted to help all children but always worried about how those with challenges would affect the well-behaved students in my classroom.

Interestingly enough, removal has negative consequences for all children, even those who are not removed. Brea Perry and Edward Morris explored this idea by observing thousands of diverse students in an urban public school for three years. They found that high levels of exclusionary discipline negatively affected the academic achievement of even the students who were never excluded. This makes sense from a child's perspective—how well would you be able to concentrate in school if your friend "disappeared" (because he was removed) and you were constantly wondering where he went, what was happening to him, and whether it could happen to you too? Perry and Morris conclude that exclusion can create a hostile environment that leads to anxiety for all children, even

PUSH PAST IT!

those not excluded, and affects math and literacy learning for everyone.

EXERCISE #1: YOUR TOP FIVE APPROACHES TO DISCIPLINE

1. On a sheet of paper, list your top five approaches to discipline—the five techniques that you use most often when facing a challenging behavior.

2. On the back of your paper, answer these questions:

   - Do your top five differ from the top fives of other members of your teaching team?
   - Do your top five align with your curriculum or teacher assessments?
   - If you are a veteran teacher, how have your top five developed and changed over the years?
   - Are your top five giving you the results you want?

Wrapping Up

Right now, you are probably saying, "Seriously, Angela? So far you've told me I can't put kids in time-out, tell them where to sit at lunch, send them to the office, confiscate toys, *or* expect them to grow out of their behavior. Now you're saying that I might have gaps in my skills and that kicking these children out of my program will make things even worse. So what in the world do you expect me to do with them?"

I'm glad you asked! In this book, I will introduce you to my PUSH PAST It strategy for dealing with challenging behaviors. This approach will help you work through your own emotions, discover the meanings behind children's behavior, find support, and create solutions as you help children improve their behavior. To lay the groundwork for this strategy, though, we have to start in an unexpected place: with you.

CHAPTER 2 ▸

Start with Your Own Self-Regulation

 Here is an image of me at five years old. Why am I starting a discussion on child development with a picture of me in a leisure suit and a butterfly collar? Because a conversation on child development outside of a meaningful connection to your own childhood is like Tuesdays without tacos, fishing without bait, Ethel without Lucy . . . well, you get the point. One simply does not work (at least not well) without the other.

Your Past Experiences Affect Your Present Reactions

You may be thinking, "Why are we talking about me? I'm not the one with the problem!" There are three reasons for starting here. First, when educators learn about children's social-emotional development without some context, they have a hard time applying that isolated information to real-life situations in a meaningful way. Second, a personal connection to a topic increases your motivation to engage with it. Third, teachers frequently struggle with understanding children's social-emotional development because they have not thoroughly processed their own social-emotional development.

So where do we start? In his book *We Can't Teach What We Don't Know*, Gary Howard states that knowing your students begins with knowing yourself. So, instead of looking at a laundry list of isolated information, we will start with your childhood because, to understand and analyze developmentally appropriate behavior, you need to understand and analyze your own image of yourself as a young child.

In another one of my favorite books, *The Courage to Teach: Exploring the Inner Landscape of a Teacher's Life* by Parker Palmer, the introduction states:

> Teaching holds a mirror to the soul. If I am willing to look in that mirror and not run from what I see, I have a chance to gain self-knowledge—and knowing myself is as crucial to good teaching as knowing my students and my subject.

> In fact, knowing my students and my subject depends heavily on self-knowledge. When I do not know myself, I cannot know who my students are. I will see them through a glass darkly, in the shadows of my unexamined life—and when I cannot see them clearly, I cannot teach them well.

How you react to a child's behavior is affected by your background: your history, temperament, and culture. It is important to be aware of how your past is constantly permeating your present. How you respond to a child's emotions depends heavily on how much you have processed your own. Therefore, throughout this chapter I am going to share my own story with you—not because I am self-absorbed and egocentric (well, that is part of the reason) but to serve as a model for self-reflection and to provide a structure for processing your own experiences.

After completing each exercise, read the case study that follows it. These examples use my own experiences to illustrate how personal history affects the way individuals react to challenging behaviors in their personal relationships with children. (We will discuss how personal history affects our professional reactions in chapter 3.)

Examining Your History with Crying, Tantrums, and Aggression

Sometimes you need to look back to understand what lies ahead. Let's begin our journey by taking a glance into your history and examining how those experiences have shaped your current opinions and reactions to some common challenging behaviors in preschoolers. Using some short exercises, we will first examine your relationships with what my mother liked to call "cuttin' up," "acting a fool," and the always-popular "clownin'."

EXERCISE #1: YOUR HISTORY WITH CRYING AND TANTRUMS

1. Think about times when you cried as a young child. What image do you have of yourself at those times?

2. On a sheet of paper, create a collage that represents that image in words and pictures.
3. On the back of your paper, answer these questions:
   • How would your parents or caregivers describe you as a baby? Were you happy or fussy? easy or hard to soothe? somewhere in between?
   • What are your family's views on crying or tantrums?
   • Do you have any memories of how your parents or caregivers responded when you cried or had a tantrum as a young child? If so, what happened?
   • How do you wish someone had responded to you as a child when you cried?
   • Personally, how do you respond to children's crying?
   • Professionally, how do you respond to children's crying?
   • How does your response change from your personal life to your professional life? Why?
   • How does children's crying make you feel? How do you manage those feelings?

CASE STUDY #1: MY HISTORY WITH CRYING AND TANTRUMS

When I was a child, I received mixed messages about crying from my family. There were times when my parents would just let me cry. I have a vivid memory from about age nine of having a downright fit when doing math homework with my father. I did not understand something he was explaining and responded by having an all-out, feet-stomping, wallowing-on-the-floor tantrum. My father just looked at me with no expression, said nothing, and waited for me to finish. I then got off the floor, relieved to have gotten those feelings out (and that he didn't say anything or slap me), and came back to my homework with more focus. But I recall other times when I cried and received typical parental threats such as, "Hush up those tears," or "I will give you something to cry about." During those episodes, I wished that my parents would realize that the more they told me to stop crying, the more it made me cry.

This discouragement of crying came from other sources, too. By age six, I had been indoctrinated into the unwritten rules of elementary-school social behavior: no thumb sucking, no tattling, and definitely no crying. I learned early on to suck it up, no matter what happened on the playground, or else get branded a crybaby. Keep in mind that most playgrounds at that time consisted of sharp-edged metal contraptions that scorched children's skin in the sweltering afternoon sun. My childhood playground was not even that fancy. It consisted of no playground equipment and a rock-hard asphalt surface to fall on. I actually remember one of my classmates being carried off on a stretcher after getting hurt there.

One unusual experience with crying also sticks in my memory. I will never forget when Mrs. Henderson, our music teacher, started crying when my fifth-grade class would not stop talking during her rendition of "Für Elise." At the time, I found it both humorous and quite empowering that we could have that much power over an adult. (Karma sorted things out years later, when my own class of ninth-grade students made *me* cry.)

HOW MY HISTORY WITH CRYING AFFECTED MY PERSONAL RELATIONSHIPS WITH CHILDREN

Fast-forward fifteen years from that music class to see me as a young parent. My husband, Reginald, and I had one baby girl who cried continually for almost two years. No lie. Since she was not our first child, we felt that something was wrong, but no one took us seriously. Just because our daughter looked healthy and happy during five-minute doctor visits or an hour-long children's party, it did not mean that all was okay. Even salt looks like sugar at first glance. After years of complaints, tests, and visits to specialists, we finally learned that our daughter had torticollis (a painful neck problem) and reflux. All that time, she had been communicating these medical issues the only way she knew how—by crying. Since this experience, I have always taken the persistent or prolonged cries of a baby very seriously.

As my children grew from babies to preschoolers, I tended to fluctuate between talking to them as if I were their inner voices and as if I had had about enough. Yes, my sympathy for crying had an expiration date. By the time my children were in preschool, I figured it was time for them to grow up. So when my children would cry or tantrum, I tended to start out with reassuring back rubs, saying, "I see you are having a hard time right now," "It's okay to cry," and "You're okay, honey." Then, if the crying persisted, I would progressively shift gears to saying, "Enough already," "There is nothing wrong with you," and "I'm the one who should be crying." If the crying still continued, I'd finally demand, "You'd better fix. Your. Face."

In all honesty, as a parent I strove (and still strive) to implement my intellectual knowledge about comforting children. All of my training and education tells me that when a child becomes upset, I should describe and validate her feelings while encouraging the expression of all feelings. Often I am proud to say that I adhere to these principles. The hard part was (and is) implementing them regularly.

EXERCISE #2: YOUR HISTORY WITH AGGRESSION

1. Think about times when you were angry or frustrated as a young child. What image do you have of yourself at those times?

2. Draw that image on a sheet of paper.

3. On the back of your paper, answer these questions:

   - What are your family's views about physical aggression (hitting, biting, spitting, throwing things, and so on)?

   - What are your family's views about verbal aggression (swearing, insults, name-calling, put-downs, back talk, and so on)?

   - Do you have any memories of how your parents or caregivers responded when you displayed physical or verbal aggression (PVA) as a child? If so, what happened?

   - How do you wish someone had responded to the PVA you exhibited as a child?

   - Personally, how do you respond to children's PVA?

   - Professionally, how do you respond to children's PVA?

   - How does your response change from your personal life to your professional life? Why?

   - How does children's PVA make you feel? How do you manage those feelings?

CASE STUDY #2: MY HISTORY WITH AGGRESSION

Growing up mainly in small-town suburbia, I did not see much aggression in my communities. My family moved from Chicago to the suburb of Hazel Crest, Illinois, when I was four and then to an even smaller town called Flossmoor, Illinois, when I was eight. I went to Catholic schools from first grade through ninth grade, and none of the parents I knew were paying all that money for their kids to go to school and fight.

So, like many children, I had my first experiences with aggression through my parents. I had a deep fear of spanking, but the only vivid memory I have of a spanking is from age eight or nine. I cannot for the life of me remember what I had done. As my father swatted me, I quickly realized that the more I screamed, the lighter the hits became, so I put on my best performance. After three or four smacks, my father suddenly stopped. But all my smugness disappeared once I looked up. The look on his face was so alarming that I realized I never again wanted to cause someone who loved me so much pain. Going forward, all he had to say was that he was disappointed in me, and I would adjust my behavior.

In terms of verbal aggression, no one in my family ever directed any profanity toward my sister or me. My mother was a Southern lady, and the worst phrase she ever used was "doggone it" when she was upset. But my father more than made up for her lack of profanity when he got angry. Still, while his vocabulary was impressive, he rarely used it, and I knew that I was never to repeat it. Both of my parents did use colorful nicknames for all our neighbors, but bullying or name-calling was never my forte. Occasionally I egged on my friend Amy when she bullied our circle of friends. That girl had a real talent for bullying that I secretly admired, so I lived out my best bullying moments vicariously through her.

My toys also affected my views of aggression. My parents had very clear ideas about the types of play experiences I could engage in, and unless it was specifically stated in a commercial that a toy was fun for girls *and* boys (good advertising, Slinky), I was only allowed to play with dolls. I could not even imagine how my parents would react if I engaged in any type of rough or dangerous play. My mother thought that walking on the living-room carpet after she had vacuumed those clean, crisp lines was not only aggressive and destructive but borderline deviant. I did try to ask for Star Wars action figures once, but when my mother said that she didn't see anything in the Barbie aisle like what I had described, I gave up. As a result, I followed the unspoken rule that I was never to engage in any play that focused on fighting or weapons.

HOW MY HISTORY WITH AGGRESSION AFFECTED MY PERSONAL RELATIONSHIPS WITH CHILDREN

Interestingly, our first child, Daniel, came into the world loving fighting and weapons. I will never forget the first time I gave him a doll. He was only a toddler at the time, and Reginald and I were trying to explain that Daniel was going to have a baby sister. Reginald was suspicious of my technique, but I explained that preschool teachers provide a variety of toys so that children can learn to be caring, nurturing adults, free of any biases or stereotypes. My innocent, cherubic little boy inspected the doll, held it curiously—and then smashed its face in. As Reginald looked on with pride, I was shocked that the fruit of my womb was capable of such aggression.

Where I saw a stick, my son saw a sword. Instead of Barney and Franklin, Daniel emulated the cool Power Rangers he heard about from the other children at preschool. Reginald and I exposed Daniel to a broad repertoire of toys, but when I refused to buy toy guns, Daniel pretended everything around him was a gun, including eating his sandwich into the shape of one while making "pshoo-pshoo" noises between bites.

At first, it was very unsettling to see my sweet little angel engage in aggressive play. Based on what I had read in child-development books, Reginald and I were doing all the right things. Now what? Were we supposed to give our two-year-old a stern talking-to about the sanctity of life?

To make matters worse, after his sister was born, Daniel started biting other children. How do you get kicked out of school at age two? (Okay, they did not kick him out—just strongly encouraged us to not bring him back.) Luckily, Daniel's biting only lasted a few months. Strategies such as reminding him to take deep breaths instead of biting took time to sink in (no pun intended).

This is a good time to point out that just like running a marathon, strategies for correcting aggressive behaviors take time to start working and require endurance. Over the next three years, Daniel's language skills grew so that he could talk about his feelings rather than bite, and he was never aggressive toward his sisters (he now had two). But his love of aggressive play intensified, and the "shooting" continued.

Ironically, as Daniel's fascination with rough-and-tumble play increased, my concerns began to decrease. The majority of the boys in his preschool and elementary-school classes loved this type of play, and they all appeared well-adjusted. Moreover, after that short-lived biting phase, Daniel never displayed any real aggression outside of his imagination. Yes, I would still sometimes cringe when he engaged in make-believe violence and made "pshoo" sounds, but should I punish him for playing?

When Daniel was in kindergarten, his teacher infuriated me. During parent-teacher conferences, she told Reginald and me to limit the amount of violent television—something that Daniel never, in fact, watched—in our home. She had a lot of nerve, stereotyping our family and our son! I am happy to say that the teacher later got to know us, and Daniel had a great year. Unfortunately, that judgment-filled conference was the first of many we endured in those tiny classroom chairs. As a teacher who used to judge parents, all I have to say is, "Well played, karma, well played."

Examining Your Temperament

According to the Early Development and Learning Lab at the University of Nebraska–Lincoln, temperament is "biologically based individual differences in thinking, feeling, and behaving in the environment." It is made up of multiple traits, as we will see in the next exercise. In and of itself, temperament is not good or bad—it is simply a good or bad match for a given environment. Temperament affects a person's behavior all through life.

EXERCISE #3: YOUR TEMPERAMENT

1. List these temperament traits on a sheet of paper:
   - Activity level
   - Distractibility
   - Regularity/predictability
   - Persistence
   - Mood

- Adaptability
- Sensory threshold (level of sensitivity to sights, sounds, touches or textures, smells, tastes, and so on)
- Tendency to withdraw from or approach new situations/people
- Intensity of emotions

2. Rate yourself for each trait on a scale of one (lowest) to ten (highest). Base your answers on your temperament at work, but feel free to create a second set of ratings for your temperament outside of work. The results make up your temperament scale.

3. On the back of your paper, answer these questions:
   - Is your temperament different at work than in your personal life?
   - How do you feel when someone has a temperament similar to your own?
   - How do you feel when someone has a temperament very different from your own?
   - Do you have any memories of how your parents or caregivers responded when you displayed certain aspects of your temperament as a child? If so, what happened?
   - How do your ratings and overall temperament compare to those of the people on your teaching team? Do you complement each other?
   - Are there some behaviors that you can tolerate more than others can because of your temperament?
   - Are there some behaviors that you cannot tolerate because of your temperament?

CASE STUDY #3: MY TEMPERAMENT

Where do I land on the scale for each of these temperament factors? As you might have guessed, I have a high activity level—I am a ten! (So much so that I wouldn't recommend giving me coffee in the morning.) I am easily distracted, very predictable, and very persistent, with a highly positive mood. I adapt to new things easily (but only at work) and have intense emotions. I tend to land in the middle of the continuum when it comes to my sensory threshold: I can tolerate most sounds, tastes, touches, and temperature changes, but I do have a lazy eye and can be overwhelmed by visual stimuli. I also land in the middle when it comes to my tendency to withdraw from or approach new situations or people. You might be surprised to know that I am shy with new people but sometimes intrigued by new situations. My temperament varies based on many factors. Whether I am a shining example or a cautionary tale is highly dependent on what time and day of the week you catch me. I start out the week with a good mood and good intentions, but sometimes by Tuesday I am exhausted. I am a morning person by nature, so most days I tend to start out upbeat and positive and then gradually become more negative and confused as the day progresses.

Interestingly, my temperament as an educator is very different from my temperament in my personal life. Professionally, I have a high tolerance for the shenanigans of other people's children. How I respond also depends on the type of behavior a child exhibits. For example, I have a low tolerance for spitting and biting. Sometimes students pick up on my temperament traits, so being animated and emotional has not always served me well in the classroom. One day, for instance, I overheard a conversation among some of my ninth-grade students about my temperament: "Yeah! You know you got her when her eyes get really big. It is hil-ar-ious!"

Later in my career, I remember being put in work groups with colleagues based on our temperaments. It was awful! The people in my groups were all so animated and perky and never stopped talking, especially when telling long-winded stories. Essentially, these people were too much like me, and I became frustrated by the lack of balance. This experience illustrates how sometimes even people with similar temperaments can clash.

HOW MY TEMPERAMENT AFFECTED MY PERSONAL RELATIONSHIPS WITH CHILDREN

Most of the time, we come into conflict not with those who are similar to us but with those who are different from us. Here is a case in point: When our children became school age, Reginald and I gave them chores to do in the mornings before they went off to school, such as straightening up their rooms, practicing the piano, and making their beds. This worked out well for our two older children, but not for our third child. Even though she was getting enough sleep, this child's morning routine consisted of 1 percent doing her chores and 99 percent sloth imitation. This, of course, led to us butting heads each and every morning.

It was not until Reginald pulled me aside that I realized that our daily conflicts were not part of some master plan by our six-year-old daughter to break my spirit. Instead, Reginald showed me that they were the product of our daughter's slow-to-warm-up temperament. He reminded me of all the instances in which she needed more time to adjust to situations, and he suggested that instead of making her adjust to my temperament, perhaps I should adjust to hers. Our discussion helped me to stop seeing our daughter's behavior as a challenge, and as a result, I accepted her true nature by letting her complete her chores after school instead of before. That situation was a good reminder that when there is a mismatch in temperament, it is the adult—not the child—who has the capacity to change and adjust.

Examining Your Cultural Lens

Anthropologist and researcher Edward Hall developed the analogy of the iceberg to explain the complexities of culture. At the tip of the iceberg are the behaviors we can easily see. But 90 percent of an iceberg is beneath the surface, and it is the unconscious part of culture that holds the beliefs, values, and motivations behind our behaviors.

What makes culture even more complicated is that one person can have membership in many cultures. For example, the teaching profession is a culture unto itself. You may also belong to cultures related to your nationality, race, religion, interests, political opinions, and more. Each culture has its own set of ideas, traditions, and values. These aspects of your various cultures may not necessarily align—nor do they need to.

EXERCISE #4: YOUR CULTURAL LENS

1. Gather your answers from Exercises #1, #2, and #3 in this chapter.
2. On a new sheet of paper, draw a line near the top (about 10 percent of the way down) to signify the tip of an iceberg, leaving enough room to write above the line.
3. On the tip of your iceberg, list your personal and professional responses to crying, physical aggression, and verbal aggression from Exercises #1 and #2.

4. On the part of the iceberg that is below the surface (the rest of the paper), list the reasons behind those responses. For example, you may believe in giving children consequences so they will grow up to be good citizens. Or you may put children in time-out because it worked for you when you were a child. On the back of your iceberg, answer these questions:

- At what age should children be given rules?
- At what age should a child be expected to feed herself with utensils?
- Is it good for babies to learn to calm themselves when they cry?
- At what age should a child be expected to sleep alone at night?
- At what age should children be allowed to make choices?
- Does holding babies make them more demanding?
- At what age should a child be weaned from the bottle or breast?
- Is it appropriate to let babies "cry it out" when they are upset?
- Does leaving a baby to "cry it out" make him emotionally insecure?
- At what age should children be toilet trained?
- Is it important for children to have a consistent schedule?
- Are tantrums a reflection of parenting skills?

CASE STUDY #4: MY CULTURAL LENS

I didn't know I was Black until I was five, when a little girl told me that I could get rid of my dark skin by washing it off. At school, I was the only Black girl in my class until middle school. For many years, I was alone to endure those awkward moments of everyone staring at me when the subject of slavery came up.

Even though my school was not diverse, my neighborhood was, and I loved getting hair tips from my Asian friends at the bus stop and got a kick out of learning the difference between Christianity and Hinduism from my next-door neighbor. I have fond memories of going to a Baptist church on the South Side of Chicago as a child and then tasting my first Communion wafer when I converted to Catholicism at age nine. I also think that my father's diagnosis of multiple sclerosis when I was two helped me appreciate those with different abilities. Because of all these different experiences with different people, I learned at an early age to change my language and mannerisms based on whom I was with.

HOW MY CULTURAL LENS AFFECTED MY PERSONAL RELATIONSHIPS WITH CHILDREN

As parents, it took my husband, Reginald, and me a while to figure out where we stood in terms of discipline. Even though I was sometimes threatened with spanking as a child, I have no clear memory of actually being spanked other than the experience I shared in chapter 1. Reginald and I weren't sure if we fit in the spare-the-rod-and-spoil-the-child camp or in the time-out bunch, so we experimented with a little of both.

With me being in the field of education, I also examined the research, such as a study by Akemi Tomoda and her colleagues that shows that children who are spanked once a month have less gray matter in the prefrontal cortex of the brain than children who are spanked less frequently or not at all. The bad news is that gray matter actually helps the brain to gain self-control. The American Academy of Pediatrics advises against spanking, and an analysis by Elizabeth Gershoff and Andrew Grogan-Kaylor of fifty years of research confirms that spanking and child abuse lead to similar outcomes. Another analysis by Elizabeth Gershoff of eighty-eight studies over sixty-two years shows that children who are spanked tend to show aggressive behavior in both childhood and adulthood.

But while Reginald and I considered information like this in our decision to stop spanking, other cultural influences also had powerful effects on our choice. As a teacher, I was always learning alternative discipline strategies, which I shared with Reginald. The more we learned, the more we moved away from spanking our children. Our African American culture also played into our decision. I was intrigued by research by Joy DeGruy and writings by journalist Stacey Patton that highlight the fact that spanking is not intrinsic to African cultures but a byproduct of historical trauma. As a result, I now am a strong proponent of positive discipline. But the strongest reason for our decision was simply that hitting our children made us feel bad.

Processing Your Experiences

These exercises may have stirred up some powerful emotions for you. While looking back helps us understand what lies ahead, Danish philosopher Søren Kierkegaard reminds us that life "must be lived forwards." Let's examine your feelings together so that we can move forward.

NEGATIVITY TOWARD CHILDREN WITH CHALLENGING BEHAVIORS (AND THEIR FAMILY MEMBERS) IS NORMAL

When I talk to educators, I frequently find that they have strong negative feelings about children with challenging behaviors and their family members. If you have spent any time working in education, you can probably relate. Why is it so hard to get past being a Negative Nancy? It's because the human brain is wired that way.

From a biological standpoint, according to Roy Baumeister and his colleagues, our ancestors' survival depended on immediate responsiveness to possible threats. As a result, negative events and information lead to more thinking, evoke more-intense responses, and are even processed more rapidly than positive emotions or rational responses. To complicate things further, negative impressions are quicker to form and harder to change. In fact, Guangheng Dong and his colleagues point out that our brains have a natural "negativity bias," or a tendency to pay most of our attention to problems. Unfortunately, as Kristen Domonell states in an article for Right as Rain by UW Medicine, the brain responds to *all* perceived dangers as if they are life-threatening, so you experience these reactions whether a child throws a chair at you or a family member gives you the side-eye. No wonder we tend to feel negative about these children and family members!

WHY ADULTS STRUGGLE WITH CHILDREN'S NEGATIVE EMOTIONS

Adults are sometimes uncomfortable with negative emotions such as sadness, anger, doubt, anxiety, embarrassment, and fear. Surrounded by these adult attitudes, children learn to suppress these emotions and miss out on learning how to properly manage these feelings. This, in turn, allows patterns of shame and denial to emerge and patterns of anger to intensify. As a result, children's social-emotional development can be truncated.

My colleague and fellow educator Jac McBride has a saying: "The whole world is three years old." This metaphor perfectly describes our struggles as adults to properly express our own emotions and empathize with those of others. Since many of us were not allowed to process our own negative feelings as children, it can trigger uncomfortable emotions in us when we see children exhibit those same feelings. As a result, instead of displaying advanced emotional control when children demonstrate challenging behaviors, we are perpetually experiencing the same fear and lack of control we had as young children. And that is the reason why when a three-year-old is having a hissy fit, it is so hard not to have one of your own.

MANAGING YOUR EMOTIONS

I, like many of you, have learned to bottle up my own negative feelings, which tends to result in them boiling over at something as minor as a two-year-old telling me no. Clearly, this is not the best way to handle my emotions, especially because in an early childhood setting, children's negative feelings will frequently be on display! Thankfully, there is a better way to keep others' emotions from provoking ours.

After years of practice, I have learned to respond to negative displays of emotion—and all the feelings that they stir up in me—with curiosity. I am definitely a work in progress, but the more I practice, the better I become at looking beyond the surface of an emotional display and directing my energies toward understanding its root cause. I often still have to stop myself from using someone else's anger or bad behavior to justify my own. But if someone displays negativity, I strive to accept that emotion, move beyond being a three-year-old, and not let it trigger any negativity in me so that I can respond with kindness. And each time I help a young child or another adult express negative feelings in positive, healthy ways, it actually helps me learn strategies to express my own feelings and develop a positive relationship with those pesky negative emotions.

Identifying Personal Biases

As you work through your emotions and learn the PUSH PAST It method, you are likely to encounter some internal resistance in the form of implicit biases. Now, I know that as soon as I mention the word *biases*, people will start to protest: "I'm not biased! How can you say that? You don't even know me!" But before you throw this book across the room or feel you have to defend your moral character, let me explain: having biases does not make you a bad person. Everyone has them. Blame it on your brain, which is biologically wired for bias. As Kathleen Woodhouse says in an article for Forbes, "If you have a brain, you're biased." In fact, biases particularly tend to surface in the mind of a teacher faced with a child who exhibits challenging behaviors, whether the teacher is conscious of it or not. However, biases get in the way of thinking objectively and dealing with challenging behaviors appropriately, so it's important that we learn to recognize and overcome our own biases.

Some biases are obvious, such as overt racism or sexism, but I would venture to say that most teachers do not hold these attitudes. In fact, implicit biases often do not match up with our professed beliefs. So what we are examining here are *implicit biases*, or biases that we do not even know we have.

These biases are especially troublesome because, even though we are unaware of them, they still can affect our behavior.

Several studies provide vivid illustrations of this point. For example, Jason Okonofua, Gregory Walton, and Jennifer Eberhardt conducted a study on a diverse group of K–12 teachers from across the United States. In two experiments, teachers were given school records labeled with stereotypical Black names (such as Deshawn or Darnell) and White names (such as Greg or Jake). The results showed that teachers are more likely to categorize Black students as troublemakers, view multiple infractions as a connected pattern, and suggest severe punishments for the offending students.

In another study, college professors and researchers Andrew Todd, Kelsey Thiem, and Rebecca Neel collected pictures of facial expressions being made by people of various ages and races and then showed the pictures to undergraduate students. Next, the researchers had the students categorize words and pictures of objects as threatening or nonthreatening. The researchers found that participants were more likely to classify pictures and words as threatening after seeing Black faces. For example, one of the pictures showed a gun. After viewing the face of a White child, participants consistently perceived the gun as a toy and put the picture in the nonthreatening category. However, after viewing the face of a Black child, participants were more likely to perceive the gun as a weapon and place the picture in the threatening category, along with words such as *violent* or *hostile*. This pattern held true even when the participants saw pictures of Black children as young as five.

A study by Amy Halberstadt and her colleagues adds more to the conversation. These researchers showed images of Black and White faces (both male and female) to teachers-in-training and asked the trainees to identify whether the facial expressions were positive or negative. Then the researchers showed the participants videos of Black and White boys misbehaving in school and asked the participants to rate the level of hostility in the misbehaviors on a scale from one (lowest) to five (highest). The results showed that the trainee teachers were more likely to misinterpret the expressions on Black faces as negative and more likely to view the misbehaviors of Black boys as hostile.

Now, after reading these statistics, some of you might be thinking, "I don't think the teachers at our school are like that," or "But Angela, I don't even see color! Can't children just be children?" If those are your experiences, that is good to hear. I wish all children had that experience. But even if you do not hold those biases, other people might. Because biases are so often implicit and therefore unconscious, as educators, we must all be on the lookout for bias so that we can help ourselves and others overcome it.

CASE STUDY #5: DISCOVERING MY PERSONAL BIASES

When I was a teacher, if I had heard about studies that revealed implicit bias against Black children, I would have gasped, shaken my head in disgust, assumed that I didn't have this bias, and gone right back to my classroom completely unaffected. After all, how could I be biased in my perception of challenging behaviors? As a Black woman, aren't I more conscious of stereotypes? As it turned out, I was not as conscious as I thought I was. I hope that being a Black woman has made me more sensitive to certain types of biases, but to then jump to the conclusion that I did not have any bias at all was a bit of a stretch. When I took stock of my own implicit biases, I received some unpleasant surprises.

As you might have gleaned from earlier sections, despite my best efforts, I was sometimes guilty of viewing children's behavior in subjective ways when it did not fit into my own perspective or past experiences. In my classroom, for example, I perpetuated gender bias and clearly disciplined children who engaged in certain types of play themes more than I disciplined children who did not. I was more comfortable with dramatic play than with any of the other learning centers in my room (such as blocks), so I devoted more of my time to setting up the dramatic-play area. When girls proclaimed in their play that "no one is my friend" and that they would not invite anyone to their birthday parties, I talked to them about friendship and called it a day. But at the start of my career, when boys started talking about superheroes, wrestling, or Power Rangers, I refused to even have conversations about those topics. Looking back so many years later, I do not think it would have been harmful to talk about the boys' interests with them.

As I worked with family members, some of their reactions to challenging behaviors deeply concerned me, sometimes leading me to make sweeping generalizations about children and their families. I cringed when I informed family members about a child's aggressive behavior and they responded by telling the child, "If someone hits you, hit them back." I felt frustrated when I told family members about challenging behaviors and they chuckled; made comments best summarized as, "It's not my kid; it's you people"; or even assured me that I would never have to worry about any hitting again thanks to *la chancla* (a term used in Hispanic culture to describe a form of corporal punishment), which neither I nor my school condoned. I often had thoughts such as, "What's wrong with these people? Can't they see that they're not helping?"

It took me many years of working with families to understand that actions and statements such as these were not part of the problem but part of family members' cultures. I realized that if 90 percent of what drives behavior is unconscious, then family members were not intentionally trying to undermine me; they were trying to support their child or my efforts. Even though I did not always agree with their actions, both of those intentions are admirable. This realization was important because research on reasoning and morality by Peter Ditto, David Pizarro, and David Tannenbaum shows that we tend to judge ourselves on our intentions and others on their actions. Moreover, researchers Alan Leslie, Joshua Knobe, and Adam Cohn also found that people are more likely to label a behavior as intentional when they consider it wrong. Once I understood the philosophy behind my judgments, I began to push myself to judge family members more positively based on their good intentions.

As these examples show, educators must cautiously check for blind spots caused by implicit bias when they work with children and family members to eliminate challenging behaviors. Implicit biases can be missed because they are often embedded within cultures and appear subtly, unintentionally, and unconsciously. From a neurological standpoint, our brains are designed to look for patterns and overgeneralize even when we think we are being impartial. This is particularly true when we are dealing with someone from an unfamiliar culture, and it makes it even more difficult to detect our implicit biases. Ryan Stolier and Jonathan Freeman studied the brain activity of participants as they viewed diverse images of faces, and they found that our brains are biologically wired to be subjective and make stereotypes even when we are not consciously doing so. Research by neuroscientist Hugo Spiers and his colleagues suggests that once those ideas are ingrained in the brain, we respond more strongly to information about individuals who appear to fit those stereotypes.

To curb unconscious biases, many White educators sometimes defer to educators of color (or ones who belong to the same cultures as the children in the White educators' care) when making decisions about discipline. However, educators who use this practice are misunderstanding the effect of implicit bias on *everyone.* We can internalize biases even toward our own ethnic groups or genders. For example, a study by Walter Gilliam and his colleagues shows that while all the teachers in the study were biased, the Black teachers tended to be even harder on Black students than on White students and to recommend harsher discipline for Black students.

SOME COMMON IMPLICIT BIASES

I realize that this information about bias could leave you feeling all sorts of emotions. Some of you might be a bit discouraged: "Oh no, Angela. I *am* biased, even though I try so hard not to be. I'm a horrible person!" Others of you might be intrigued, while others of you might be skeptical or even indifferent: "Well, I never had those experiences." However you are feeling, just hear me out.

Remember, you are not bad or evil for having implicit biases. Everyone has them. But implicit biases can get in the way of clear and fair thinking when you face challenging behaviors, so you need to decide how to deal with those biases. The first step to overcoming implicit biases is to become aware of them. So now we will examine some common implicit biases that adults confront when dealing with challenging behaviors.

"WELL, I TURNED OUT OKAY"

I have heard this phrase all too many times in discussions: "I experienced such and such a situation as a child, and I turned out okay; therefore, this situation should not be an issue for this child, and she will be okay too." Do you recognize any of these variations?

- "We had nothing when I was growing up, but I never acted like these kids do."
- "I got a spanking whenever I mouthed off, and I'm fine."
- "My parents fought all the time, and I turned out okay."

This train of thought represents a cognitive bias. Psychologists Amos Tversky and Daniel Kahneman have studied cognitive bias and claim that people often make arguments based on flawed reasoning. In this case, this argument oversimplifies the problem, erroneously draws the same conclusion about situations that are completely different, and does not account for factors that may affect the results in each situation.

Even though I have used the "I turned out okay" argument myself, I have to admit that I am probably not the most objective person to make an assessment of whether I am okay. I mean, I would like to think I am okay, but I am sure you can find other people who would say otherwise. Besides, what does *okay* even mean? It might signify different things to different people. In other words, is any individual truly objective enough to assess whether an experience has injured or damaged her? Can she really see a wide enough picture to know whether her life would have been better with or without a certain event?

If you are having a hard time letting go of "I turned out okay," consider these questions:

- Are we all using the same standard to measure whether someone is "okay"?

- If we are okay, does that mean we have no desire to further improve?
- You were able to tolerate that experience or situation, but does that mean everyone is?
- Is it possible that you were able to tolerate a particular situation because of supports that are not available to everyone?

You are just one example. What about all the people who are not okay?

- Are you able to explore an idea beyond your own personal situation? Can something be important even if it does not affect you?
- Would you want to go to a doctor who still treats every ailment with leeches? If medicine, technology, fashion, and hairstyles can evolve, can ideas about children and their behavior evolve?

It is true everyone views the world through her own philosophical prism, but to never extend your thinking beyond yourself can limit your perspective. Taking one experience and generalizing it to everyone also has drawbacks. Scientific research and new ideas and information give us opportunities to understand perspectives outside of ourselves, explore the evolution of ideas over time, and use what we learn to help the children we serve.

ANECDOTAL EVIDENCE VERSUS OTHER SOURCES

Another common implicit bias often sounds like this:

- "Time-out always made me behave. Why shouldn't it work for kids nowadays?"
- "My grandma always says that babies have to 'cry it out' so they learn to fall asleep on their own."
- "That strategy would never work. My cousin tried it with his kids, and now they argue with him about everything!"

Of course, you and your experiences are unique, and those experiences make an enormous difference to your teaching practice. On the other hand, what would happen if you tried to make a cake using only flour and milk? The result might be edible, but it would not be much of a cake (certainly not very tasty).

Just as in baking, to effectively work with young children, we need to incorporate various ideas in the right proportions into our practices. I do think our experiences and feelings are important and valid. And yes, I too have had some colorful and entertaining conversations with my friends and family over the years, many of them involving observations of other people's children at the local grocery store and proclamations about the shortcomings of today's world and its impending apocalyptic end. But if someone from the other side of the world saw the same events, would she have the same thoughts? Could researchers draw the same conclusions from a well-conducted study? My Uncle Harry's theories on childhood emotional regulation might include some useful insights, but they probably should not have as much influence on my practice as, say, two hundred research articles that include data gathered from twenty countries over three decades. We put limits on our learning when we restrict ourselves to only taking lessons from personal feelings or experiences.

Also, keep in mind that seemingly contradictory ideas can coexist. For example, you can value children being able to handle the pressure of the real world *and* value children expressing strong emotions. These ideas are not mutually exclusive. Valuing research does not mean you have to completely dismiss your own experiences or conversations at your dining-room table.

PUSH PAST IT!

THE HAZARDS OF NOSTALGIA

After hearing new ideas or when dealing with challenging behaviors, you may find yourself reminiscing about how we did things "back in the day." Let's take a moment to understand the psychology behind these feelings.

Nostalgia is a sentimental emotion that makes you long for the past. Ironically, this longing for the past is one way we cope with challenges in the present. Nostalgia is a psychological tool that provides security in times of uncertainty. When a child has challenging behaviors, it can provoke feelings of anxiety in adults, and we can find comfort in wrapping ourselves in a blanket of memories.

But the sense of warmth and comfort we feel from nostalgia can become a hindrance if we are not careful. Intellectually, we may know that both the past and the present contain good and bad elements. But if you look at only what was good about the past and only what is bad about the present, your view has lost its balance. Clinging to the past can be a useful coping mechanism, but it can become counterproductive when those thoughts become our sole focus, are used to avoid what is occurring now, or cause us to miss out on gaining new strategies or experiences. Focusing on the past can potentially divert our attention from solutions that are actually under our control in the present.

To maintain balance and avoid getting stuck in unproductive thinking patterns, remember that elements of the past have led us to the present and that life is a mixed bag no matter what time you are in. Also remember that what is happening now does not have to compete with what happened in the past. The past and the present are not in conflict with one another.

Wrapping Up

This chapter has given us a lot to think about. If this information is not fitting into your existing paradigm, I understand. I have had years to study, process, and act on this information. Personally, I tend to go through the five stages of loss when accepting a new idea, and you might be experiencing some of the same feelings:

1. **Denial:** "This is bogus."

2. **Anger:** "I hate this stupid book."

3. **Bargaining:** "Well, if I try, the children might start engaging in activities."

4. **Depression:** "Why can't this be easier?"

5. **Acceptance:** "What have I got to lose? What I'm already doing isn't working."

Whatever stage you might be in, I encourage you to keep going. If you are willing to acknowledge and process your own emotions, you will have much greater success in dealing with the challenging behaviors in your classroom. So take a deep breath, pat yourself on the back, and let's move on to the next step in the process.

CHAPTER 3

Thinking about Challenging Behaviors in a Professional Context

Now that you have processed your own emotions and acknowledged the effects they have on your present actions, how do you feel? Hopefully you feel calm and unburdened and now have the energy to begin focusing on how to help the children in your care.

Defining Your Professional Self

The information and exercises in this chapter will help you understand how you are currently reacting to challenging behaviors as a professional. This work builds on the emotional processing we did in chapter 2, further helping you understand where you are right now and where you want to go.

After completing each exercise, read the case study that follows it. These examples use my own experiences to illustrate how personal history affects the way individuals react to challenging behaviors in their professional relationships with children.

EXERCISE #1: YOUR PROFESSIONAL IMAGE

1. What is your image of yourself as a professional? Use words and pictures to create a collage.

2. On the back of your paper, answer these questions:

   - How well does this image match the professional image you want to have of yourself?

   - How well does this image match the professional image you want others to have of you?

   - What gaps exist between where you are now and where you want to be as a professional?

ADULT BEHAVIOR AND ATTITUDES AFFECT CHILDREN'S BEHAVIOR

Take a moment and think of a recent trip. It doesn't have to be a long one. For example, my last trip to Wal-Mart was an all-out adventure, full of a wide range of emotions: fear as I waded through the sea of shopping carts that never seem to make it to the corral, shock as I averted my eyes from particularly revealing fashion choices, and frustration when I saw only two out of thirty checkout lanes open. More often than not, even the most memorable, cherished family vacations still contain negative elements, and so does working with children. It is important to embrace all aspects of that journey. Every teacher longs for a classroom full of happy, perfectly regulated children who always follow instructions and play calmly with each other, but few (if any) teachers can say they have achieved this dream. (If you have, I want to meet you.) So we as educators have two options: we can struggle for the ideal and constantly become frustrated because we cannot reach it, or we can recalculate what a peaceful classroom looks like and find joy and fulfillment even in our imperfect experiences.

What do I mean by a peaceful classroom? Mahatma Gandhi, Dorothy Thompson, Ronald Reagan, and wrestler Hulk Hogan are all credited with variations of this quote: "Peace is not the absence of conflict but the ability to cope with it." In the same vein, a peaceful classroom does not rely on the absence of sadness, anger, envy, or even frustration. Every emotion will make its way into the classroom at some point. Instead, a peaceful classroom relies on adults' abilities to cope with all feelings. If adults know how to cope appropriately, they can help children learn to do the same.

Of course, coping appropriately is easier said than done, especially when it feels as if a child seems to be going out of his way to aggravate you. As a consultant, I often ask teachers what they think is the reason behind a student's challenging behavior. Many of them respond with statements such as, "To bother me," or "To ruin my day." I know the feeling! Not so long ago, my husband questioned whether the little preschoolers in my classroom were trying to destroy me. It took time for me to grow as a professional and realize that spite was actually not the reason behind most challenging behaviors and that it was not my job to make children with those behaviors pay for what they had done. Actually, it was an interaction with one of my own children's teachers that taught me the most about how to adjust my professional viewpoint.

CASE STUDY #1: FRUSTRATED TEACHER, FRUSTRATED CHILD

I will never forget a particular meeting that Reginald and I had at our son's school. Daniel was *that* kid, the one who always seemed to have a conflicted relationship with his teachers. When Reginald and I met our three daughters' teachers at school open houses, we were greeted with good cheer: "Hello, Mr. and Mrs. Searcy. What a pleasure to meet you." But when we visited Daniel's teachers, we were met with icy stares and stiff, awkward conversations.

When Daniel was in sixth grade, Reginald and I decided that it would be beneficial for Daniel to join in any school meetings about his progress. So the three of us went to parent-teacher conferences together that year. At the meeting with Daniel's language-arts teacher, she declared, "I can't do anything with him. I'm done." Mind you, this was said in front of my twelve-year-old child.

Afterward, I asked Daniel how he felt about his teacher's comments. I can still hear his response: "Well, if I don't know what to do, and she doesn't know what to do—I'm sunk!" To this day, I hold Daniel's perspective close to my heart. If he had known what to do, he would have done it! If this despair came from a twelve-year-old, what must a two- or three-year-old feel?

In the end, it all turned out okay. Daniel has since graduated from college and gone on to graduate school. (Did I mention that his father and I are beyond proud?) But I wish Daniel's teachers could have understood him better so we could have more positive memories to look back on.

CHILDREN NOTICE SPEECH, ATTITUDE, TONE, AND MORE

Daniel's teacher reminds us of a crucial point that is easy to forget. Even though we often feel (much to our frustration) that children are not paying the slightest attention to us, they notice much more than we may think. They pick up on not just the words we say but the way we say them, our body language as we speak, and even more. The messages we send through all these means can have unintended consequences.

As we discussed in chapter 2, it is normal to feel negative toward children with challenging behaviors. However, those feelings often prompt adults to give children negative labels, which in turn can affect a child's development and life outcomes into adulthood. For example, research shows that young children who are labeled aggressive tend to carry those difficulties into adolescence. Kenneth Dodge found that children who are labeled aggressive tend to get caught in a downward spiral; and research by Jeffrey Lamont, Deborah Perry, and their colleagues shows that these children are likely to endure continual rejection from peers, punitive interactions with teachers, and school failure.

Let's take a moment to examine how the relationships between adults and children influence later development. In one study, Richard Fabes and his colleagues examined the relationship between children's social competence and their parents' reactions to the children's negative emotions. The researchers note that when parents demonstrate verbally (such as, "If you start that crying, you'll have to go to your room," or "You're overreacting") or in other ways that they feel uncomfortable with or upset about their children's emotions, children have difficulty regulating their emotional expression and have decreased abilities to engage in socially competent interactions. Nicole Perry and her colleagues discovered that college students who recall receiving punitive responses to negative emotions as children have more anger-management issues as adults. Along those same lines, a study by L. Alan Sroufe, Nancy Fox, and Van Pancake shows that children whose caregivers are unresponsive have a constant need for adult approval, attention, and contact that interferes with other developmental tasks, such as peer interactions. Conversely, infants who have responsive caregivers are more autonomous by the time they attend preschool.

Adults must remember that children do not come "fully assembled." Children learn what to do through relationships with adults. It is only when adults acknowledge and label emotions and model appropriate calming strategies that children gain the skills that will help them become capable, independent adults.

Analyzing Your Current Professional Practices

All teachers have their own sets of professional practices for dealing with challenging behaviors. Some teachers yell, some teachers lecture, and some teachers simply ignore the behavior. Before you can improve your practices, you need to clearly understand what you are already doing. The next several sections provide information, exercises, and questions to help you analyze yourself and your current professional habits.

FOLLOWING PROFESSIONAL GUIDELINES

The first ground rule for any strategy that attempts to address challenging behavior is to follow the professional guidelines for teachers in your area. These principles provide a starting point and help you ensure that whatever strategy or strategies you use are compliant with ethical and legal standards. Professional organizations such as your country's or region's educational association provide codes of ethics to adhere to when dealing with challenging behaviors. For example, the National Association for the Education of Young Children (NAEYC) in the United States has developed standards for those working in early childhood education. Additionally, state, provincial, or local licensing standards and quality-rating systems can provide further guidance.

If you use a published curriculum in your program, the curriculum materials may include additional guidelines for addressing challenging behaviors in a way that harmonizes with the curriculum. These recommendations can help you plan and can influence your decision making throughout the PUSH PAST It process. They also help all members of your team stay consistent. Because PUSH PAST It and most curricula are research based, the two systems should complement each other.

IDENTIFYING YOUR PROFESSIONAL VALUES

We all have both personal and professional values. Professional values are not specific to an individual and are embodied in workplace guidelines, professional and licensing standards, and ethics. Frameworks such as teacher-child assessment, evidence-based curricula, and program standards help define our professional values and guide our day-to-day interactions with children.

Even though we should acknowledge our personal values, professional values must take precedence in the workplace and guide our decision making there. This is not an easy undertaking, however, and the ability to prioritize different values at different times is a skill that we have to acknowledge, practice, and cultivate. Whatever your gut reactions to challenging behaviors may be, effective educators are aware of and put aside personal feelings that might be not be congruent with the professional demands of the workplace or the well-being of young children.

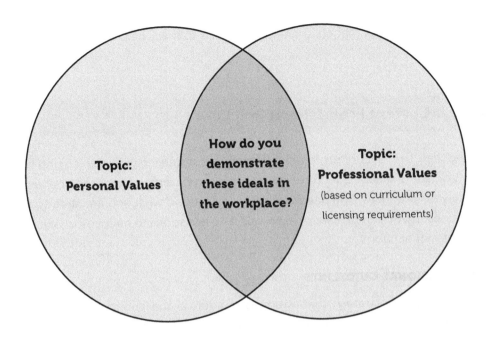

**Topic:
Personal Values**

How do you demonstrate these ideals in the workplace?

**Topic:
Professional Values**
(based on curriculum or licensing requirements)

EXERCISE #2: PERSONAL VALUES VERSUS PROFESSIONAL VALUES

1. On a blank sheet of paper, draw a Venn diagram similar to this one, and fill in each space.

2. On the back of your paper, answer these questions:

   - What are some potential or current conflicts between your personal values and your professional values?
   - When faced with these conflicts, how can you make sure you are fulfilling professional obligations?

You can use this exercise as a reflective tool to create an ongoing skill-building routine. At the start of every staff meeting, training session, or meeting of your professional learning community, try picking a particular focus—such as discipline, feeding, or time management—and fill out this Venn diagram for that topic to facilitate self-reflection and discussion. Over time, using this tool will become a habit of mind.

CASE STUDY #2: MY PERSONAL VALUES VERSUS MY PROFESSIONAL VALUES

I come from a very traditional, two-parent, middle-class family. I was raised on classic Midwestern values: your parents weren't your friends or your playmates, children didn't have opinions, and children were to be seen and not heard. Often, adults prepared children for the harshness of life by being harsh themselves.

Yet my upbringing did not automatically determine my professional values. I am naturally playful and genuinely get a kick out of the funny stuff that children say, so I like talking with them and hearing their opinions. Occasionally I wondered if I was preparing my students for the harsh world ahead if I was not being harsh myself, but I usually dismissed that idea.

HOW MY PROFESSIONAL VALUES AFFECTED MY PROFESSIONAL PRACTICE

My professional values mesh well with key values of the early childhood profession, and during my teaching years, this match enabled me to better implement those priorities in my practice. For instance, I valued (and still value) play and enjoyed designing a playful environment—a perfect fit for a field in which playtime is at the center of children's learning. While other teachers complained about weekly lesson planning, I enjoyed thinking about the new adventures I would explore with the children each week. My interest in conversing with children helped me support their language development. In short, where some teachers saw work, I saw an opportunity to work my magic.

IDENTIFYING YOUR PROFESSIONAL ATTITUDES TOWARD TEMPERAMENT AND CULTURE

While I was working as a behavior specialist, I was asked to work my magic on a playgroup for children with special needs. The therapists who ran the group described an adorable little nonverbal two-year-old, whom I'll call Nathan, who was tearing up the group each week. On the day we had arranged, I came into the classroom and asked which child was Nathan. One of the therapists said, "Don't worry. Just wait; you'll see." The only thing I noticed were highly engaged children interacting with one another and the toys throughout the room.

The playgroup was off to a great start—that is, until one therapist exclaimed loudly, "It's time for circle time!" The result was immediate. Have you ever seen a tiny child knock everything off a shelf with one swoop? Well, Nathan did it. I suddenly was caught in a tornado of toys and even chairs flying in the air. The chain reaction was also immediate. Some of the children joined in and started throwing things, others began to cry, and a child with autism started to spin. It took several minutes to restore order in the classroom.

To begin our "magical" journey, I helped the therapists complete a temperament scale (similar to the one you filled out in chapter 2) for Nathan. He was two years old but was unable to speak. According to my developmental assessment, usually by the end of age two, children have a vocabulary of about forty to fifty words. Nathan also had a low sensory threshold, was sensitive to sounds, and had difficulty adapting to new situations and tended to withdraw from them.

What about Nathan's chair throwing? How did that fit into this puzzle? When a tiny two-year-old is able to throw chairs, it is not a sign of strength but a sign of *fear*. When I hear stories that start with, "Have you ever seen a child flip over a wooden table or push a heavy cabinet?" that tells me that the child is receiving a rush of adrenaline. Adrenaline is released by the adrenal glands when the brain perceives physical or emotional danger. This hormonal release, though useful when fighting predators, gives us all a glimpse into this child's perspective: "I'm not angry—I'm afraid."

If you are now thinking, "A simple announcement about circle time shouldn't lead to a response like *that*," you might be judging Nathan's behavior based on your temperament and knowledge of the situation as an adult. Looking at the situation from a two-year-old's eyes, the therapists and I realized that the transition to circle time—a sudden loud announcement followed by an abrupt change in activities—was frightening and uncomfortable for Nathan. We changed the transition to turning down the lights, singing the group's cleanup song very softly, and having one adult move very close to Nathan during the transition to whisper that Nathan was safe and could wear earmuffs if the singing was too loud for him. After cleanup was finished, I would turn on a flashlight and whisper a chant: "Where is circle time? Where is circle time?" Then I would lead the children around the room "looking" for circle time with my flashlight until we eventually arrived at the carpet.

At the carpet, we added visuals and manipulatives to support Nathan, who otherwise might not have been able to sustain his attention because of his auditory sensitivities. We also gave him the option of continuing to wear earmuffs to muffle some of the potentially loud circle-time activities. I also created a short story using pictures that showed Nathan holding his finger to his lips if things were too loud for him.

This all occurred in April, and when I came back in June, Nathan (who was now about to turn three) was leading the other children to circle time using the flashlight. That same day, I felt a great sense of accomplishment because when I got a little too excited at snack time and my voice rose, my little friend came very close to me, looked me in the eye, put his finger to his lips, and told me to "shhhh." To top it all off, this child never wiped a shelf clean again!

EXERCISE #3: YOUR PROFESSIONAL ATTITUDES TOWARD TEMPERAMENT AND CULTURE

1. Look back at the temperament scale you created in chapter 2. On the same paper but using a different color, assess the temperament of a child in your care who exhibits challenging behaviors.

2. On the same paper, use a third color to assess a child in your care with whom you get along well.

3. On the back of your paper, answer these questions:

   - What do you notice about the differences between you and the two children you assessed?

   - How do other children in your care rate on the scale?

   - How do you adjust when there is a mismatch of temperament between you and a child, between you and a coworker, or between you and a child's family members?

   - How does your response correlate to the cultures to which you belong?

HOW MY ATTITUDES TOWARD CULTURE AFFECTED MY PROFESSIONAL RELATIONSHIPS

Scottish philosopher and economist Adam Smith used the term *invisible hand* to describe how something unseen can drive our behavior. Although he most famously used the phrase to discuss economics, my culture also functioned as an invisible hand, shaping my life and everyday interactions without my awareness.

When I did a self-assessment, all my diverse experiences fooled me into believing that I was not culturally biased when I worked with children, their family members, and my colleagues. Looking back now, I realize that I probably was not the best person to assess this trait in myself. I often found myself in conflicts with family members and coteachers that arose or got worse because I acted in ways that reflected my unconscious cultural attitudes:

- I became frustrated when I told family members about their children's behavior challenges and they did not take my concerns seriously. Some family members would even laugh about how they would play-fight with the child at home or how the child might have learned inappropriate behaviors from movies or video games. Because I had been raised in a home where play-fighting was unthinkable and where certain standards of behavior were expected regardless of what fictional characters did, I could not fathom why my students' family members did not appear concerned about their children's behavior.

- Of all the responses from skeptical family members, one infuriated me the most: "He doesn't act like that at home." Argh! I was a professional who had studied and worked with children for years—did these people doubt my word? Or did they think I would violate my personal and professional values by lying about their child?

- If I had a disagreement with one of my coteachers in the classroom, it sometimes got so bad that we would give each other the silent treatment and talk to each other through the children: "Go tell Ms. Smith I need the glue." After all, it was better to not talk than to argue, right?

It was not until later in my career that I began to uncover my cultural biases by participating in a guided activity at a presentation. First, I wrote down the initials of ten nonrelatives whom I trusted. Then I organized these people by their diversity. For this exercise, diversity included not just race and ethnicity but also gender, education, sexual orientation, disability, profession, socioeconomic class, and marital status. Interestingly, most of the people I trusted were educators, middle class, and highly educated. I realized how much I was interacting with only people who were similar to me. Perhaps this narrow circle was limiting my perspective. Furthermore, how I viewed misbehavior or conflict had a lot to do with my experiences and mindset. That mindset, in turn, was derived from my culture.

That activity allowed me to shift my thinking. Now I saw interactions with people who opposed my ideas not as conflicts but as conversations that helped me learn about different cultures and perspectives. I realized that when I let disagreements bring me into conflict with family members, children, or colleagues, my anger was only silencing my message and creating more division. Being angry at others didn't change their behavior or the circumstances, but it did change *my* behavior and often worsened situations. Why be upset at something I could not control? I did not have to accept or agree with a person's every action to accept that person.

Now when I hear something from a family member or coworker that clashes with my values and unsettles me—such as, "Kids don't need to have rules until they are twelve"—I take a tip from author Lori Deschene and "practice the pause." For example, I might stop and take a sip of water to give myself time to think. This helps me to slow myself down and refrain from jumping to conclusions. When I do this, I can observe family members instead of evaluating them, support a need instead of picking a side, and be empathetic even when I do not understand why a family member is doing something. It took a lot of weight off me to realize I didn't need to agree with family members, only support them.

CASE STUDY #3: AGREEING WITH VERSUS SUPPORTING A FAMILY

To illustrate this point, let's go back in time to 2005. I was working as a therapist then, and I provided treatment and support to children and families as a home visitor. One of these children was a little girl whom I'll call Sarah, whose behavior was . . . how can I say this delicately . . . out of control! I struggled to get this child to concentrate on any task for more than a second. In search of a cause, I inquired with Sarah's mother, whom I'll call Aimee, about Sarah's sleep routine. Aimee responded that Sarah's routine consisted of no routine. Sarah was regularly up until the wee hours of the night, watching TV and going back and forth between her room and her older siblings' room. I talked to Aimee over and over about how to create a bedtime routine for Sarah, to no avail.

As our therapy sessions continued, if we had an appointment in the evening, Aimee would occasionally ask me to stay for dinner. I didn't want to stay. I didn't want to eat. I was so frustrated with both Sarah and Aimee! But I wanted to build a relationship with this family, so I would stay and eat a few bites to be polite and then go on my way. As I continued this practice, I found out that Aimee took great pride in her garden. So did I, so we had some things in common.

After a few months, I began to notice an improvement in Sarah's behavior. When I told Aimee that Sarah's teacher and I were finally seeing our classroom strategies pay off, Aimee stated that she had started implementing a sleep routine with Sarah a few weeks ago, based on the strategies I had shared. I was shocked! I had simply accepted the home situation for what it was, thinking that neither Sarah nor Aimee was ever going to change. I realized that the more conversations Aimee and I had had and the more our relationship had grown, the more I had moved into the circle of people whom Aimee trusted, and she had become willing to try my ideas.

IDENTIFYING YOUR PROFESSIONAL ATTITUDES TOWARD DISCIPLINE

What does *discipline* mean, exactly? The word *discipline* comes from the Latin word *disciplina*, which means "instruction" or "teaching." This concept differs from many traditional ideas about discipline, which focus on punishing children when they behave in unacceptable ways. By contrast, *positive discipline* focuses on strategies designed to guide children and teach them acceptable ways to behave.

EXERCISE #4: YOUR PROFESSIONAL ATTITUDES TOWARD CRYING

On a sheet of paper, answer these questions:

- How do you typically respond when children cry? Do you want to respond that way?
- What is your level of tolerance for crying? Does crying hit a nerve for you? What about for other members of your team?
- Do you worry about spoiling children by picking them up each time they cry?
- Do you worry about not meeting other children's needs because your time is taken up with one child who tends to cry?
- Think back to your responses in Exercise #1: Your History with Crying and Tantrums in chapter 2. How does your response to crying correspond to your own upbringing?
- Does that response change from your personal life to your professional life? Why?
- Does your response to crying align with professional codes of ethics, frameworks, or quality rating systems?
- Does your response to crying align with your curriculum? Is your curriculum research based?
- Does the time of day or day of the week affect your response to crying?
- Does crying trigger negativity in you?
- Do you have a positive relationship with crying?
- Are there stressful conditions in your work environment that are not conducive to properly responding to crying?
- How can lesson planning help you respond to crying?

CASE STUDY #3: MY PROFESSIONAL ATTITUDES TOWARD CRYING

I have already mentioned my inconsistent responses to my own children's tears, but interestingly, my approach as an educator is very different. During my years as a teacher and as a therapist, I had a high tolerance for crying children, regardless of what was going on in my life or what time of day it was. I like to call it the OPK (other people's kids) effect. When working with OPKs, I would typically respond to crying calmly, repeating, "It's okay—you're going to be all right," giving gentle touches, and even holding a child on my hip if he was small enough. I was so unfazed by crying that other teachers would bring their inconsolable students to my classroom.

HOW MY ATTITUDES TOWARD CRYING AFFECTED MY PROFESSIONAL PRACTICE

I was once asked to support a preschool teacher (whom I'll call Bahar) who had a child in her class who would not stop crying (whom I'll call Ciara). The crying started each morning with the daily drop-off, and not only did Ciara have difficulty with this separation, but so did her mother (whom I'll call Ellen). Ellen would linger for so long, uncertain whether she should leave, that it seemed to put Ciara in a state from which she could not recover.

When I asked Bahar what her goal was for Ciara, Bahar responded that it was for Ciara to "stop it." As you know, I have a high tolerance for crying, but I could see how frustrated Bahar—who was wonderful with Ciara, by the way—was feeling. I gently reminded Bahar that "stop it" was not on her list of teaching goals for children's learning and development. According to her program's curriculum and assessment system, the learning goal that applied to this situation was for Ciara to effectively manage separations and engage in positive relationships with caregivers. Those were the skills that Ciara needed our help to learn.

To support Ciara (and Ellen) with these goals, Bahar and I came up with several strategies. First, Bahar asked Ellen to bring in a photo of herself. Bahar had previously created a visual schedule for her classroom's daily routine, and she added the photo of Ellen to the schedule. At each transition, Ciara moved the photo down to the next activity. This technique helped her understand how much longer it would be until she would see her mother again. To teach Ciara the skills she needed, Bahar created a song to the tune of "If You're Happy and You Know It": "If you're sad and you know it, dry your eyes. . . . If you're sad and you know it, hold my hand," and so on, listing a different strategy for dealing with sadness in each verse. (Adaptations of "If You're Happy and You Know It" are especially useful for teaching children appropriate behaviors. We will discuss more ways to use this tool in later chapters.)

EXERCISE #5: YOUR ATTITUDES TOWARD AGGRESSION

On a sheet of paper, answer these questions:

- How do you typically respond when children demonstrate physical or verbal aggression (PVA)? Do you want to respond that way?

- What is your level of tolerance for PVA? Does PVA hit a nerve for you? What about for other members of your team?

- Think back to your responses in Exercise #2: Your History with Aggression in chapter 2. How does your response to PVA correspond to your own upbringing?

- Does that response change from your personal life to your professional life? Why?

- Does your response to PVA align with professional codes of ethics, frameworks, or quality rating systems?

- Does your response to PVA align with your curriculum? Is your curriculum research based?

- Does the time of day or day of the week affect your response?

- Does PVA trigger negativity in you?

- Do you have a positive relationship with PVA?

- Are there stressful conditions in your work environment that are not conducive to properly responding to PVA?

- How can lesson planning help you respond to PVA?

CASE STUDY #4: MY PROFESSIONAL ATTITUDES TOWARD AGGRESSIVE PLAY

When I first began my career as a teacher, I was determined not to allow any aggressive play under my watch. So I started out with a rule against playing "guns" or "fighting" in my classroom. No discussion. End of story. But after the birth of my son, I realized that this type of play had more to do with saving people than with hurting them. Later, based on my experience at my son's school, I realized that I didn't want to shame children for acting out all elements of their experiences, and I didn't want to put limits on their imaginations or play themes. After all, playing "house" can lead down some dark roads as well (remember, children notice—and share with their teachers—much more than we think), but I didn't limit that type of play.

HOW MY PROFESSIONAL ATTITUDES TOWARD AGGRESSIVE PLAY AFFECTED MY PROFESSIONAL PRACTICE

Instead of stifling types of play I wasn't comfortable with, I began to pull these types of play into positive directions when I saw things heading somewhere unsafe or unsuitable for young children. If the children played cops and robbers and started "shooting," I would ask the children what other things police do, or I would start a conversation about all the community helpers who mend hurt people. If the children played ninjas and began "karate fighting," I would start a dialogue about the people of Japan and bring out a map. Play wrestling led to discussions about the shiny belts that the winners wear. Even when the children pretended to be flesh-eating zombies, I was unfazed and moved the discussion toward types of food we actually eat or toward dental care. Play is the perfect opportunity to explore and understand all types of people and concepts in the world.

Spoiler alert: children play! My son helped me realize that play explores a wide variety of situations and emotions, whether they are real or imagined. As a teacher, I had to become comfortable with, plan for, and have positive responses to all types of play. Aggressive play is now a signal to me that I should move close to the children and provide suggestions to expand the play in positive directions rather than shut it down. When play becomes aggressive, it is also a good time to ask questions. Sometimes children engage in aggressive play because they have witnessed some type of violence, need mental-health services, or are being exposed to violent media. Each "pshoo-pshoo" is an important opportunity to talk about peaceful ways to solve problems and to help children make sense of and process what they may have witnessed in real life or on TV.

CASE STUDY #5: MASON AND JAMIA

During my time as a preschool teacher, I particularly struggled with a certain child in one of my classes (previously mentioned in chapter 1), whom I'll call Mason. I had seen aggressive behaviors before, but this was different. Mason repeatedly bit a girl whom I'll call Jamia—the sweetest, smallest, friendliest child in the classroom—for no apparent reason. The more it happened, the more I disliked Mason. Because nobody ever asked me what I thought and it is not socially acceptable to call a three-year-old a serial killer, I bottled up my feelings and followed the advice of my administrator and our outside consultant to try to stop the biting. But, as I mentioned earlier, no strategy worked, and the situation climaxed with Jamia in the hospital and a lot of angry parents at the school.

HOW MASON AND JAMIA AFFECTED MY PROFESSIONAL PRACTICE

It was not until several weeks after this incident, when I learned that Mason had post-traumatic stress disorder, that I finally stopped being angry at him. Instead of wondering what was wrong with him, I wondered what had happened to him to affect him so deeply. As it turned out, Mason had witnessed repeated domestic violence. I had known that his mother was in treatment for drug addiction, but since she was recovering, I had not considered how the past was still influencing Mason's present.

In the context of his experiences, Mason's behavior finally made sense. In his mind, it kept him safe to bite anyone who came near him. He did not know another way to respond, even in a new, safe environment with children his age. And because sweet little Jamia was the only child who kept trying to be Mason's friend—and therefore kept coming close to him—he kept biting her.

Once I changed my thinking and began to feel empathy for Mason, I realized that I needed to change my approach to interacting with him. I began staying close to him and warning him when someone came near so that he would not feel threatened. I learned that forcing Mason to look in my face or make eye contact would cause him to escalate his behavior and injure me. Instead, when I needed to talk to him, I would bend down to his level and approach him from the side or even speak softly in his ear from behind. Before my realization, it had seemed like a ridiculous waste of time to use trays or painter's tape to define space and make sure Mason had enough room. Now I saw these activities as essential strategies. And as I changed my approach, Mason changed his behavior.

Mason and Jamia teach us several critical lessons:

1. As adults, we have to process negative feelings in healthy ways, or our anger will grow and resentment will develop. It is normal to feel upset with children who have challenging behaviors, but we cannot stay upset. Anger and resentment are like roadblocks that hinder our higher-order thinking and problem solving. If you do not have a positive relationship with a child, no strategy will work.

2. Always look past what is happening to see *why* it is happening, and accept that the why might not fit into your current logic or experiences. I never experienced this type of aggression as a young child myself, so when I see it in young children now, I always wonder what they could be experiencing outside of school.

3. Dealing with aggressive behaviors is somewhat like taking a Rorschach test. In this test, a psychologist holds up an abstract inkblot, asks the patient what he sees, and determines the patient's emotional functioning based on his answers. In my case, the way I saw the situation with

Mason affected my social and emotional responses to his behavior. My perceptions influenced how I evaluated possible interventions ("a waste of time" versus "essential") and how I carried them out. As a result, Mason's functioning was only as good as mine.

4. If tiny little Jamia could keep trying, so can I. Ever since then, I have always striven to emulate the spirit of that sweet, small, friendly child.

Cleaning Up Your Act

By now, you've probably realized that your students are not the only ones who need to unlearn some behaviors. As long as your own unhelpful behaviors hold you back, you will not be able to help the children in your care resolve their challenging behaviors. The good news is that now we are going to learn how to clean up these messy situations! Don't worry. The steps to cleaning up your act are much like the steps in doing your laundry.

ADULT BEHAVIOR LAUNDRY LIST

1. Sort out your feelings.
2. Repair rips in your relationship.
3. Figure out the care instructions.
4. Put behaviors in the meaning-making machine.
5. Choose a cycle.
6. Be patient during the trying time.

For now, we are only going to focus on the first three steps in this process. Anyone can do them. (We will examine the other steps in later chapters.)

STEP 1: SORT OUT YOUR FEELINGS

On good days, teaching can be a walk in the park. On other days—well, let's just call it Jurassic Park. On those days, people seem to forget that problem solving is both an intellectual and an emotional enterprise. All too often, too much attention is given exclusively to the intellectual side of the process. When was the last time anyone asked you about your feelings when children in your classroom were acting out their strong feelings? If you're like me, the answer is never!

Remember how cute I am when I smile? Go to that place— because I just bit the kid next to me and ate three blocks.

PUSH PAST IT!

As we have already discovered, personal reactions affect professional actions. Educators not only manage children but also manage the emotions that those children trigger. Interestingly, no one seems to want to acknowledge teachers' emotions outside of a side conversation. But because adult emotions and behavior ride in tandem with and even can predict children's behavior, I propose that those pesky adult emotions should move to the forefront of our discussion.

To achieve balance, all emotions are a needed and necessary part of our lives. Being able to accept and talk about these feelings is healthy. Our built-in tendency to focus on the negative, however, can be a hindrance. When educators, parents, and therapists focus on what is going wrong, they are accessing the most primitive part of the brain, or the emotional brain. As I said earlier, a certain amount of negativity is normal, but if these feelings are allowed to linger in your brain, they can alter your thought process. It is okay to be emotional, but it is not okay to stay emotional. Your first instincts may be your most emotional thoughts, but unfortunately, they are typically not your most logical.

To problem solve, it is important to have a balance between cognition and emotion. Adults who work with and in the best interests of young children have to be able to constrain their emotions, suspend judgments, and make objective decisions. Just because young children are at the mercy of their emotions does not mean that adults should be. So before beginning any strategy for curbing challenging behavior—including reading the rest of this book—it is important to first acknowledge and sort out any negative emotions you feel about a child, a family member, or even your coworkers so that those feelings do not throw your thinking out of balance.

So when a child bounces through the door and you are thinking, "Not today"; when a child is swearing at you like a sailor and calling you every name in the book; when your heart is racing and your body is tense; or when you have a letter of resignation ready in your bag and start thinking, "Start something with me today, and all I have to do is date this letter and turn it in, and you won't have me to push around anymore!"—all that pain and frustration is your signal to push. Push yourself to think of the positives about this child. Push yourself to examine this child's perspective. Push yourself to remember that obscenities may be the only words this child knows to express his feelings. Push yourself to wonder if those awful names are the ones this child is called at home. Push yourself to count to five while you inhale and exhale deeply. And at the end of the day, push yourself to have a good cry, let it all out, and ask for help—because in your heart of hearts, you know that there is no other job for you than this one.

Pushing yourself is never easy! As I taught myself to do it, I often found that I needed to cool down before I could push forward. There are many ways to do this. Some educators recommend breathing deeply, cooling off with a fan, counting to five, having a good cry (outside the classroom), venting to a friend, praying, meditating, eating a snack, or drinking a glass of wine (at home!). I like to call these *cooling-down strategies* because they make you "chill" enough to push yourself when things get too hot.

EXERCISE #6: YOUR COOLING-DOWN STRATEGIES

1. On a piece of paper, draw an outline of a thermometer.

2. Instead of writing numbers along the side of the thermometer, list cooling-down strategies that will help you relax so that you can push yourself when children demonstrate challenging behaviors.

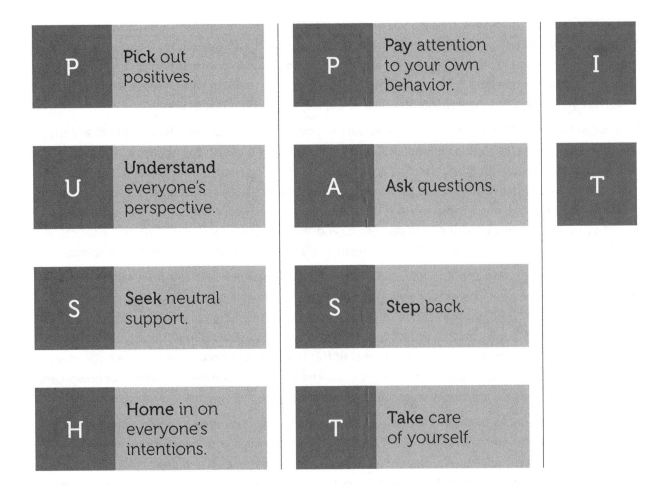

P	Pick out positives.		P	Pay attention to your own behavior.		I
U	Understand everyone's perspective.		A	Ask questions.		T
S	Seek neutral support.		S	Step back.		
H	Home in on everyone's intentions.		T	Take care of yourself.		

PUSH PAST IT

In those moments when you face challenging behaviors, pushing yourself is crucial. But what exactly does *push yourself* mean? It is more than simply forcing yourself to be logical when your emotions want full control, though that is an important element. This is where PUSH PAST It comes in. PUSH PAST It is an acronym for a cognitive process that moves your brain from your initial reaction to a higher level of thinking so you can problem solve.

Keep in mind that PUSH PAST It is not a one-and-done activity! It is a method that you must practice and repeat until it becomes an integrated thought process that you can quickly engage when you encounter challenging behaviors.

EXERCISE #7: PRACTICING PUSH PAST IT

1. Think of a child, family member, or coworker with challenging behaviors. Using the PUSH PAST It Handout in appendix A, write down your negative feelings about that person or those people at the bottom of the page.

2. Go through the process of PUSH PAST It by writing down your applicable thoughts for each letter on the handout:

   • **Pick out positives:** Write at least one positive thing about the child, family member, or coworker.

PUSH PAST IT!

- **Understand everyone's perspective:** Describe the situation from the perspective of the child, family member, or coworker. Be honest with yourself about how the other party probably feels.

- **Seek neutral support:** List the people you have talked to about this situation. Consider whether they are truly neutral or whether they simply echo your own thoughts. If they are not neutral, list some other people who might be more helpful to talk to.

- **Home in on everyone's intentions:** Based on what you wrote down for *U*, write what you think the child, family member, or coworker is trying to accomplish with the challenging behavior. Is the child really out to ruin your day, or is he desperately trying to express a need? Is the family member genuinely trying to harm the child, or do you actually agree with the family member's intentions but not his actions? Is your coworker intentionally being difficult, or is he having a hard time in his personal life? Have you asked any of these people lately how they are doing?

- **Pay attention to your own behavior:** List your physical and emotional reactions to the challenging behavior.

- **Ask questions:** Educators should always respond to challenging behavior with curiosity. Brainstorm questions that could help you find the reason or reasons behind the challenging behavior. Is the child getting nutritious food, adequate sleep, and proper hygiene? Could a family member be upset at a situation rather than at you or be uncooperative because of a bad previous experience with school? Is he taking out unrelated frustrations on you or dealing with difficult life events? Is your coworker stressed out?

- **Step back:** Pause. Take time to really look at this situation and think deeply about it. Write down any insights that come to you.

- **Take care of yourself:** List all the ways that you are taking care of your own mental health.

3. Now look again at the thoughts you wrote at the bottom of the page. Apply logic to those negative statements and rephrase them into positive thoughts, ideas, or questions that can help you work with the child, family member, or coworker. Write the new versions at the top of the page.

Here's an example of how a filled-out handout might look:

- **Negative feelings:** "Jorge is driving me crazy! Every day, I have to deal with him grabbing toys from other children. His parents never answer the phone or return my calls. They're just too lazy to teach him to say *please* and *thank you* and use other basic manners."

- **Pick out positives:** "Jorge has a nice smile. His parents bring him to school, so they must value education."

- **Understand everyone's perspective:** "Jorge is likely feeling confused or scared because he's new to our school. His family just moved and both parents have new jobs, so they're probably overwhelmed."

- **Seek neutral support:** "My coteacher listens and gives me encouragement, but Jorge is driving him crazy too. Maybe I should talk to my director for some neutral ideas."

- **Home in on everyone's intentions:** "Is Jorge just being selfish when he grabs toys from others, or is he trying to communicate something that he can't yet verbalize? Do his parents really not care whether he has good manners, or do we just not agree on what good manners are or when children should learn them?"

- **Pay attention to your own behavior:** "When Jorge grabs toys from other children, my heart beats fast, and I feel anxious."

- **Ask questions:** "What could be going on in Jorge's life and in his parents' lives to make them act this way? Is Jorge upset because he had to leave a familiar school? Are his parents ignoring my calls because they feel too busy to deal with one more situation?"

- **Step back:** "Now that I think about it, Jorge's sleep schedule might be out of whack because he's not used to his new bedroom yet."

- **Take care of yourself:** "As much as I can, I do my lesson planning at school so I don't have to think about it at home. I go for a walk every day after dinner. I make plans with friends each weekend so I have something to look forward to."

When you rephrase your original negative thoughts in the balloons at the top of the handout, they might look something like this:

- "Jorge is driving me crazy!"
  - ➔ "This is a tough situation, but I want what's best for Jorge."
- "Every day, I have to deal with him grabbing toys from other children."
  - ➔ "He's only three. He doesn't know how to share yet."
- "His parents never answer the phone or return my calls."
  - ➔ "I'll keep trying and figure out how to effectively communicate with this family."
- "They're just too lazy to teach him to say *please* and *thank you* and use other basic manners."
  - ➔ "I wonder what this family's home life is like."

STEP 2: REPAIR RIPS IN YOUR RELATIONSHIP

Don't you hate it when you discover a tiny hole in your best jeans or a tear in the seam of a favorite T-shirt? If you don't do anything about it, the damage can become even worse after the garment goes through the washer and dryer a few times. Relationships with the children in your care are like fabric: they have some flexibility, but under too much stress, such as when most of your interactions involve challenging behaviors and punishments, they can rip. Your relationship with an individual child will undergo even more stress as you help him eliminate his challenging behaviors, so before you attempt any strategies to modify his behavior, you need to first repair the relationship.

CASE STUDY #6: WARM-FUZZY FIASCO

Many years ago, I was consulting with a preschool teacher whom I'll call Deja. She stated that one child in her class, whom I'll call Ryder, hit and kicked other children and teachers and refused to listen. I asked when the behavior had started, and Deja stated, "It happens every day, starting as soon as Ryder walks in." As we talked about the situation, I learned that Ryder's temperament made him active and eager to engage with new people. He could have strong negative emotions but also strong positive ones.

One of the consultants on my team, whom I'll call Lucille, went to Deja's classroom to model what we called the warm-fuzzy strategy, a technique used to build strong teacher-student relationships. When Ryder came in, Lucille praised him for walking into the room properly and gave him a piece of cotton (a warm fuzzy). Ryder smiled and responded positively. Lucille asked Ryder if he could behave at breakfast and said that if he did, she would give him another warm fuzzy. This type of exchange repeated throughout the day, and by the end of the day, Ryder had so many warm fuzzies that he needed a small bag to hold them all. None of his challenging behaviors occurred that day.

Deja was so excited! She couldn't wait to try this strategy herself. She went home and even colored her warm fuzzies and made a special bag for them.

The next day, Lucille watched as Deja praised Ryder for walking in so nicely and eagerly gave him a warm fuzzy. Ryder looked at the warm fuzzy, dropped it, stepped on it, spit on it, and ran away. Deja cried, "What am I doing wrong?" Lucille later told me that at that moment, she realized that Deja had a conflictual relationship with Ryder. Given the fate of the wet, flattened warm fuzzy, Lucille and I knew that no strategy Deja tried would change Ryder's challenging behaviors until the teacher-student relationship was repaired.

Deja spent the next two weeks working on her relationship with Ryder. She greeted him at the door, diligently played with him, stayed close to him (he was still hitting, mind you), and tried to get to know him better before trying the warm-fuzzy strategy again. Ryder's behavior was an ongoing challenge, but Deja's story reminds us how important it is to repair your relationship with a child before trying to change the child's behavior.

WHY YOUR RELATIONSHIP WITH THE CHILD IS CRUCIAL

Research shows that Deja's struggle is not unique. An analysis by Gregory Marchant, Sharon Paulson, and Barbara Rothlisberg demonstrates that supportive social environments and relationships with teachers predict higher levels of student motivation and achievement. Another study by June Zuckerman suggests relationship building as a strategy to help chronically disruptive students. A study by Pamela Garner and her colleagues shows that warm and supportive teachers are associated with improved student learning outcomes. Conversely, Pervin Demirkaya and Hatice Bakkaloglu point out that in preschoolers, problem behaviors tend to foretell conflicted relationships between students and teachers. To make things even harder, problem behaviors also negatively affect these relationships. No wonder the cycle of challenging behavior is difficult to break!

If you are reading this book, your relationship with a child has probably sustained some damage. So how do you go about repairing that relationship? According to research by John Gottman and Robert Levenson, there is a crucial ratio of positive and negative moments in strong relationships: five positive interactions for every negative interaction. Those relationships are the foundation on which strategies for addressing challenging behaviors can stand.

To build such a foundation, commit yourself to spending two consecutive minutes per day with that child for two weeks. During each session, connect with the child in positive ways. (It often helps to plan these interactions in advance. See appendix B for a useful planning sheet.) For example, point out what the child is doing right. Talk with him and call him by name. Make eye contact. Play with him. Ask him to help you. Read to him. Hug him. Let him choose which activity to do first. Let him tell you about his interests. Tell a joke and laugh with him. Sit with him at lunch or snack. Let him choose an activity that you can do together. Each of these acts, along with others that you come up with, is another "stitch" to close the holes in your relationship.

When mending a garment, have you ever pricked yourself with a needle or cut yourself with scissors? Just as in Deja's story, it may hurt deeply if your kindness is not well received by a child at first. Keep trying. You might need to start with a simple "safety-pin" strategy—just staying close to the child to keep everyone safe. As you spend time with the child, not only do you "stitch up" the damage, but you also make "alterations" to your relationship as you open up new perspectives and close down negative thoughts.

CASE STUDY #7: THE PAPER-CLIP CHALLENGE

Now, I know that some of you are raising your eyebrows. You are not alone. When I recently shared these ideas with a teacher whom I'll call Linh, she was flabbergasted. "Spend more time with this child?" she said. "Are you kidding? This child already takes up all my time!" But when I asked Linh to reflect on the type of time she spent with this child (whom I'll call Kelly), she realized that all her time with Kelly was spent redirecting Kelly. It wasn't the positive, relationship-repairing type of time that Kelly needed.

To stay positive, Linh implemented an unusual strategy based on a technique described by self-improvement author James Clear. She put ten paper clips on her collar first thing in the morning as a tangible way to measure her level of positivity. Each time she said something negative to Kelly (such as, "Kelly, no," "No, thank you, Kelly," or "Don't do that, Kelly!"), she took off a paper clip. On the first day, Linh had no paper clips left by 9 a.m.! She realized how negative she was being and knew she had to repair her relationship with this child.

Linh started by changing how she talked to Kelly. Instead of saying no, Linh tried reframing her words as a question, such as, "Is that what you should be doing?" or "What is the rule?" These questions not only helped Linh be more positive, but they also helped her increase her level of instructional supports because she was now both guiding behavior *and* prompting Kelly to build her thinking skills.

Linh learned that what she put into Kelly was what she got out of Kelly. Instead of saying, "No, thank you," Linh began telling Kelly what *to* do: "Walk," "Be gentle," "That chair is for sitting," and so on. As a result, Linh was shocked to realize that Kelly was better able to comprehend her directions. Linh also noticed that when she used a larger variety of words, so did Kelly.

Once Linh had repaired the relationship and her strategies began to work more effectively, she realized that she suddenly had more time to do other things in the classroom. You see, everyone has twenty-four hours in a day. But it is how you intentionally use that time that helps you become more effective.

STEP 3: FIGURE OUT THE CARE INSTRUCTIONS

Before you wash any garment, you need to read the tag inside it that details the care instructions for that item. Is it hand-wash or dry-clean only, or can you simply toss it in the washer? Does it need pretreatment to keep the colors from bleeding? Can it go in the dryer? If you disregard the instructions and follow your own plan, you may still end up with a clean item—but it might no longer be its original color or size. And those clothes are no fun to wear (accidental pink socks, anyone?).

In the same vein, educators must take time to look inside a child with challenging behavior to know how to care for him. What are his strengths? What are his interests? This information can guide you to the most effective strategies for helping the child change his behavior. (We'll learn more about choosing strategies in later chapters.)

CASE STUDY #8: FIGURING OUT CARLOS'S CARE INSTRUCTIONS

While working as a consultant, I assisted a teacher whom I'll call Emma, who had great concerns about a child whom I'll call Carlos. Carlos was withdrawn. He rarely, if ever, talked and was very shy. Emma wasn't sure what he knew or how to assess him.

The first question I asked was, "What does Carlos like?" Emma stated that every day he wore a shirt with John Cena, the wrestler, on it. She wasn't sure if Carlos had a closet full of these shirts or if his mother was handier with the wash than those happy housewives from the 1950s. "But I can't use that!" Emma said. "I don't want to encourage wrestling in my classroom."

I suggested that we use Carlos's interest in a positive way to help him build his self-help skills. I copied pictures of John Cena (with clothes on!), and Emma placed them in the dramatic-play area with the dress-up clothes. The result was amazing. Carlos was so excited to see his favorite wrestler that he began to talk. As he began to open up more and more, it turned out that he could add and subtract well beyond his years.

Wrapping Up

In all honesty, I am still growing as a professional. My logic and my emotions are in constant debate. The skills associated with PUSH PAST It and cleaning up one's act are easy to describe, but that does not mean that they are easy to implement—even for me. I have found that working through challenging behaviors involves just as much working on my professional self as it involves working on children. However, each challenging experience has helped me strengthen my skills in PUSH PAST It, cleaning up my act, and more. In turn, my improved skills have helped me better navigate later sticky situations.

As a professional, your effectiveness depends heavily on the quality of your relationships and on your level of reflectiveness. The PUSH PAST It technique provides a reflective space between you and your emotions, freeing up room in your brain for new strategies and other perspectives. By cleaning up your act, you can repair your relationships with children and lay the foundation for implementing strategies that will help these children change their behavior.

CHAPTER 4

Working with Family Members

CHILD: I'm going to tell my momma and daddy on you!

ME: ~~If your momma and daddy were so smart, they woul-~~

~~Tell yo' momma *and* yo' daddy—in fact, give me that phone so I can tell them mys-~~

~~Your momma and daddy don't run this clas-~~

~~Don't [clap] let [clap] this preschool demeanor fool you! I am from the same hood you fr-~~

I would love to talk to your wonderful family!

Can you relate?

It can be hard to work with family members during difficult situations with children. Sometimes family members display behaviors that are just as challenging as their children's! However, it is not in the best interests of any child to have her family members and her other caregivers in conflictual relationships. This chapter explores how to manage your feelings about family members, how to communicate effectively even when family members have challenging behaviors, and what to do when family members refuse to or cannot help you address their child's behavior.

EXERCISE #1: FAMILY-MEMBER BEHAVIORS AND YOUR FEELINGS

1. Take a piece of paper and divide it into three columns.

2. In the first column, list all the things family members do and say that drive you crazy.

3. In the second column, write down how these behaviors make you feel.

4. For now, leave the third column blank.

Using PUSH PAST It for Family Members

As Exercise #1 illustrates, just as when we encounter challenging behaviors in children, our first thoughts about family members with challenging behaviors are usually our most emotional thoughts, not our most logical. If your emotions are running high after completing Exercise #1, try some of the cooling-down strategies you listed in chapter 3 before you continue reading.

For some educators, difficult interactions with family members cause even more frustration, anger, and pain than difficult interactions with children. It can be very liberating to release all your negative feelings about an entire family by filling out the PUSH PAST It Handout (see appendix A) for that family. For this use of the handout, consider these statements and questions:

- **Pick out positives:** People are more than their problems, and every family has something positive to offer.

- **Understand everyone's perspective:** You might know that it is impossible for you to take a thirteen-month-old to the bathroom every hour (yes, family members have asked me to do that) when you have a whole classroom of toddlers under your care, but that child's family members may not have experience in a busy classroom. If family members ask their child, "Is your teacher lying?" the question may be a reflection not on you but on a previous teacher who did not seek the child's best interests. Family members might drag their feet on filling out paperwork because they are uncertain about what you will do with the information or are embarrassed about their own struggles with literacy.

- **Seek neutral support:** Don't we all have that coworker who is super supportive? When we share our problems, she showers us with phrases such as, "That family are the crazy ones, not you!" and "Are you serious?" Yes, it feels good to be affirmed, and we often bond through these moments, but do those statements really help us solve problems? You can vent to your coworkers if you desire, but also counsel with a neutral party, someone who will not pick sides and will help you gain a more balanced perspective.

- **Home in on everyone's intentions:** Are these family members trying to become your archenemies? Even though it may feel this way, most family members just want the best for their children. Because we as educators also want the best for children, we and family members usually have the same intentions. We just pursue them in different ways.

- **Pay attention to your own behavior:** What is your body language when you speak to family members? What is your tone? It is not always about *what* you say, but it is always about *how* you say it.

- **Ask questions:** What might this family be going through? Is everything okay at work? Is a family member sick? Are family members in conflict? Are they reacting in a certain way because of their own experiences with school?
- **Step back:** Sometimes taking a step back helps you to respond instead of react. An intentional pause creates time and space for thoughtful consideration so that insights can come to you.
- **Take care of yourself:** Sometimes we stress ourselves out about things we cannot control. Family members are one of those things. Instead of trying to control family members, focus on connecting with them.

Recall that PUSH PAST It is a constant process, not a one-and-done exercise, so you may need to repeat this activity every so often for a particular family.

CASE STUDY #1: "THE SPOILED KID"

I once worked with a group of teachers who all had conflicts with a particular child, whom I'll call Addison. They had labeled her "the spoiled kid" because her mother (whom I'll call Hanna) gave in to whatever Addison wanted, such as buying her toys whenever she demanded them. While I did not approve of the nickname, I understood the teachers' frustration, as Addison would throw tantrums when she did not get her way in the classroom.

Weeks later, during a home visit, a social worker learned that Hanna had been abused as a child and was trying to break the pattern of abuse for Addison. As soon as we heard this story, the teachers and I realized why Addison was "spoiled." Now that we understood Hanna's intentions, we were better able to support this family. We gave Hanna suggestions for ways to show love and support other than simply giving in to Addison's demands. These new strategies helped Hanna break the pattern of abuse by learning healthy ways to both show love to Addison *and* teach her how to behave appropriately. In turn, this process helped Addison change her behavior. But family members should not have to disclose something so personal for educators to employ empathy.

CASE STUDY #2: SOMETIMES YOU CAN ONLY LET GO

At one of my workshops, a teacher whom I'll call Mariana expressed frustration because the mother of one of her students did not have any rules in her home. As a result, the child struggled with following classroom rules, and Mariana wondered how she could tell the mother to establish some home rules. I reminded Mariana that her responsibility was not to tell the mother what to do but to find out whether the mother even had the capacity to try new ideas. Sometimes parents are not ready to accept suggestions, especially if they already feel overwhelmed. In these cases, all educators can do is let go of what they cannot control and focus on what they *can* do.

EXERCISE #2: FROM CHALLENGES TO HOPE

1. Retrieve the chart that you started to fill out in Exercise #1.
2. In the third column, reframe the items from the second column into positive thoughts that can help you work with family members. This is similar to what you did on the PUSH PAST It handout, but now you are thinking about all families instead of one particular family.

Here are some examples:

- "Why are you calling me a liar?"
  - → "I wonder how I can build trust between us."
- "This family is crazy!"
  - → "This family must be struggling."
- "This parent is in denial."
  - → "My role is not to get parents out of denial but to support them when they are going through it."

Some Commonly Misinterpreted Family-Member Behaviors

Before I had children of my own, I often felt frustrated by certain behaviors among the family members of my students. To me, these actions seemed careless at best and downright rude at worst. Didn't these people care? Or were they trying to make my life difficult? However, as my own experience as a parent illustrates, there is often another side to challenging family-member behaviors—one that has nothing to do with apathy or malice.

TARDINESS

When I was a teacher, I often reminded family members to bring their children to school by 9 a.m. Otherwise, I would have to disrupt circle time to greet late children and family members, get breakfast for these children, and get them adjusted into the classroom. All of this would really frustrate me. Why couldn't these family members handle something as simple as getting their children to school on time?

Then I had my own children.

To be precise, my husband, Reginald, and I have four children. In 1995, when our oldest was born, I thought I would have the whole parenting thing in the bag. I had years of experience as a teacher, degrees in education and child development, and a specialization in infant studies. But by 1998, Reginald and I had three children under the age of five, and as a result, I don't remember anything from 1995 to 2002. Reginald and I call them the lost years. People ask us things such as, "Don't you remember that movie?" or "Do you remember that TV show?" and we say no. Repeatedly. If it wasn't on public television, we missed it. My memories of this time are a hazy blur of crying, snot bubbles, and little people screaming, "I want the blue cup, not the red cup!" And sick children. All. The. Time. In fact, a study by Carrie Byington and her colleagues shows that families with four children have at least one family member with a virus for *58 percent of the year.* (That statistic goes out to all my colleagues who thought I was lying when I said my kids were sick.)

Yet recurring sickness was only part of the problem. Constant sleep deprivation left Reginald and me exhausted. Add on the struggle to get our children to brush their teeth and put on their clothes each morning, and the daily routine was sometimes so daunting that I thought our family would never be on time to anything again. But to my surprise, this early-morning chaos eventually turned into calm as our children developed language, fine-motor, and social and emotional skills. Today, all four of our children are very punctual.

Until I became a parent, I didn't realize how hard it is for a young family just to get out the door every morning. I now know that it can take years for a family to establish routines, discipline strategies, and relationships. Not only are young children developing their immune systems, but they are also learning motor skills, the concept of time, the ability to see someone else's point of view, and more—all of which can slow down the morning routine. So now I help educators and family members understand that young children's behavior is a reflection of age and development, not a reflection of child-rearing abilities or a sign of how children will behave as adults. And I applaud family members for getting their children to school at any time of the day.

NEGLECTED NEWSLETTERS AND PROJECTS

As a teacher, I used to feel very insulted when I would see my precious newsletters squished at the bottoms of children's bags or art projects crushed beyond recognition. I had worked hard on those things—and in the case of art projects, so had the children! Why couldn't their family members take care of such important objects?

Then I became a parent.

With four children, our house often seemed to be floating in a sea of mostly white school papers. Reginald and I were often overwhelmed by all the permission slips, flyers, notes, and more. Some papers had bright colors, which I initially thought might indicate what kind of information was on them—pink for notices about sickness? green if we owed money to the school?—but there was no method to the madness. And do you know how many art projects four children can accumulate in a week? We could only fit so many toothpick-and-marshmallow sculptures in our house. Something had to go. As a result, many an art project got flattened at the bottom of a bag (preserving them on the way home from school was not exactly a high priority), and countless newsletters ended up in the trash without being read.

These experiences taught me that ignored flyers and destroyed artwork typically signaled a lack of time and space, not a lack of caring, on the part of family members. To make sure that any important information still made it home, I verbally told family members about it, posted it on a dry-erase board, and stuck little reminders in children's cubbies. As for the art projects, I stopped taking it personally.

WHAT'S THE RUSH?

There were no cell phones when I was a teacher, but even at that time, family members still seemed in a rush to drop off their children and in a rush to leave. How rude! Even if they had to hurry off to work, couldn't they at least say hello or ask how their children were doing in class? I could not understand it.

Until I had children myself.

Once our children were old enough to attend school, I usually dropped them off each day, but on one particular day, my husband had to do it. Later that day, I asked him how the drop-off had gone. He said, "Fine." Not wanting to miss a detail of our children's lives, I pushed him to share specifics—and then I realized in horror that there were none. He had just dropped the children off without talking to any of their teachers and raced out of there!

Appalled, I asked, "Why did you do that?"

Reginald answered, "I felt really uncomfortable around all those little tiny chairs and tables. And, to put it bluntly, I didn't have good experiences with teachers as a kid, so I feel awkward around them. I couldn't get out of there quick enough."

I was blown away hearing all of this. But as I thought about it, things began to make sense. Reginald is 6'5", so all that small furniture—which felt completely comfortable to me—must have seemed very uncomfortable to him. I am a teacher, so I had always felt right at home speaking with my children's teachers. But given Reginald's history, no wonder he had no interest in such conversations.

It had never occurred to me that the reasons family members rushed out of my classroom had nothing at all to do with rudeness or with me but a great deal to do with their comfort levels and personal histories. After hearing Reginald's story, I realized that my classroom setup told everyone, "This is a place for small children only." If we want family members to stay in our classrooms and talk to us, we have to have spaces that are inviting for them. I recommend that every classroom have a comfortable adult-sized chair where family members can sit. In my own classroom, I also placed baskets full of useful items, such as takeout menus for local restaurants, coupons, and train schedules, near my parent sign-in sheet. When family members had something to stay for, I learned, they would stay in the room longer and talk to me.

Communicating

Even though we often think we know what family members are thinking ("They just don't want to admit that there's a problem"), there is no way to truly know anyone's inner thoughts without communication. Healthy communication seeks to help both parties connect to and understand (not control) one another. It is important to have regular communication with family members and build strong relationships from the beginning. Even if you do not have this type of connection before a challenging behavior arises, you can still successfully communicate with family members about the behavior. If you seek support from your colleagues, put yourself in family members' shoes, think about their individual strengths, and try to learn more about their needs, you will be on the road toward meaningful conversations.

GENERAL TIPS

ACKNOWLEDGE FAMILY MEMBERS' STRENGTHS

You may have heard of the trick of starting a conversation with a strength. If you begin conferences with family members by mentioning a child's positive attributes, you are already using this strategy. Wonderful! But have you ever considered starting with an observation of a family member's strength? For example, you could say, "I noticed that Shanice comes to school every day! You must really value education." This technique can help you begin building trust with family members right away.

ASK BEFORE YOU TELL

Before you do any telling about a child's behavior, you need to do some asking. Use questions to sandwich information so family members do not feel that you are simply lecturing them.

- Start with a question to open up dialogue. You might ask, for instance, "What do you already know about separation anxiety?" or "What have you noticed about Bobby at home?"

- During the conversation, listen without judging whether what family members are saying is right or wrong. When it is your turn to talk, focus on making objective, fact-based statements. For example, instead of saying, "Bobby is clingy and was sad all day," state specifically what you saw him do and heard him say: "I noticed that Bobby screamed several times today and stayed close to his teachers."

- End with a question that keeps the dialogue open: "What are you thinking about the information I've shared with you?"

AVOID GIVING UNSOLICITED ADVICE

Before offering suggestions, ask family members whether they would like your advice: "Do you need ideas about this? I have some." This way, family members feel that they have a choice in the matter, and you are not forcing information on people who are not ready for it. If family members are unsure of what they need, present a menu of options: "Well, what do you need right now—advice? to ask questions? a hug?" Here are some more ideas you could offer:

- Advice from another professional, such as a pediatrician or a speech therapist
- Advice from other families who have experienced the same issue
- Time to process the information, with follow-up at a later date
- Referral to a support group for people who are dealing with the same issue
- A listening ear

COMMUNICATION CONUNDRUMS

As hard as you try to have good relationships with your students' family members, you and they will not always see eye to eye. When you find yourself in a sticky situation with a family member, use these questions and tips to help you keep communication flowing as you work through the difficulties:

- **What is your own perspective on the conflict?** What do you believe? Why do you believe this? Are your ideas grounded in research about children and families? Are your ideas facts or simply your own thoughts?

- **What is the family member's perspective?** Do you correctly understand the family member's belief? What is the context for that belief (past experiences, culture, temperament, historical factors, and so on)? Are you accepting of—though not necessarily condoning—all beliefs? As mentioned before, ask open-ended questions to make sure you understand, such as, "Tell me about Zion's sleep schedule," "What do you already know about how children adjust to new situations?" or "What would you like to see happen with Erika when you drop her off each day?". As family members explain their viewpoints, listen without judgment about whether what they are saying is right or wrong.

- **Validate the family member's beliefs.** Unless a child is in danger, it is not your responsibility to tell a family member what to do or how to think about something. Affirm the family member's ideas and wishes: "I see why this is important to you." Consider the family member's intentions—even if her actions are not evidence based, is her intention to help the child?

- **Look for common ground.** A family member and I may disagree about spanking a child, for example, but in the end, we both want to instill discipline in that child. Sometimes even if we disagree, we can find common ground to build on: love for the child, desire for the child to grow into a well-adjusted adult, and so on.
- **Being effective in working with children means being effective in working with adults.** It is unhealthy for a child to see the adults she cares for in a constantly conflictual relationship. Effective education involves shared decision making with family members.
- **Family members' actions do not always match their values.** I may value healthy eating and still eat pizza and doughnuts. A family member might be disengaged but still value a good education for her child.

In some cases, family members refuse to acknowledge that there is a problem, or they even try to blame you for the issue. When a family member insists, "Well, she doesn't act like that at home," or "It's not my kid—it's you people," you may be tempted to roll your eyes. Don't. Yes, the family member could speak more kindly, but keep in mind that her level of emotion might differ from yours; she may feel a need to defend her child against seemingly unfair accusations. But as educators, our professionalism dictates that we model calm behavior. Also, as you can explain to family members, there are multiple reasons why children might act differently in the home than outside of it.

For one thing, the environment affects children's behavior, and the home environment may not have as many demands, transitions, or people as a school or child-care environment does. For instance, a child might have more challenging behaviors on Mondays because she does not have a regular schedule on weekends and resists coming back into the highly structured classroom environment. While you cannot force that child's family members to create a schedule, you can adjust your schedule. Instead of getting into a power struggle, you might make fewer demands on the child on Mondays and have a cot ready in case she needs an extra nap. After all, if you refuse to change, how can you expect family members to change?

Additionally, part of the issue stems from the fact that the child's self-regulation skills are still developing, or emerging. Children often exhibit emerging skills inconsistently. Critically, Elena Bodrova and Deborah Leong point out that until young children master the abilities to focus their attention, manage their emotions, and control their behavior, they gain control through "other regulation," or adults helping them regulate themselves. Therefore, a child's behavior might look vastly differently based on the adults she is with and the level of support they provide for her emerging skills. You and your fellow educators may have different expectations of and ways of interacting with this child than her family members do, so she might indeed behave differently in each place. In fact, maybe this child's family members are using a strategy at home that might work at your school or center.

In short, if a family member claims that a challenging behavior does not happen at home, believe her. Then figure out what is different at home that could inform your approach to addressing the behavior.

Even if you feel that a family member is in denial, it is not the end of the world. Aren't we all in denial about something? (Come on, forty is not really the new thirty!) Denial is a normal coping mechanism that we all use to deal with change—it is not a sign that the family member does not care about her child. If you do think a family member is lying to save face, that tells you something about your relationship with that person. Work on building trust with her so that you can become her partner in helping the child improve his behavior.

4: Working with Family Members

Sometimes it seems that no matter what you do, family members simply refuse to help you address their children's challenging behaviors. However, I never have met a family member who is thinking, "I can't wait to mess this kid up!" Remember that everyone has complex reasons behind her behavior, and family members are no different. In general, I assume that family members are doing the best they can. Here are some common reasons why family members might be less than helpful in addressing their children's challenging behaviors:

- If family members do not see a behavior at home, they may be skeptical about whether it actually exists in another setting.
- A study by Selma Fraiberg concludes that family members often interact with their children in counterproductive ways because they are unconsciously reenacting their own childhood trauma. Keep in mind how the past might be permeating the present.
- Family members might value education or discipline but struggle with acting on these values (in much the same way as I value a healthy lifestyle but struggle with implementing it regularly).

Let's now examine some of the more complex reasons for a lack of family-member support.

DISAGREEMENT ABOUT WHETHER THE BEHAVIOR IS A PROBLEM

In some cases, family members see no need to address a behavior that you perceive as challenging. They may cite reasons such as, "She's just being a kid," "She'll grow out of it," or "It's not hurting anyone." These attitudes can be frustrating, but they need not defeat you. You do not need to make family members see everything from your perspective. Your goal is to meet family members where they are and build relationships with them from there. As you do so, their understanding of your perspective—including the reasons why you want to address their child's behavior—will grow.

STRUGGLES WITH ADDRESSING THE BEHAVIOR AT HOME

Occasionally, family members feel that they cannot do anything about their children's challenging behaviors. Some family members I have worked with, for instance, live in homes in which they are not the final decision makers. They may want to try new strategies, but they encounter opposition from spouses, partners, or other adults in their households. Alternatively, family members might feel too busy or overwhelmed to deal with the behavior or that the behavior is too entrenched to change.

NOT UNDERSTANDING THE ISSUE

Poor support from family members can often indicate a lack of clarity about the situation. Perhaps a family member does not understand child development or typical behavior and therefore does not recognize the problem. Also consider whether your explanations about challenging behaviors might be confusing. To avoid this problem, use objective statements and avoid terms such as *bad day* or even *good day* when describing behaviors. Instead, state what exactly you saw the child do or heard her say.

To assist all family members—even those whose children do not have challenging behaviors—on an ongoing basis, create classroom or bulletin-board displays with information about social and emotional stages and strategies for addressing common challenges. This practice helps family members understand normal development and offers them ideas to try if an issue arises.

HESITANCY ABOUT NEW IDEAS

Remember, you already have some idea of what to do to address challenging behaviors. You may already have strategies in your toolbox and know professionals in the community who can provide other needed services. But much, if not all, of this information is unfamiliar to family members. Sometimes introducing new ideas or services to family members can be like suggesting a blind date to a skeptical friend:

> TEACHER: I've got someone I want you to meet.
>
> FAMILY MEMBER: What? Who?
>
> TEACHER: The mental-health specialist.
>
> FAMILY MEMBER: *What*? I don't need a mental-health specialist! Are you trying to say my kid has mental issues?
>
> TEACHER: This person is super nice! He can help you with your child! And *girrrrl*, he has services!
>
> FAMILY MEMBER: Look, I don't care how nice he is! I'm not looking for anyone! I don't care what kinds of services he's got! My kid doesn't even have a problem!
>
> TEACHER: But the strategies you've got are no good for you or your child. This guy could really help you!

If family members refuse to acknowledge a problem or to pursue any solutions, give them time to process what you have suggested. I am probably the only person on Earth who still has an AOL account, because that was my first email address and sometimes family members contact me there years later for support. At the extreme end of the spectrum, one of those emails came from family members who were finally moving forward with services ten years after I had first suggested them. Ten years! But no matter how long it takes, I let family members know that I will always be there for them and their children. The point is not to make family members conform to my timeline but to help them along their journey. Whatever that journey is, I will support them through it.

Obviously, if children or family members need classroom strategies or professional services, we would rather not have them wait ten years to accept them! The best way I have found to speed up this process is to connect the family members with other families who have successfully used those services or strategies. It is normal for family members to be skeptical of some service or strategy they have never heard of—this is actually a strength. They will probably have concerns about the proposed strategies and services, so they may appreciate hearing both information about those processes and wisdom from people who have tried them. By helping the new family connect to an experienced family, you provide a powerful support to encourage the new family to follow through with addressing the behavior.

WHEN A FAMILY IS FALLING APART

Once I PUSH PAST my emotions about family members, I often discover that they are not unhelpful by choice—they genuinely cannot help me address their child's challenging behavior. If they could, they would. But they may be lacking in social skills themselves or going through their own crises. Frankly, the most unhelpful family members are frequently the ones in need of the most help themselves.

CASE STUDY #1: A FAMILY IN CRISIS

I will never forget the day when I made a home visit to a family with four children under the age of six: a set of ten-month-old twins, a three-year-old, and a five-year-old. The family lived in a lovely home. However, when the mother (whom I'll call Nia) and I went into the family room, I saw food, clothes, diapers, and toys strewn in all directions. A few minutes later, as Nia and I talked, I was shocked to spot a syrup-logged waffle sliding down a table. I thought, "What is the proper etiquette in this situation? Do I grab the waffle? Or do I pretend not to see it—or the rest of this mess?" Ultimately, I did my best to ignore the waffle, cringing inwardly the whole time.

A few weeks later, when I arrived for another visit, I noticed that Nia not only had to unlock the door but also had to push a large chair from behind it to let me in. When the five-year-old told me how having the chair behind the door would keep her father out, I knew I had to talk to Nia about getting help.

Of course, I thought, "How do I even approach such a sensitive subject with Nia?" In search of ideas, I reflected on a time when I had been in crisis. What would I have needed to calm my fears and encourage me to seek support? I also consulted my colleagues, put myself in Nia's shoes, thought about her individual strengths, and asked her about her needs. Together, all these strategies helped me have a meaningful conversation with Nia, and she did eventually seek help from social-work and mental-health services.

IMPORTANT NOTE

According to *The Neglected Child: How to Recognize, Respond, and Prevent* by Ginger Welch, Laura Wilhelm, and Heather Johnson, educators and child-care providers are legally obligated to report neglect and abuse, even if they only suspect that it is happening. *The Neglected Child* provides excellent guidance and resources for responding to these situations.

Wrapping Up

Remember, your goal is to support children and their families. You do not need to evaluate or agree with family members' choices. The goal of any healthy relationship is not to control family members or even to give them information. It is to understand their perspectives so that you can give them the appropriate supports.

Now that we have processed our feelings about family members, the next leg of our journey involves exploring the differences between developmentally appropriate behavior and challenging behavior. As always, it starts by assessing you.

CHAPTER 5

Developmentally Appropriate Behavior for Children Ages One through Six

Sometimes the issue may not be that a child has a challenging behavior at all. Sometimes the issue is that an adult has an incomplete or inaccurate understanding of how children typically behave at a certain age, also known as *developmentally appropriate behavior*. This chapter will help you "get real" and realistic with your expectations by explaining what developmentally appropriate behavior looks like for children ages one through six and how to interpret behavior as communication.

How Much Do You Know about Developmentally Appropriate Behavior?

Misconceptions about the capacities of young children are common, even among teachers and caregivers. Take this self-assessment to test your knowledge about what young children really can and cannot do.

EXERCISE #1: TEST YOUR KNOWLEDGE OF DEVELOPMENTALLY APPROPRIATE BEHAVIOR

For each statement, write your answer on a sheet of paper. Answer *T* if the statement is true; answer *F* if the statement is false. **Note:** All ages are approximate.

1. T/F Most children fully master the ability to share by age two.
2. T/F Between ages three and four, most children can begin to tolerate being apart from a family member in a familiar environment.
3. T/F By age two, most children can resist the desire to do something that a caregiver has told them not to do.
4. T/F By age eight, most children can see multiple points of view in a conflict.
5. T/F By age three, most children can solve their own social problems.
6. T/F By age five, most children can understand and follow directions with five to six steps.
7. T/F Between ages three and four, most children can use three-to-four-word sentences.

ANALYZING YOUR RESULTS

Here are the answers for the self-assessment:

1. False. According to the report *Tuning In: Parents of Young Children Speak Up about What They Think, Know, and Need* from Zero to Three and the Bezos Family Foundation, children begin to develop sharing skills between ages three and four.
2. True, according to the Government of Western Australia Department of Health
3. False. Zero to Three and the Bezos Family Foundation explain that children learn to resist taking a prohibited action when they are between ages three and a half and four.
4. True, according to "Social and Emotional Growth" by PBS Parents
5. False. "Social Development in Preschoolers" from the American Academy of Pediatrics states that children are just beginning to develop the ability to solve social problems between ages three and four and often need help from an adult.
6. False. According to Johns Hopkins Medicine, five-year-old children can follow directions with three steps (not five or six).
7. True, according to the Raising Children Network (Australia)

How did you do on the exercise? Were you surprised? Are you comfortable with your current level of knowledge about what is developmentally appropriate behavior for young children?

GET REALISTIC ABOUT WHAT CHILDREN CAN DO

Let's now explore exactly what is reasonable and unreasonable to expect from children ages one through six. Before we get started, we need to remember a few key points:

- Like the plot of an action movie, development does go through predictable stages. But children are complex and unique, and some areas of development are easier to observe and understand than others.

- Not all aspects of child development progress at the same rate. For example, the same child could show above-average cognitive development but below-average social-emotional development for his age. Even the most gifted children are not uniformly good at everything.

- Similarly, children with special needs or a history of trauma (see chapter 6) are not uniformly delayed in all abilities. Such a child might be one age chronologically but a lower age developmentally in certain areas. For example, he could be four years old chronologically but show the cognitive development of a two-year-old. Children who have experienced trauma may be so good at changing their behavior to survive different environments that it might take many observations for educators and therapists to understand what these children actually know and can do.

CASE STUDY #1: TEACHING TEACHERS ABOUT EMERGING SKILLS

When our son was in elementary school, Reginald and I once attended a meeting with several of Daniel's teachers. Daniel had been struggling to follow directions at school, and the teachers asked me if he followed directions at home. I said yes. One teacher looked at me empathetically, put her hand gently on mine, smiled, and said, "Of course he does." Then she winked at the other teachers while writing "mom in denial" on her notepad. Ouch!

I had to explain to the teachers that Daniel's skill in following directions was still emerging and that the supports in the home environment helped him exhibit this skill there. He followed directions better in small groups, and his family was naturally a smaller group than his class. Furthermore, I always bent down to Daniel's level when giving him a direction, made sure he made eye contact with me, and required that he repeat back my direction to ensure his comprehension.

Developmentally Appropriate Behaviors for Children Ages One through Six

All too often, we view the behavior of young children through a school-age lens rather than an early childhood lens. These lists of age-appropriate behaviors for children ages one through six are taken from HealthyChildren.org (maintained by the American Academy of Pediatrics), the Centers for Disease Control and Prevention, and "Your Six-Year Old" by PBS Parents. These developmental checklists can act as your very own crystal ball, helping you predict how a child might behave in a given situation so you can plan accordingly. However, the magic only works if you know the children you care for and where they are in their development. As you read these lists, keep in mind the many nuances to an individual child's development: his abilities, his home situation, any stresses or trauma in his life, his temperament, and so on.

ONE-YEAR-OLDS

COGNITIVE DEVELOPMENT

- Find objects even when hidden
- Play two to three minutes with a toy
- Imitate familiar gestures

LANGUAGE DEVELOPMENT

- Babble
- Use single-word sentences, such as, "Mama!"
- Respond to simple requests

A study by Julia Irwin and her colleagues examined how being "late talkers" as toddlers affects children's social skills. Their results show that late-talking children have lower social engagement and compliance and tend to be more withdrawn. It makes sense that language-skill acquisition affects social-skill acquisition. This study shows how developmental domains are interdependent and influence one another.

PHYSICAL DEVELOPMENT

- Walk alone
- Grasp a crayon
- Clap

Teachers who work with toddlers may notice that once children start moving independently, they do not want to stop! Do you ever wonder whether every child in the toddler room has attention deficit hyperactivity disorder (ADHD)? It may feel that way, but according to the *Diagnostic and Statistical Manual of Mental Disorders*, fifth edition (DSM-5), clinical terms such as *hyperactivity* were created to describe the behaviors of school-age children or adults and do not apply to young children. Rest assured that it is normal for toddlers to be in constant motion and exhibit boundless energy as they test their newly acquired motor skills.

Not only is the toddler period critical for motor development, it also lays the foundation for good neurological development. In her book *Smart Moves: Why Learning Is Not All in Your Head*, neurophysiologist Carla Hannaford states, "Physical movement, from earliest infancy . . . plays an important role in the creation of nerve cell networks, which are actually the essence of learning." So the next time your fitness tracker says that you taught in the toddler room for five miles, keep in mind that while all this running around is exhausting for you, it is normal for the children.

SOCIAL-EMOTIONAL DEVELOPMENT

- Aware of self as separate from others
- Play near other children
- Respond to emotions of others
- Like to be within sight and sound of a caregiver

Infants and toddlers have a short list of ways to communicate to get their needs met: moving; using facial expressions; vocalizing, such as by cooing or screeching; and crying. As children develop, they make a slow and gradual transition from crying to using words.

Of course, all babies and young children cry at least sometimes. But what is considered a normal amount of crying? In search of answers, Dieter Wolke, Ayten Bilgin, and Muthanna Samara analyzed research on babies up to twelve weeks old from around the world. While every baby is unique, the average total amount of fussing and crying for the infants in this study ranged anywhere from 48 to

170 minutes per day. By ten to twelve weeks old, these babies cried an average total of 68 minutes per day.

To learn more, Malla Rao and his colleagues at the National Institute of Health in Norway and Sweden studied whether crying had any adverse effect on child development. Their results suggest that children with excessive, prolonged crying that persists beyond three months of age have poor fine-motor development and lower IQ scores as they grow. Research by Ricardo Halpern and Renato Coelho also links excessive crying in infancy to later diagnosis of ADHD and struggles in adapting to preschool. In other words, excessive crying might be a sign of a bigger problem.

In separate studies, researchers Cynthia Stifter and Tracy Spinrad conclude that excessive crying leads to less-regulated babies. Moreover, studies by Jane Brazy; Stephen Butler, Mark Suskind, and Saul Schanberg; Christopher Coe; Cynthia Kuhn, Stephen Butler, and Saul Schanberg; and Allan Schore show that letting a baby "cry it out" can elevate blood pressure and decrease oxygenation in the brain, inhibit growth hormones, weaken the immune system, and destroy neural connections. Eminent trauma researcher Bruce Perry (senior fellow of the ChildTrauma Academy in Houston, Texas) points out in "Incubated in Terror: Neurodevelopmental Factors in the 'Cycle of Violence'" that the developing brain is very sensitive to stress and that excessive crying might lead to an overactive stress-response system. In short, adults need to help children learn to calm themselves in healthy ways. Letting them "cry it out" does more harm than good.

If you are like me, you are probably thinking that this advice totally flies in the face of what your Great-Aunt Bertha said about spoiling babies. Those thoughts are understandable because until recently, many understandings of babies and young children were based on rudimentary research. For example, as Philip Boffey and Helen Harrison point out in separate articles in *The New York Times*, many infants and toddlers had to endure cancer care, treatment for serious burns, and even surgery without painkillers or anesthesia as recently as the late 1980s because of a widely held medical assumption that babies did not feel pain. Then new research by physicians Kanwaljeet Anand and Paul Hickey showed that withholding these medications resulted in more infant stress, difficulties, and deaths—and as a result, medical practices changed.

This study is just one of many examples illustrating the idea that no matter how long we have been in a field, there is no end to the knowledge we can obtain. Once you think you know everything there is to know about something, you put a ceiling on your knowledge. Ideas are always evolving. New research and the advent of new technology, such as magnetic resonance imaging (MRI) and positron emission tomography (PET) in the late twentieth century, have led to new understandings of human behavior and child development. So while your Great-Aunt Bertha based her ideas and practices on the information that was available in her time, we now know so much more, and we need to base our own ideas and practices on current information.

TWO-YEAR-OLDS

COGNITIVE DEVELOPMENT

- Engage in imaginary play
- Activate cause-and-effect toys, such as a jack-in-the-box, and know how they work
- Will give one out of many, such as choosing one toy from a pile and handing it to an adult

Many teachers who work with infants, toddlers, and two-year-olds hesitate to "give in" to children's crying, clinging, or tantrums because they fear being manipulated. However, young children do not have the cognitive faculties to manipulate others, because manipulation requires advanced planning skills and the ability to see someone else's point of view—capacities that children this age have not yet mastered. Even though it feels as though two-year-old Taquan is trying to destroy you, he honestly does not have the slightest idea how his behavior is emotionally affecting you and your lesson plan or what time his father has to be at work. No, your observations do not lie. Taquan *does* cry to get your attention and *does* fall on the floor like a limp noodle when he does not want to stop playing. But he is not capitalizing on your sympathy or secretly plotting your demise. His actions are simply a sign that he has observed and remembers how you respond to his behavior—in other words, he understands cause and effect.

You may still be skeptical, so let's look at the research. Thomas Suddendorf, Mark Nielsen, and Rebecca von Gehlen conducted experiments with three- and four-year-olds to find out whether young children have the cognitive capacity for future planning. Their results show that four-year-olds can anticipate needing an item in the future, but younger children cannot exhibit this skill. Other research by Daniela Kloo, Josef Perner, and Thomas Giritzer confirms that the abilities to predict another person's reaction and to understand other people's knowledge, emotions, and intentions in social situations—concepts that together are often called *theory of mind*—are just beginning to emerge at the end of preschool, when children are between ages four and five.

LANGUAGE DEVELOPMENT

- Experiment with communication
- Can say about thirty to forty words
- Respond to simple commands

Early childhood is a critical period for language development. Young children love to repeat novel words—for better or for worse. In his book *Why We Curse: The Neuro-Pyscho-Social Theory of Speech*, psychologist Timothy Jay explains that children learn swear words along with all other words as a part of normal language acquisition. In fact, he adds, children can repeat profanity as soon as they can speak.

However, even if young children use swear words in grammatically correct places with the appropriate tone, they do not actually know what they are saying. To understand this concept, let's briefly examine the theories of Swiss psychologist Jean Piaget, whose book *The Origins of Intelligence in Children* includes a framework explaining the different stages of cognition in human development.

PIAGET'S STAGES OF COGNITIVE DEVELOPMENT

- **Sensorimotor stage (birth to 2):** Infants and young toddlers learn by grasping, sucking, listening, and watching. They discover that they can affect the world around them through their actions. They are egocentric and cannot see things from any perspective but their own.

- **Preoperational stage (2 to 7):** Older toddlers and young children are beginning to think symbolically, using words and pictures to represent objects. They are rapidly developing their language skills. They continue to be egocentric and struggle to see things from others' perspectives.

- **Concrete operational stage (7 to 11):** Children this age are beginning to think logically, but they are very literal in their understandings. For example, if a seven-year-old hears someone say, "It's raining cats and dogs outside," the child may run to the window expecting to see poodles and Russian Blues falling from the sky. At this age, children are beginning to be able to see things from another's perspective.
- **Formal operational stage (12 and up):** Adolescents and adults can think abstractly, see things from various perspectives, and reason through hypothetical problems.

As this framework shows, a two-year-old assumes that everyone around him sees things the same way he does. Because his perspective-taking abilities are still emerging, he has a limited capacity to anticipate another person's reaction. So even though he can use swear words, he does not fully understand why they might offend others. Jay also points out that children do not begin to consider what might be good and bad until about age four. Thus, if young children observe adults using profanity when they are angry, the children may copy this behavior not because they want to cause offense but because they have learned that swearing is what people do when they get angry.

This is why it is important to react appropriately to the language that young children use. Language exploration is normal, and all children use the words that get the most attention. In my practice, I have noticed that this is especially true of children with special needs. Their thought processes go something like this: "If I am only capable of saying a few words, I am going to use the ones that will guarantee a reaction." For any child who uses profanity, take a deep breath and try not to overreact. Instead of viewing this situation as a problem to solve, take advantage of the opportunity to teach him the proper vocabulary for expressing his emotions.

PHYSICAL DEVELOPMENT

- Kick a ball
- Jump with both feet
- Put tiny objects in a small container

SOCIAL-EMOTIONAL DEVELOPMENT

- Show a wide variety of emotions
- Express affection
- Can have wide emotional shifts

As any teacher of two-year-olds can attest, behaviors such as hitting, pushing, and kicking are commonplace among this age group. Remember that, as Richard Tremblay and his colleagues point out in "Do Children in Canada Become More Aggressive as They Approach Adolescence?" it is developmentally appropriate for physical aggression to appear at the end of infancy. Thus, some aggression is a natural occurrence as children journey down the path of development. Young children are in the process of developing the social-emotional, cognitive, physical, and language skills associated with good behaviors. As educators and family members, we must both give children space to explore and teach them acceptable ways to behave.

THREE-YEAR-OLDS

COGNITIVE DEVELOPMENT

- Make mechanical toys work
- Match object in hand to picture in book
- Play make-believe
- Sort objects by shape and color
- Complete three- and four-piece puzzles
- Understand concept of *two*
- Copy a circle with pencil or crayon
- Turn book pages one at a time
- Build towers of more than six blocks
- Screw and unscrew jar lids or turn door handles

Have you ever tried to play hide-and-seek with a three-year-old? You may be chuckling right now because you usually have to pretend that you cannot see the child! Children this age are not great at hiding because they are still developing the ability to see a situation from someone else's point of view.

Josef Perner, Susan Leekam, and Heinz Wimmer confirm that high-level perspective-taking skills are limited in children aged three and under. Furthermore, as noted by Carol Westby and Lee Robinson and by Jill de Villiers and Peter de Villiers, at about age eighteen months, children begin to realize that others might have different emotions, likes, or dislikes than they do. But only older preschoolers can understand that two people might see *the same thing* differently. It is not until elementary school that children begin to develop the capacity to predict others' responses and how they might be thinking or feeling.

LANGUAGE DEVELOPMENT

- Understand the concepts of *same* and *different*
- Have mastered some basic rules of grammar
- Follow instructions with two or three steps
- Can name most familiar things
- Understand words such as *in*, *on*, and *under*
- Say own first name, age, and sex
- Name a friend
- Say words such as *I*, *me*, *we*, and *you* and some plurals, such as *cars*, *dogs*, and *cats*
- Talk well enough for strangers to understand most of the time
- Carry on a conversation using two to three sentences

Do you ever feel that you are constantly repeating instructions in your classroom and yet the children still do not do what you ask? Christopher Chatham, Michael Frank, and Yuko Munakata of the University of Colorado at Boulder wondered why children often do not listen or follow directions.

They found that, compared to school-age children or adults, preschoolers have weaker abilities in following directions. During the experiments described in the study, preschoolers slowed down and exerted mental effort when presented with directions. Preschoolers are slowly developing the abilities to remember what happened previously, plan, and predict the next step in a process. So the preschoolers in your classroom are indeed listening, but they cannot execute your directions as quickly or easily as an older child or adult could.

As a teacher, I often felt frustrated when children struggled to follow my instructions. I thought, "Why are you behaving as if this is brand-new? We just did this yesterday!" But to a three-year-old, each day *is* brand-new. How young children store information is different from how older children and adults do it, and because young children react more slowly, they need more time to process directions. So instead of thinking that children just aren't listening, allow them extra processing time, and focus on reinforcing their understanding and supporting their listening skills (which we will discuss further in chapter 7).

PHYSICAL DEVELOPMENT

- Climb well
- Run easily
- Pedal a tricycle
- Walk up and down stairs, one foot on each step

In her research, June Zuckerman has studied strategies for preventing and managing classroom discipline problems, and she explains that lessons designed to prevent the likelihood of challenging behaviors in the classroom "[feature] . . . novel, brains-on, and/or hands-on activities." The structure of the brain corroborates these findings. Robert Sylwester's book *How to Explain a Brain* shows that the structure of the brain known as the *cerebellum*, which is chiefly associated with movement and balance, is also essential in the learning process. Half of all the neurons in the brain are stored there.

Many educators hesitate to incorporate movement into their teaching practices because they have outdated images of learning that include children seated at their desks, staring at chalkboards, and scribbling furiously on worksheets. However, now that we have the technology to see how the brain works, it is clear that all people are biologically wired to learn through interaction and involvement.

SOCIAL-EMOTIONAL AND SELF-REGULATION DEVELOPMENT

- Copy adults and friends
- Show affection for friends without prompting
- Take turns in games
- Show concern for a crying friend
- Understand the ideas of *mine* and *his* or *hers*
- Show a wide range of emotions
- Separate easily from parents or guardians
- May get upset with major changes in routine
- Dress and undress themselves

Richard Tremblay's article "Development of Physical Aggression from Early Childhood to Adulthood" shows that physical aggression tends to peak in young children at about thirty to forty-two months of age, with boys exhibiting higher frequencies of these behaviors. So if you are looking for a calm, quiet, peaceful classroom full of compliant, self-regulated three-year-olds, you might have unconsciously internalized the romanticized classrooms often shown on television or in movies. In real life, challenging behaviors are typical (and, for some behaviors, at their most frequent) among this age group.

FOUR-YEAR-OLDS

COGNITIVE DEVELOPMENT

- Correctly name some colors
- Understand the concept of counting and may know a few numbers
- Approach problems from a single point of view
- Draw a person with two to four body parts
- Begin to have a clearer sense of time
- Follow three-part commands
- Begin to copy some capital letters
- Recall parts of a story and state what they think will happen next
- Engage in fantasy play

At the age of four, the capacity to take someone else's perspective is just emerging; it will not be fully developed until about age ten or eleven. If a child has a language delay, this ability to take another's perspective could be delayed even further. Typically, according to researcher Sandra Crosser, it is not until school age that children can fully understand the effects of their words on others and anticipate others' reactions. When you hear phrases such as, "You're not my friend," or "You can't come to my party," it is a sign that children are maturing. Of course, we want children to continue to mature in how they speak to each other. We'll explore how to support those skills in later chapters.

LANGUAGE DEVELOPMENT

- Know some basic rules of grammar, such as correctly using *he* and *she*
- Sing a song or say a poem from memory, such as "The Itsy Bitsy Spider" or "The Wheels on the Bus"
- Tell stories
- Can say own first and last name

Verbal aggression is a natural progression from physical aggression. Teachers often tell young children to "use your words" to get them to stop hitting or engaging in other types of physical aggression. While this phrase is not meant as an invitation to swear or use other forms of verbal aggression, technically a child *is* using his words when he engages in these behaviors. They show that the child is reducing his use of physical aggression, is picking up on more acceptable ways to interact with others, and is beginning to use other tools to express himself and his emotions. Essentially, he is *saying* bad things instead of *doing* bad things. The next step is to teach him the right words to use.

PHYSICAL DEVELOPMENT

- Hop and stand on one foot for up to five seconds
- Go up and down stairs without support
- Kick a ball forward
- Throw a ball overhand
- Catch a bounced ball most of the time
- Move forward and backward with agility
- Draw a person with two to four body parts
- Use scissors
- Draw circles and squares
- Begin to copy some capital letters

At this age, children still need movement to learn. Many authors—such as neurologist Carla Hannaford, Gail and Paul Dennison, and Marilee Sprenger—describe how movement enhances learning and memory, strengthens neural connections, and helps build the foundation for better brains. In her book *Becoming a "Wiz" at Brain-Based Teaching*, Marilee Sprenger argues that movement should be a part of every lesson because it allows a classroom to run smoothly with less stress. Play provides the freedom of movement that is essential for learning and development.

SOCIAL-EMOTIONAL AND SELF-REGULATION DEVELOPMENT

- Interested in new experiences
- Cooperate with other children
- Play "mom" or "dad"
- Increasingly inventive in fantasy play
- Dress and undress themselves
- Negotiate solutions to conflicts
- More independent
- Imagine that many unfamiliar images may be "monsters"
- View themselves as whole people with bodies, minds, and feelings
- Often cannot distinguish between fantasy and reality

Young children do not yet have a firm grasp of reality. Many four-year-olds still believe Santa Claus and fairies are real. So when you ask little Brandy if she hit Tyson (which you just saw her do) but get an answer of, "No," or "Batman did it," Brandy might not be intentionally lying. She may be imagining that she did not hit Tyson, just as when she imagines that she is not wearing a large white T-shirt but a doctor's coat in the dramatic-play area. The study "Social and Cognitive Correlates of Children's Lying Behavior" by Victoria Talwar and Kang Lee shows that children have the capacity to make up stories and even lie, but they have limited moral comprehension of lying and incomplete depth of understanding about other people's thinking and how a lie might affect others. Children's grasp of these concepts, however, grows with their cognitive development.

FIVE-YEAR-OLDS

COGNITIVE DEVELOPMENT

- Count ten or more things
- Draw a person with at least six body parts
- Print some letters or numbers
- Copy a triangle and other geometric shapes
- Know about things used every day, such as money and food

LANGUAGE DEVELOPMENT

- Speak very clearly
- Tell a simple story using full sentences
- Use future tense—for example, "Grandma will be here"
- Say own name and address

In her book *Whispers through Time: Communication through the Ages and Stages of Early Childhood*, author L. R. Knost describes whining as a win. She defines whining as a child's attempt to avoid having a meltdown and to self-regulate by using words. Though whining can be infuriating, remember that it is a more advanced skill than physical aggression and is actually a sign that a child is maturing.

PHYSICAL DEVELOPMENT

- Stand on one foot for ten seconds or longer
- Hop and possibly skip
- Do a somersault
- Use a fork and spoon and sometimes a table knife
- Can use toilet on own
- Swing and climb

Educators often think of movement as a gross-motor activity. However, movement should be an important part of every learning activity for this age group. In an article from *Educational Leadership*, Robert Sylwester states, "Mobility is central to much that's human—whether the movement of information is physical or mental. We can move and talk. Trees can't. Misguided teachers who constantly tell their students to sit down and be quiet imply a preference for working with a grove of trees, not a classroom of students." What a good reminder to all of us that the traditional sit-down-and-be-quiet approach to learning is not suited for young children.

As a former teacher, I realize that too much movement in a classroom full of five-year-olds can become chaotic and unsafe when not executed properly. So I suggest keeping movements small and quiet. Here are some ideas:

- Use learning centers to keep children moving and engaged. Have the children rotate in groups from center to center, each of which has a different task that groups complete together.
- Ask each child to gently tap a friend's hand when they hear a certain letter sound.

- Instead of directing the children to raise their hands when they want to answer a question, tell them to stand on one foot.
- Have the children form a single line facing you. Explain that you will tell the children some statements. Ask them to take one step forward if they think a statement is true and one step backward if they think it is false.
- Toss a beanbag to the student who will answer the next question.
- Play Sneaky Addition. Write a number (for example, 5) on the board. Give each child a number, and then instruct each child to tiptoe as quietly as he can, looking for a partner who has a number that he can add to his own number to make a total of five.

SOCIAL-EMOTIONAL AND SELF-REGULATION DEVELOPMENT

- Want to please friends
- Want to be like friends
- More likely to agree with rules
- Like to sing, dance, and act
- Are aware of gender
- Can tell what is real and what is make-believe
- Show more independence (for example, may visit next-door neighbors alone—adult supervision is still needed)
- Are sometimes demanding and sometimes very cooperative

If you feel that your day is a blur of "You're not my friend" statements and endless arguments about how many children can be in the same area, keep in mind that this is normal. Young children do not yet have the capacity to work disagreements out peacefully without the help of adults. The best way for children to learn to get along and resolve conflicts is for adults around them to model these behaviors. In many classrooms I work with, the adults make problem solving a job so that the children can share in the responsibility. Taking turns as the "problem solver of the day" can support children in acquiring new skills.

Around age five, children enter kindergarten and encounter both an increase in academic demands and the expectation that they should meet those demands with less adult support. These new circumstances can lead to conflicts and so-called noncompliance. But the word *noncompliance* paints a misleading picture of the situation because it suggests that a young child is in complete control of his behavior and is willfully disobeying. However, we know that young children's self-regulation skills are emerging, not mastered. These facts together indicate that young children do not actually have the capacity to be noncompliant. If they are not doing as an adult directs, the adult must find other ways to support the children in complying with the instructions.

SIX-YEAR-OLDS

COGNITIVE DEVELOPMENT

- Show rapid development of mental skills
- Count up to two hundred

- Count backwards from twenty
- Understand the concepts of odd and even numbers
- Represent numbers on a number line or with written words
- Use increasingly sophisticated strategies to solve addition and subtraction problems
- Count the sides of shapes to identify them
- Combine shapes to create new ones
- Give and follow directions for moving around a room or on a map
- Continue to straddle the world between make-believe and reality

Age six signifies the beginning of middle childhood. At this age, children show significant improvements in their abilities to sustain attention, plan, set goals, look at situations from different points of view, and control their impulses. However, these skills develop slowly, so children still need support from adults. According to neuropsychologist Maureen Dennis, these skills emerge in gradual stages, fully maturing in late adolescence.

LANGUAGE DEVELOPMENT

- Learn better ways to describe experiences
- Pronounce words clearly
- Use complex grammatical forms accurately
- Language skills become increasingly sophisticated
- Vocabulary rapidly increases
- Language moves beyond communication to provide a foundation for learning, including the development of independent reading skills

Language skills play an increasingly important role in the social-emotional domain as children grow and develop. Consequently, children with language challenges are vulnerable to social-emotional struggles. Researchers Holly Craig and Julie Washington found that children with language delays have a more difficult time engaging with and interacting with other children of the same age.

PHYSICAL DEVELOPMENT

- Run in various pathways and directions
- Manipulate own bodies by jumping and landing, rolling, and transferring weight from feet to hands to feet
- Coordination still developing, so skills such as throwing, catching, kicking, and striking are still emerging

As with earlier ages, learning at this age is enhanced by interaction and movement. Movement, in fact, releases chemicals in the brain that enhance learning. Author Marilee Sprenger explains that these chemicals are vital for boosting learners' attention spans and help improve their memories.

SOCIAL-EMOTIONAL AND SELF-REGULATION DEVELOPMENT

- Talk about thoughts and feelings
- Have less focus on themselves and more concern for others

- Show more independence from parents and other family members
- Start to think about the future
- Understand more about their places in the world
- Pay more attention to friendships and teamwork
- Want to be liked and accepted by friends

At this age, children can wait for a turn, and there are more moments where logic prevails. You can finally play musical chairs or Duck, Duck, Goose without all the children ending up crying! Six-year-olds are beginning to understand how their words and actions affect others, but they may still struggle with bullying and excluding others from social situations. Though six-year-olds are becoming much more adept at navigating social situations and expressing their emotions, they still need prompting and support from adults when solving social conflicts.

Even though a child's ability to run or see is fully developed by age six, his self-regulation skills need much longer to grow. In a study of nine hundred children ages eight through twenty-two, Graham Baum and his colleagues found that skills such as staying on task and making good decisions steadily increase with age. It is important to remember where six-year-olds are on this journey and that they have quite a distance to go before they master these skills.

Behavior *Is* Communication

My wonderful colleague Gillian McNamee describes hitting as a child's first language. I am not sure if it is really the first, but it definitely lies somewhere between crying and talking. Challenging behavior is similar to Morse code, but instead of a series of dots and dashes, you must interpret a series of hits and bites! Although these behaviors may seem to defy logic, they always have meaning. Sometimes that meaning is relatively ordinary (such as, "I'm sleepy" or "I'm hungry"), and sometimes it is equivalent to an SOS. Challenging behaviors also provide clues to what children know and what skills they need to learn. At first, these messages can seem as unintelligible as Morse code is to an untrained observer, but with practice (including learning to manage your own behaviors), you can learn to detect and interpret these messages.

A wonderful colleague of mine, Pamela Green of Ananda Montessori, describes the *mis-* in the word *misbehavior* as what she is missing in a child. I think that the *mis-* sometimes arises because adults misunderstand what children are and are not capable of doing. For instance, I have met teachers who were alarmed that babies were crying or two-year-olds were not sharing. I had to remind these teachers to get realistic about the skills of the children in their care.

When teachers misunderstand typical misbehavior, it can be a sign that they are stressed or need to PUSH PAST It so they can think logically. At other times, a challenging behavior is developmentally appropriate but becomes overwhelming because it happens frequently or is accompanied by extreme emotions. Many of you are likely reading this book because that statement describes your situation. Beginning in chapter 6, we will learn how to address these difficulties. But first, we must finish laying the foundation that will help us implement that process successfully.

Wrapping Up

Now that you know more about young children and their development, you can start to predict what challenging behaviors are likely to happen among the children in your care, when they might occur, and how you can prevent them. For example, if you work with two-year-olds, you now know that they cannot share, so you could add more toys to the environment or create calming baskets (see chapter 9) for the inevitable tantrums. I worked with one teacher who put pinwheels in each learning area in her classroom and used them to teach the children to take deep breaths when they felt angry. Another teacher, who works with three-year-olds, changed her verbal prompts. Because three-year-olds are egocentric, she realized that it was not helpful to ask them, "How do you think you made your friend feel?"

One therapist I trained, who works exclusively with children ages zero to three, used her new knowledge about child development to better serve her clients. For instance, she realized that she needed to add more movement to her therapy sessions, so she put puzzle pieces or blocks around the room. Then the children could crawl or move to find them and assemble a puzzle or tower with her. In another case, this therapist worked with family members who were trying to teach a child not to bite by biting the child back. Using her increased knowledge of developmentally appropriate behavior, the therapist explained that a young child does not have the cognitive capacity to realize, "Ow! That hurt when Mom bit me. It probably hurts her when I bite her. I guess I shouldn't bite anymore." This explanation helped the family members realize that responding with words such as "gentle touches" would be more effective to help the child stop biting.

CHAPTER 6

Understanding the Role of Trauma in Behavior

Have you (or has a child you know) ever squirted out the entire contents of a tube of toothpaste? What happened when someone tried to put the toothpaste back into the tube? You likely discovered that it was impossible to get everything back in—and even if some toothpaste made it back, it was not the same as before. Similar things happen to children who experience trauma. In their book *The Boy Who Was Raised as a Dog, and Other Stories from a Child Psychiatrist's Notebook*, Bruce Perry and Maia Szalavitz make this observation about the effects of trauma on children and their behavior:

> "Because new situations are inherently stressful, and because youth who have been through trauma often come from homes in which chaos and unpredictability appear 'normal' to them, they may respond with fear to what is actually a calm and safe situation. Attempting to take control of what they believe is the inevitable return of chaos, they appear to 'provoke' it in order to make things feel more comfortable and predictable. . . . As one family therapist famously put it, we tend to prefer the 'certainty of misery to the misery of uncertainty.'"

Sometimes the meaning behind a behavior is more than what you can observe in a classroom. Just as you needed to process your own background to understand where you are coming from, now we need to process the backgrounds of children with challenging behaviors. Many of these children have experienced trauma. Once we understand where they are coming from, we can determine how to help them.

Defining Trauma

The Center for Substance Abuse Treatment compares living with trauma to perpetually living as a character inside a scary, suspenseful movie. If simply watching a two-hour film can leave us jumpy and unable to sleep for days on end, imagine the intense physiological arousal that lingers in a child after trauma. She experiences life anxiously sitting on the edge of her seat, clutching the arm of the person next to her while nervously waiting for something to happen.

This analogy explains why ordinary interactions and everyday items, smells, touches, and sounds can trigger challenging behaviors. For children who have been exposed to trauma, these seemingly benign occurrences are reminders of intense fear or sadness. In the face of such terror, survival instinct takes over and often manifests itself as challenging behaviors.

We'll discuss this connection in a moment. First, we need to examine what trauma looks like for young children.

WHAT IS TRAUMA?

When I first heard the term *post-traumatic stress disorder*, I initially thought of veterans returning home from war-torn countries. After all, the word *trauma* itself typically conjures images of suffering a serious injury, being abused for years, witnessing a horrific event, or having a similarly devastating experience. But to a young child, trauma encompasses more than you might expect.

To better understand trauma and its implications, let's revisit the work of renowned trauma expert Bruce Perry. In his report *Stress, Trauma, and Post-Traumatic Stress Disorders in Children: An Introduction*, he defines trauma as a onetime event, such as a car accident, a medical procedure, or a natural disaster, or a series of ongoing events, such as physical or emotional abuse, neglect, or community or domestic violence, that impairs the body's stress-response system. Here are some examples of types of trauma. Many come from a list developed by the Substance Abuse and Mental Health Services Administration:

- Community violence
- Political violence
- Interpersonal violence, such as homicide or suicide
- School violence or bullying
- Domestic violence
- Physical, emotional, and sexual abuse or assault
- Neglect
- Natural or manmade disasters

- Medical trauma from a serious accident
- Illness or medical procedure
- Refugee trauma or forced displacement
- Household dysfunction, such as having a family member incarcerated, substance abuse, or mental illness
- Acts of terrorism
- Military trauma, including a loved one being deployed and the stress from trauma experienced by the deployed person
- Traumatic grief or separation
- Mass violence
- Historical trauma that affects communities for generations, such as the lingering effects of slavery on Black people in the United States

Put more simply, to a young child, trauma is any event or series of events in which she feels threatened. Trauma that occurs in childhood is often referred to as *adverse childhood experiences* (ACEs).

EFFECTS OF TRAUMA

In *Stress, Trauma, and Post-Traumatic Stress Disorders in Children*, Bruce Perry explains how our brains and bodies are designed to spot danger and respond to it. If faced with a stressful situation, our bodies go into *fight-or-flight mode.* Fight-or-flight mode describes a biochemical reaction that results in increased heart rate and respiration and the release of stress hormones. These hormones, such as adrenaline, make us strong enough to handle any trouble that gets in our way.

Fight-or-flight mode is not necessarily a bad thing. Perry argues that controlled amounts of tolerable stress are a part of child development. *Tolerable stresses* are often short-lived and are mitigated by caring adults. However, when the human body is in fight-or-flight mode for prolonged periods or when the stress is unpredictable, reaches a high level, or feels overwhelming, this mode becomes harmful.

Unfortunately, this is exactly what happens when babies and young children suffer trauma. Some people argue that infants and young children are too young to be affected by stressful events, but as the National Scientific Council on the Developing Child explains, this is not the case. Early experiences shape the brain. Because early childhood is a period of rapid brain growth and development, young children's brains are more sensitive to external experiences than adults' brains are. To survive ACEs, children's brains are not working as they should. In fact, "the regions of the brain involved in fear, anxiety, and impulsive responses may overproduce neural connections while those regions dedicated to reasoning, planning, and behavioral control may produce fewer neural connections." These children experience *hyperarousal*, or a heightened sense of anxiety, meaning that they are always on high alert, even when they are in safe environments. Significant adversity in the form of trauma can lead to lifelong mental- and physical-health challenges, and the amount of trauma a child experiences and the duration of the event (or events) influence the level of impact.

Look at it this way: Everyone has a "danger dial" in her brain. For a child who has experienced trauma, this dial is always turned up to the highest setting, even when real danger is no longer present.

How Trauma Manifests in Young Children's Behavior

In *Stress, Trauma, and Post-Traumatic Stress Disorders in Children*, Bruce Perry notes that even two children with an identical diagnosis of post-traumatic stress disorder could look completely different and have very different sets of behaviors. Responses to trauma depend on the individual child, her family members, the nature of the event, its duration, and the community in which the child and family live. Some reactions to trauma might occur immediately following an event, while others occur as delayed reactions.

This list (based on a fact sheet created by the American Counseling Association's Traumatology Interest Network) provides some common ways in which young children respond to trauma. Remember, most children exhibit some or all of these behaviors at one time or another, so the behaviors do not, in and of themselves, indicate that a child has experienced trauma. The key is to look at the intensity and frequency of behaviors, the context of a child's family and community, and whether these behaviors interfere with normal day-to-day functioning.

- Bed-wetting or wetting pants
- Withdrawal
- Anger or aggression
- Tantrums or outbursts
- Separation anxiety or fear of being alone
- Startle or aggressive response to sudden or loud noises
- Excessive crying
- Sleep challenges
- Fussiness
- Stomachaches
- Headaches
- Regression (acting like a younger child), such as baby talk or loss of self-help skills
- Thumb sucking
- Not listening or following directions
- Play that reenacts trauma
- Avoidance of everyday things that remind the child of the event
- Asking the same questions repeatedly
- Loss of concentration
- Inability to focus on a task or directions
- Lack of usual responses to typical daily events
- Heightened arousal or intense reactions
- Throwing chairs or other large objects (may be a sign of adrenaline release and fight-or-flight mode being active)
- Irritability
- Mood swings

Remember, when a child is behaving aggressively, crying excessively, or demonstrating some other challenging behavior, it is a sign that the child has a need that no adult has identified or addressed. Adults must look at the whole child within the contexts of school or child care and home to understand what is missing and to fill those gaps. If you are missing what a child needs from you, then you are missing an important part of the story.

CASE STUDY #1: THEY DON'T FORGET

As a consultant, I worked with an Early Head Start teacher, whom I'll call Carmen, who had a set of two-year-old twins in her classroom. According to Carmen, the twins cried excessively, were clingy, and had difficulty with transitions and listening. They did not talk much at all, even for two-year-olds, and never seemed to pay attention to any activity Carmen presented.

At this point in my career, I had learned to respond to challenging behavior with curiosity, so I began asking questions. After several queries, Carmen mentioned as an afterthought that as infants, the twins had had a brief separation from their parents because of neglect, during which time they had lived in foster care and with family members. But Carmen stated, "They're back with their parents now. There's no way they even could remember not being with them. After all, they're only two." However, with my understanding of trauma, I knew differently. I explained to Carmen that the twins definitely remembered the separation: they were telling us so with their behavior.

As Carmen and I worked with the twins, they still hardly talked or paid attention to activities until one day when I visited the classroom and showed them a picture of a baby crying. They both paused and stared at the photo for longer than I had ever seen them look at anything. I asked, "Do you feel like this?" and one of the twins nodded.

Carmen was finally convinced that the twins needed her support. She realized that she had to slow down transitions, use pictures to talk about feelings, and accept that the twins needed to be very close to her most of the time. When I came back a few weeks later, their behavior had become more manageable because Carmen had become more understanding, responsive, and realistic with her expectations.

CASE STUDY #2: UNDERSTANDING MASON

Remember Mason from chapter 3? Even though I was an experienced teacher by the time I had him in my class, I had never encountered challenging behaviors that really stumped me. At the time, it honestly felt as if Mason was behaving badly for no reason. In retrospect, I now recognize some flaws in my thinking about the situation.

First, saying that Mason had no reason for his behavior would imply that I had evaluated and eliminated every possible reason for why a child might behave that way. Given the infinite number of potential reasons, that conclusion was illogical.

Second, I did not adequately factor in Mason's history or lifestyle when considering why he might act the way he did. At the time, I knew that Mason's mother was in a drug-treatment program, but I did not consider how that situation was affecting his behavior. I even wonder now if Mason had been exposed to drugs in the womb. I also knew that Mason's family had previously been in shelters and homeless. But at that time in my career, I thought that he was too young to remember those difficulties and that he should be okay because he was in a safe place now. In reality, I underestimated the lingering effect of these experiences, and I did not understand the psychological symptoms of a mental-health disorder.

Mason taught me that the real reasons behind a challenging behavior may have nothing to do with how the behavior appears on the surface, perhaps even defying logic. This realization propelled me to learn about developmental trauma and helped me understand how the reasons behind a challenging behavior can go beyond one's scope of knowledge or experience.

CASE STUDY #3: DEVELOPMENTAL TRAUMA IN AN INFANT

During one of my educational workshops, the subject of children's crying came up. Upon my proclamation that teachers should do everything they can to hold "that hollerin' baby," one of the teachers (whom I'll call Celia) responded with an eye roll. As a presenter, I live for the moments when participants finally wipe those polite smiles off their faces and feel comfortable enough to keep it real.

I embraced Celia's feelings and encouraged her to share what was on her mind. Celia went on to describe a baby in her classroom, whom I'll call Janie, who cried all the time. I listened and responded with curiosity. As it turned out, Janie was going through a lot:

- Janie's mother was a teenager.
- The mother's entire family was in poverty and had been for generations.
- A family member was going through cancer treatments.
- Janie had been born prematurely.

After hearing all of Janie's life circumstances, I wondered whether her behavior was an expression of developmental trauma. *Developmental trauma* is harsh adversity that occurs when children experience a great deal of stress and the adults in their lives either cause or do not try to decrease that stress. Perhaps Janie's teenage mother was so overwhelmed with raising a young child and having a sick family member that she was experiencing maternal depression and had become unresponsive. A pattern of unresponsiveness could lead to infant neglect, which in turn could affect Janie's development. The family's pattern of poverty across several generations also has a name: *transgenerational trauma*. Transgenerational trauma is unacknowledged suffering that is passed down from one generation to the next. For example, families living in poverty are often isolated in one area or region. According to an analysis of neighborhood poverty by Elizabeth Kneebone, Carey Nadeau, and Alan Berube, that isolation can lead to less access to quality healthcare, housing, and schools and more exposure to high levels of crime. When a family cannot escape this environment, poverty affects each family member and the family as a whole and takes a cumulative toll generation after generation.

Upon hearing more about the context of Janie's environment, I was not the only one concerned. Each person at the workshop looked at me, then at each other. Then we all unanimously decided, "Celia, you've got to hold that baby." We also asked about the other children in Celia's care, and it turned out that while all of them lived in poverty, the other children did not have as many challenges to overcome. As a result, even though all the children cried, they did not all cry with the same frequency or for the same length of time.

After talking this out, even Celia realized that everything Janie was going through was just too much for anyone, let alone a baby, to bear. We all sat together and helped Celia make a plan for how she could provide physical and verbal comfort to Janie throughout the day.

PUSH PAST IT!

- Instead of letting Janie wait for comfort when she cried, Celia or her coteacher would respond quickly as a way to limit crying.
- Celia and her coteacher would work as a team and position themselves in the classroom so that they could be responsive to Janie.
- We discussed the times of day at which Janie cried the most and planned for those times. The more planning Celia and her coteacher did, the better able they were to act swiftly when the situation presented itself.

This story is a good example of why you cannot create solutions to challenging behaviors without understanding the depth of the situation. This example also illustrates the cumulative toll of adversity. Everyone reading this book has experienced some type of adversity. But the amount and intensity of adversity matters. Was it short-lived or long-term? Was it mild, or was it so intense that it had lingering consequences? Did you have a loving support system during that time, or did you face the adversity mostly or completely alone? The answers to these questions make a huge difference in what long-term effects the experience had on you. The same is true for young children.

While you cannot control what happens to a child outside of your classroom, you can make a difference while the child is with you. All children need and deserve responsive caregivers. Responsiveness is *not* about giving every child the same thing. Responsiveness is about fulfilling every child's needs based on her unique life circumstances and individual characteristics. That responsiveness can sometimes require unusual actions, such as in the next case study.

CASE STUDY #4: CALMING CHASE'S TANTRUMS

Have you ever seen a preschool child throw a chair? swipe all the materials off a shelf? hit the teachers? A child in the foster-care system, whom I'll call Chase, began showing these behaviors after a holiday break. His teacher, whom I'll call Shania, was soon at her wits' end.

When I asked Shania about what triggered the behavior, she stated that Chase acted up all day. So I asked, "If you could eliminate only one behavior, what would you eliminate?" Shania chose to work on Chase's tantrums at lunch. He refused to sit with the other children at the lunch table, insisting on being allowed to eat in the library instead. If asked to sit anywhere else for lunch, he would destroy the classroom.

See if you can relate to the exchange that followed:

> Me: If you don't mind me asking, is it possible that Chase can sit in the library to eat lunch? He has a paraprofessional who'll sit with him.
>
> Shania: He has to follow the rules. He has to learn to sit at the table like everybody else.
>
> Me: I know rules are important to you. I agree that teaching children rules is important. But I'm wondering whether Chase is having difficulty adjusting to the changes in his schedule that happened during the holiday break. He's in the foster-care system for a reason, and changes in his routine might have triggered this behavior. If it prevents a tantrum, is it possible that he could eat in the library?
>
> Shania: Angela, I'm not catering to this one child. If he eats in the library, everyone will want to eat in the library.

ME: I see your concern. You're right to worry about how the other children will respond. But I'm also keeping in mind that the trauma Chase experienced in the past might be affecting his behavior now. He has a mental-health issue that the other children do not have. Perhaps we can explain that to the children in simple terms. For example, we can say, "Sometimes when people are upset, they need to be alone." I would emphasize how the other children can sit at the table and it's fun to be there. I also wonder whether Chase has just become too sleepy and hungry after holding it together for the morning; perhaps the time of day is also a trigger. We could try to see whether the other children might coax Chase to sit with them at the table. Or perhaps he could have one friend sit with him. What are you thinking?

SHANIA: That little boy is going to jail if he can't follow rules. I am old school. I can't cater to this one child. What kind of classroom are we running nowadays where the children tell the teacher what to do? Back when I was coming along, children followed rules.

ME: I see your worries about being too permissive and what that might lead to in the future. But keep in mind that this is a Head Start program. Our curriculum encourages us to have rules but also to make accommodations for children with special needs. Chase is just three years old, after all. What if he were in a wheelchair or blind, for example? Wouldn't you make accommodations if a child had a disability? Well, Chase has a mental-health issue.

SHANIA: Angela, that little boy ain't blind! Oh well . . . I guess we can try.

We ended up letting Chase sit in the library, but we also implemented several strategies to help him cope with all he was feeling and to support him in joining the group:

- Shania used visuals of emotions to help Chase express his feelings. When he was overwhelmed and unable to verbalize what he felt, he could point to the appropriate visual to communicate.

- Together, Shania and Chase created a book about sitting with friends at lunch that included Chase's picture. It was a great way to strengthen their relationship, and it was a great literacy, art, and math activity.

- Shania positioned Chase on the end or at the outer corner of the table when he ate with his friends so that he could have extra space.

- Shania and some of the children would sing a song to the tune of "Row, Row, Row Your Boat":

Sit, sit, sit at the table,

Eating with your friends!

Sit, sit, sit at the table,

Eating with your friends!

After a period of using these strategies consistently, Chase eventually went back to sitting at the table.

But can you relate to Shania? Did you ever just want to bypass all these strategies and go back to the "good old days" when children just did as they were told? As we discussed in chapter 2, nostalgia can be a hindrance to problem solving. If we take off our rose-colored glasses and think logically, I think we can all remember instances of not all children doing as they were told. This type of thinking, while comforting, only distracts us from solving the issues at hand and implementing useful strategies.

Turning Down the "Danger Dial"

When a child is in fight-or-flight mode, her "danger dial" is on the maximum setting. When a child has experienced trauma, her dial tends to get stuck on maximum, even once she is safe. Because children are still learning to manage their emotions, they need help from adults to turn down their dials. Here are some ideas to help you recognize this state in the children you care for and, in turn, help them dial down from fight-or-flight mode.

Signs that my danger dial is stuck	What I might need to help me dial down
Fast breathing	Deep breathing
Rapid heart rate	A touch on my chest
Tense muscles	Help relaxing
Narrowed vision	Visuals to help me focus
Sweating	Help cooling off
Pale face	A look in a mirror to notice this sign
Flashbacks of original trauma	Reminders that I am now in a safe place
Clinging or withdrawing	Being close to adults, support from a peer buddy
Short temper/releases of adrenaline	Adults predicting and preventing or limiting frustrations
Repeatedly asking questions	Adults repeating the answer without being annoyed
Demanding more attention	Planning times in the daily schedule to give the child attention—for example, give the child a high-five or a hug at each transition

Wrapping Up

Facing trauma in young children can be frightening, saddening, and even frustrating when it causes children to have challenging behaviors. The good news is that with your new understanding of trauma and how it can show itself in young children, you can help the children in your care. Now that we understand one of the major reasons behind challenging behavior, we can begin analyzing specific types of challenging behavior—and what we can do about them.

CHAPTER 7

Analyzing Specific Challenging Behaviors

Now that we have discussed the need for better methods of discipline, pushed past our emotions, repaired and strengthened

our relationships with children and family members, and studied what developmentally appropriate behavior and trauma look like in the children we care for, we are equipped to begin taking on the challenging behaviors themselves. Remember the Adult Behavior Laundry List from chapter 3? In this chapter, we learn how to do step 4.

ADULT BEHAVIOR LAUNDRY LIST

1. Sort out your feelings.
2. Repair rips in your relationship.
3. Figure out the care instructions.
4. **Put behaviors in the meaning-making machine.**
5. Choose a cycle.
6. Be patient during the trying time.

Put Behaviors in the Meaning-Making Machine

Did you know that most behavior plans fail because teachers arbitrarily pick strategies without taking into account the meaning or reasons behind a challenging behavior? If you spilled grape juice on your favorite green shirt, you wouldn't simply dump bleach on the stain and hope for the best. The bleach might remove the juice, but it would take the color with it, leaving your shirt with an ugly brown splotch and you with nothing to wear for your dinner date on Friday. Yet we often tackle challenging behaviors this way, simply selecting any strategy out of desperation without knowing whether it is a good match for the problem we are trying to solve.

Thankfully, there is a better approach. It requires a bit more work than simply searching "remove grape-juice stains from clothes" online, but the results can be even more effective. Just as we spent chapter 2 finding the *whys* of your reactions to challenging behaviors, we need to find the *whys* of the children who are exhibiting those behaviors. I like to call this process the *meaning-making machine*. Regardless of the types of stains on individual garments, all clothes have to go through the washer at some point to get fully clean. Similarly, regardless of what specific challenging behavior we are dealing with, we have to carefully consider the context in which it occurs and the factors that affect it so that we can discover the meaning behind that behavior—and, eventually, how to change it. Let's do that now for some common types of challenging behavior.

Physical Aggression

Physical aggression includes behaviors such as hitting, biting, pushing, throwing objects, kicking, spitting, and so on. As we discussed in chapter 5, this behavior is developmentally appropriate for young children, so it is normal to see some physical aggression in your classroom. However, just because a behavior is developmentally appropriate does not mean that we want it to continue!

We tend to attribute physical aggression to anger. However, even if a child is angry, that is only part of the problem. Psychologists often refer to anger as a secondary emotion, meaning that to eliminate anger, one must eliminate the emotion or action that preceded it.

EXERCISE #1: UNCOVERING THE REASONS FOR PHYSICAL AGGRESSION

On a piece of paper, write down all the possible reasons why a child might exhibit physical aggression. This is harder than it sounds because the reasons can vary based on the child, the classroom, and the situation. Here are some possibilities:

- To gain attention
- To avoid a transition or person
- To satisfy a physical need, such as a child who bites because he is teething
- To satisfy a sensory need, such as a child who bites to satisfy a need for oral input
- To express strong negative emotions, such as frustration, sadness, or anxiety
- To communicate when language skills are limited
- To cope with a physical problem

In my career, I have worked with many children whose challenging behaviors stemmed from this last reason. For example, as a therapist, I worked with a child who threw things and hit others. Someone eventually discovered that this child could not see well, and she stopped all physical aggression when she got glasses. While I was working as a consultant, I encountered a child who would tear up the classroom after lunch. In this case, the child had an allergy to dairy and felt sick after drinking milk—an easily solved problem. I also knew another child who would become physically aggressive right before nap time, and it turned out that the child had a sleep disorder and needed medication. I wish all my cases were so easy! As a result of these experiences, when I suspect that physical aggression might be related to a physical problem, I systematically start with the most serious possibility and move down to the most benign. Hearing, vision, sensory, medical, dental, and allergy issues are just some of the potential factors that could contribute to physical aggression.

As these examples show, the reasons why a child might exhibit physical aggression are as varied as children themselves are. Moreover, there may not be just one factor behind a challenging behavior. A child could show physical aggression for all the reasons listed here, several of them, or just one of them. To gain more information, let's look at home, environmental, and other factors that might cause a child to behave this way.

FACTORS THAT AFFECT THIS BEHAVIOR

HOME FACTORS

I cannot tell you how many times I have been called in as a mental-health consultant to deal with physically aggressive behaviors, only to find out about the birth of a new baby in that child's home. Based on a comprehensive review of research, Brenda Volling explains that following the birth of a sibling, children tend to respond with decreases in affection and responsiveness toward caregivers. Moreover, further research by Brenda Volling and her colleagues shows that levels of problem behaviors after a sibling's birth depend on how securely children are attached to their caregivers.

While a new sibling is a common factor, many other challenges and adjustments at home can also trigger physical aggression. For example, many children who show physical aggression are feeling the effects of family members' unemployment, the loss or absence of family members, family members working long hours, family members' separation or divorce, or food and housing insecurity. Interestingly, research by Emory Cowen and colleagues shows that resilient children in urban communities who exhibit good mental health and social problem-solving skills during stress also have family members who exhibit good mental health and coping strategies during stress. On the other hand, stressful home situations can be particularly challenging for children when the adults in their families do not possess good coping skills themselves. As educators, we should not expect all family members to know how to deal with stress or support their children.

Though educators cannot necessarily change what is happening in children's home environments, they can fill a void and help prevent physical aggression by teaching coping skills regularly to all children and by supporting their family members. I suggest placing small calming baskets with sensory items, such as bubbles, playdough with lavender extract, and sensory calming bottles, in each learning area throughout the preschool classroom. It is also a good idea to make small calming bags for family members who are under a great deal of stress.

ENVIRONMENTAL FACTORS

As we learned in chapter 5, physical aggression is common in young children, particularly when certain environmental factors are present in the classroom. For example, young children often become physically aggressive when they are waiting in line with nothing to do or when they are forced to share before they are ready. Adults need to observe people, characteristics, and situations in the classroom to determine what tends to trigger physical aggression—and then plan ahead. To continue our examples, adults could try making wait times active and keeping multiples of toys in the classroom.

CASE STUDY #1: BRAIN-BASED LEARNING, ENVIRONMENT, AND PHYSICAL AGGRESSION

My own research about physical aggression provides some important insights on environmental factors that contribute to this behavior. My experience as a neuro-developmental specialist involved studying and implementing brain-based learning (BBL). In her book *Becoming a "Wiz" at Brain-Based Teaching*, Marilee Sprenger explains, "Understanding and applying how the brain functions, how memory works, and what the brain needs is what makes a classroom brain-based." With that idea in mind, I noticed that physically aggressive behaviors were sometimes the byproduct of ineffective classroom practices that were mismatched to the maturity level of the students.

Previous research corroborates this observation. For example, a study by Judy Hutchings and her colleagues shows that in classrooms with children ages three to seven, teacher training in classroom management yields significant reductions in off-task behavior (both for individuals and for the whole class) and in negative child feelings toward teachers. *Classroom management* refers to an adult's ability to organize students' time, attention, and behavior, potentially providing the external regulation that children need to meet the situational demands of the classroom. Another study by Virginia Vitiello and her colleagues notes that characteristics of the classroom setting are just as important as child factors in predicting children's positive or negative behavior. Instead of only focusing interventions on the child, this study shows that minor modifications to the structure of the preschool classroom lead to less negative engagement in young children. Similarly, Maureen Conroy and her colleagues reviewed strategies to reduce challenging behaviors and found that changing the classroom environment was effective in reducing challenging behaviors. And another review of behavior interventions by Wendy Machalicek and her colleagues shows that adapting the classroom and adapting instruction are both effective in decreasing challenging behaviors in children with autism. Given all these results, I wanted to better understand how BBL affects physically aggressive behaviors in young children.

According to the book *12 Brain/Mind Learning Principles in Action* by Renate Caine and her colleagues, there are three essential components of BBL. I discovered that these elements are also evident in the three domains of the prekindergarten version of the *Classroom Assessment Scoring System*, or CLASS, an observation tool used to assess quality interactions in infant through twelfth-grade classrooms that was developed by Robert Pianta, Karen La Paro, and Bridget Hamre. The following table compares the two systems.

CLASS domains	BBL essential components
Emotional support	Relaxed alertness: creating the optimal emotional climate for learning
Classroom organization	Orchestrated immersion in complex experience: creating optimal opportunities for learning
Instructional support	Active processing of experience: creating optimal ways to consolidate learning

Consequently, I decided to use the CLASS tool to measure BBL in racially diverse Head Start classrooms. The higher the CLASS score for a particular classroom, the more BBL was taking place there. By comparing each classroom's score to the number of behavior-incident reports from that room, I hoped to see whether BBL had any effect on physically aggressive behavior among the children. As it turned out, this hypothesis was correct. The higher a classroom's CLASS score in emotional support and classroom organization, the lower the number of behavior-incident reports from that room, and vice versa. Here are some of the types of behaviors among these teachers that led to fewer physically aggressive behaviors in children:

- Adults joining in play with children and displaying positivity in the form of smiles or positive words
- Adults displaying low numbers of negative behaviors, such as yelling or anger
- Adults being aware of children who might need extra support, responding quickly, and even planning for that assistance or attention ahead of time
- Adults allowing children to take the lead or make choices
- Adults being proactive to prevent behavior problems from occurring in the first place
- Adults having interactive transitions and hands-on, multisensory learning activities

These results extend existing knowledge of how teacher behavior can either increase or decrease physically aggressive behaviors in children. Although we cannot control the behavioral influences that our students experience outside of the classroom, our levels of emotional supports and classroom organization are variables within our sphere of influence.

IMPLICATIONS OF CASE STUDY #1

Some of you are probably thinking, "Angela, I already have classroom organization and provide emotional support. So now what?" It is important to note that CLASS primarily looks at teacher behaviors and is unique in that it measures how much organization and how many emotional supports a classroom provides. In other words, CLASS not only measures interactions between teachers and children but also the frequency and depth of those interactions. More specifically, even if challenging behaviors still occur, it does not mean that teachers did not provide any classroom organization or emotional supports. It means that they did not provide the right amount or type of classroom organization and emotional supports. For example, a teacher might place pinwheels or visuals around the room to encourage children to take deep breaths when they are upset, but the teacher might not use this excellent strategy consistently.

CASE STUDY #2: STRATEGY DOSAGES

When a child demonstrates physical aggression, we want to apply a large dose of a particular strategy frequently. Look not only at *what* adults are doing but also at *how much* they are doing it. If I give you half a dose of medicine when you need a full dose, will you get better? No matter how great a classroom might be, elements such as the day of the week (how often has your emotional stamina *not* been completely depleted by the time Friday rolls around?), the time of day (as a teacher, I was often just hanging by a thread in the afternoon), how many children are in your care (don't you just love how you can be the teacher you always imagined when there is a bad-weather day and only three children show up for class?), and the adults on your team (being crazy alone is not as much fun) all affect the dosage levels. So instead of thinking, "I tried that!" start considering how much you tried an idea and at what frequency.

For example, I was providing consultation with a teacher and observed how often she used positive words to tell a child what to do and how often she used negative words, such as *no* or *stop*. When she used negative words, it actually led to the child exhibiting more aggression. As a result, I suggested using more positive words. She replied, "I do use positive words." I agreed, "Yes, you do, but not all the time." The teacher went on to describe all the times she used positive words. I agreed with those observations and told her that I hoped she could implement that strategy more frequently. Many times I find that teachers, therapists, and family members are implementing great strategies—just not frequently enough to make the behaviors stop.

OTHER FACTORS

Keep in mind that children do not need to see physical aggression to begin using it. In the article "Development of Physical Aggression from Early Childhood to Adulthood," Richard Tremblay notes that children do not necessarily learn physical aggression from their environments (that is, they can figure out how to use it on their own). Instead, "children learn *not to use* physical aggression through various forms of interaction with their environment." This finding emphasizes the importance of how adults and other children respond to physical aggression. If children are seeing this behavior at home, school or child care is an even more important place to learn other strategies and forms of interaction. For example, if you overreact to hitting by displaying an exaggerated frown, a child might begin to hit more in order to fill a need for attention. Or if you respond by yelling, a child might take the cue from you that yelling is how to respond when you are upset. If you let children defend themselves against physical aggression by being physically aggressive in return, it will only reinforce the use of aggression.

So when a child is physically aggressive, try to take a pause before responding to the madness. This millisecond breather will allow you to respond to the child instead of reacting. If there is no imminent danger, for example, I might count to ten, rub my hands with lotion, take a sip of water, look up to the heavens, or recite a few lyrics from Bon Jovi's song "Living on a Prayer."

This practice can help you make sure you are not hovering and overreacting to everything. For example, after attending one of my workshops, one teacher (whom I'll call Victoria) described how influential it had been for her to follow Lori Deschene's advice and "practice the pause." Victoria described an incident in her room in which one child (whom I'll call Collin) had moved toward the head of another child (whom I'll call Domingo) with a block. Instead of reacting, Victoria "[practiced] the pause" and decided to change her approach. Instead of removing Collin and asking why he was touching someone with a block—the way she typically reacted to this type of situation—she asked, "What are you doing with that block?"

Collin replied, "Giving Domingo a haircut."

Victoria was shocked. The child she was always removing did not have bad intentions. He just wanted to play! Because the block was very close to Domingo's head and could cause injury, she responded by showing Collin how to give a "haircut" by pretending to touch Domingo and holding the block above, not on, Domingo's head.

On the other hand, sometimes danger is imminent and there is no time for such rituals. When I was a therapist and working with multiple children who showed high levels of physical aggression, I learned to respond quickly to incidents but also to stay neutral and keep my composure. If I did not, I could cause the behavior to escalate, which could cause injury to other children or to me. During this time, I learned to pause when a child was upset, "listen" to his body language, and be cautious about how I entered his personal space during a challenging moment. I also learned how to develop a positive relationship with physical aggression and not let someone else's aggression result in me exhibiting any of my own.

Verbal Aggression

Verbal aggression includes children saying unkind phrases, such as, "I'm not your friend," or "You can't come to my party," or using profanity. Psychology professor Timothy Jay reminds us that the use of profanity is a normal part of language acquisition. As stated in chapter 5, verbal aggression is a sign that children are understanding words and exploring language. However, adults still need to understand the reasons behind this behavior so they can help children learn more appropriate ways to communicate.

EXERCISE #2: UNCOVERING THE REASONS FOR VERBAL AGGRESSION

On a piece of paper, write down all the reasons why a child could exhibit verbal aggression. Here are some possibilities:

- To gain attention
- To imitate adults
- To express anger or frustration
- Child has an involuntary tic
- To express a physical need, such as fatigue or hunger
- Child is about to have a tantrum

As you look at your list, remember that a child could display this behavior for one of those reasons, several of them, or all of them. But if you focus on what a child *says* to express anger (or whatever emotion he is feeling) instead of focusing on the *source* of the anger, you are paying attention to the wrong thing. The more you understand the emotions or events that led up to the verbal aggression, the better you will be able to predict and plan for future occurrences and to teach the child alternative words for those emotions or situations.

FACTORS THAT AFFECT THIS BEHAVIOR

HOME FACTORS

It is inevitable that children will hear verbal aggression at home at some point. Whether they hear it from TV, a song, or their sweet Oma when she gets riled up, children not only pick up the words themselves but also the tones and situations in which these words are used.

Interestingly, the greatest harm seems to come not just from profanity alone but from frequent amounts of verbal aggression directed toward children. In a study exploring the association between verbal aggression by parents and social problems in children, Yvonne Vissing and her colleagues explain that children who experience frequent verbal aggression from parents have higher rates of physical aggression and social challenges. Another study by C. Ruth Solomon and Françoise Serres shows that verbal aggression toward children results in lower self-esteem.

When a child uses verbal aggression in your classroom, it is important to stay curious. Ask yourself, "Are these the only words directed toward this child at home? Are these the words this child is called?" Imagining this type of home environment helps to move our thoughts from our own emotional reactions to compassion for the child.

ENVIRONMENTAL FACTORS

Adults and peers should not draw unnecessary attention to any type of challenging behavior, but it is particularly important with verbal aggression. Did you ever have a behavior become contagious in your classroom? Verbal aggression is especially prone to this phenomenon—as soon as you say, "Don't say that word," everyone starts to say it! This happens because adults draw so much attention to the wrong thing and not enough attention to the right thing. Young children are still developing the capacity to understand language and might be attracted to the words that get the most attention. They are also learning how to describe their emotions and only have a limited number of words mastered. As a result, certain words and phrases can contain hidden messages. Here are some examples to consider.

What the child says	What the child might actually mean
"Don't look at me."	"I'm ashamed." "I don't want to draw attention to myself."
"You're not my friend."	"I'm frustrated with you right now."
"I hate you."	"I hate this situation." "Maybe saying this will get your attention or get me out of this classroom."
"I don't want to go to sleep."	"I'm afraid of the dark or of being alone on my cot or in my bed."
"I don't know."	"I don't yet have control over my behavior, so I don't know why I did what I did, because logic and reasoning don't guide my decision making yet."

CASE STUDY #3: IGNORING SHIELDS

I once worked with a school-age program in which one child, whom I'll call Ricky, used profanity frequently. Interestingly, it was the other children's reactions to the profanity that gave me pause during my observation. After Ricky used an expletive, his peers' sassy, over-the-top replies ("*Ohh-hh*! You're using bad words!" or "I'm telliiing!") were actually just as disruptive as the profanity and seemed to reinforce it by giving Ricky the peer attention he was craving.

In this case, the teachers and I curbed the behavior by teaching the other children to use what we called ignoring shields. (I got the idea from the "Teasing Shield" video in "Preschool Module 2: Social Emotional Teaching Strategies," created by the National Center for Pyramid Model Innovations.) Each child created a shield with art materials. They then used their shields to "protect themselves" from bad words by holding them up and not saying anything when Ricky used profanity. Once the children were praised for using their shields, they began to just ignore the bad words. As a result, Ricky began to use them less frequently. The teachers also tried to fill Ricky's need for attention in positive ways by giving him jobs and responsibilities in the classroom.

This experience provides several valuable lessons. First, if you focus your attention only on the child with the challenging behavior, you might be missing an easy solution. Second, by involving the whole class in our strategy, we were able to not only work on the challenging behavior but also teach important concepts to the other children. The ignoring shields taught the children that responding to a behavior is not always necessary and helped them develop the skill of ignoring bad behavior. (This, of course, does not apply 100 percent of the time—there are times when it is very necessary to tell a teacher. Each situation is unique, so be cautious not to overgeneralize a strategy to all behaviors or all situations.)

Lying

From a developmental perspective, as we learned in chapter 5, children's elaborate tales are rarely a cause for concern. According the American Academy of Child and Adolescent Psychiatry, young children are still learning the distinction between what is real and what is imagined, and the part of the brain that helps young children to make good choices is not fully mature yet. Lying is an indication that children are beginning to comprehend the thoughts and motivations of others and how those might be different than their own. In the study "Development of Lying to Conceal a Transgression: Children's Control of Expressive Behavior during Verbal Deception" by Victoria Talwar and Kang Lee, researchers asked children ages three through seven not to look at a toy while the researchers left the room. While most of the children could not resist the temptation, three-year-old children were less inclined to lie when the researchers returned. About half of the three-year-olds confessed, while most of the children over age three lied. The lies demonstrate that these children recognized that what the researchers wanted (for the children not to peek) was different from what the children wanted (to peek). However, when the children who lied were asked about their transgressions, they did not have the verbal skills to maintain their lies and gave themselves away upon questioning, demonstrating that children under the age of eight are not skillful liars.

EXERCISE #3: UNCOVERING THE REASONS FOR LYING

On a piece of paper, list all the reasons why a child might lie. Here are some ideas:

- Child likes to tell stories
- To avoid an undesired adult reaction
- To impress someone

Having said these things, remember that young children do not have the cognitive skills to carry out diabolical master plans of deceit. Even if a child under the age of seven lies to cover up a behavior, his cognitive skills will not allow him to make up a story sophisticated enough to deceive others or withstand questioning. As children's perspective-taking abilities develop, they slowly become more understanding of how lying can negatively affect others.

FACTORS THAT AFFECT THIS BEHAVIOR

HOME FACTORS

A teacher once asked me why parents believe their children, even when they lie. Well, because research (as we've seen) shows that very young children tend to not lie intentionally or lie well, it makes sense that their parents believe them. Nonetheless, I understand how this phenomenon can irritate educators. For instance, when I was a teacher, a student claimed that I pulled his arm aggressively and hurt him. While I was frustrated, I did not stay upset for long because I knew that I had not pulled the child's arm. My child-care program had security cameras, and after viewing the video footage, the child's family realized that he had made the story up. But even if there had been no cameras, this child did not yet have the cognitive ability to maintain a convincing lie, so a neutral person questioning the child would have revealed my innocence just as well.

ENVIRONMENTAL FACTORS

Certain circumstances in the classroom can encourage children to make up stories. When I was a teacher, I would always try to make sure that I was with another teacher whenever possible. For instance, if I had ten children by myself, I would combine my classroom with that of another teacher who was supervising a small number of children.

If children are intentionally lying, that is also my cue to reflect on my reactions. If a child is lying to escape a punishment, perhaps that punishment is making things worse and adding to the child's challenging behavior instead of eliminating it. So ask yourself these questions:

- Is my response singling out this child?
- Is my response shaming the child?
- Is my response so exaggerated or negative that the child feels uncomfortable?
- Is my response teaching the child the skills that I want him to implement in place of engaging in the problematic behavior?

The American Psychological Association defines *bullying* as "intentionally and repeatedly [causing] another person injury or discomfort . . . [using] physical contact, words, or more subtle actions." Bullying is not just mean words or actions but *intentional* mean words or actions. To do this purposefully, a child has to be able to correctly interpret the thoughts and emotions of others. Children three and under have great difficulty with these skills, so they actually cannot bully.

Now, you may be thinking, "Humph! Angela, you obviously haven't met the three-year-old bullies in my classroom!" Let's see what researchers have to say about this type of behavior among very young children. Maria Vlachou and her colleagues argue that what you are seeing in your classroom with children three and under might be better classified as "unjustified aggression," in which children are victims of aggression that does not have a clear cause or motive. This type of behavior might be the result of a child misinterpreting an emotion or behavior from another child, such as one child mistaking another child's touch for a push. This type of behavior can also happen as children test limits. For example, at the school where I currently consult, a teacher recently described an incident in which one child stepped on another child's block tower just to see how the second child would react.

As we learned in chapter 5, the ability to predict another person's reaction is just beginning to emerge at about age four, and along with this skill can come bullying. According to Vlachou and her colleagues, because of young children's limited language and cognitive skills, bullying at this age is less sophisticated than it is among older children, and it is usually a reaction to something another child says or does. For example, if Xavier wants to play with Regina in the house area and Regina refuses, Xavier might respond with, "You're not my friend."

EXERCISE #4: UNCOVERING THE REASONS FOR BULLYING

On a piece of paper, list all the reasons why one child might bully another child. Here are some possibilities:

- To gain attention
- To get a toy
- To gain control over another child or a play situation

If you can remember specific bullying incidents in your classroom, try to think about what preceded the incidents. That reflection will point you in the right direction when you consider your interventions. We will explore this idea in more detail when we look at environmental factors, but first, let's explore home factors.

FACTORS THAT AFFECT THIS BEHAVIOR

HOME FACTORS

Some children have social conflicts with others because this is their first experience with a large group of children outside the home. Other children bully because they have previously had difficulty with peer relationships. Judy Dunn and Shirley McGuire explored the association between early home experiences and relationships at school, and they note that children who are highly aggressive toward their siblings also tend to have challenging relationships with children outside their families. Interestingly, in their exploration of other family risk factors, Linnea Burk and her colleagues point out that children who are victims of bullying tend to have high levels of family conflict and anger directed toward them in the home. Put another way, both the children who bully *and* the children who are bullied tend to be experiencing problems at home.

ENVIRONMENTAL FACTORS

The classroom environment can affect the likelihood of bullying. In a study of preschool aggression, Jennifer Adams explains that bullying typically takes place during unstructured free play, recess, and transitions. To prevent this problem, educators should maintain good supervision of the classroom at all times (for example, never sit with your back toward any area of the room where children are) and move around the classroom during free play, spending time in each play area to intercept bullying in the places where it begins.

Some of you may hesitate to implement that last idea, and I understand why. Over my years as a teacher, I had to learn to "let go of the table" during free play. Early in my career, I would sit at a table during the entire free-play time, coaxing children to come make something with me to send home to their family members, while my assistant watched everyone else. Looking back, I realize now that this practice contributed to bullying incidents. Because I was distracted and my assistant had a whole classroom to supervise, we were bound to miss problematic interactions among children.

Yet walking around and art projects are not mutually exclusive. Now I encourage teachers to set art materials out so children can make things on their own during free play while the teachers walk around to various areas. As teachers play with and talk to children throughout the classroom, they can stop bullying where it starts.

Because transitions are also bullying-prone times, I also suggest pairing up children as transition buddies and making transitions into fun activities with songs or games. Most classrooms I work with have transition bags or boxes with items such as books or magnetic drawing toys. These objects keep children so busy during transitions that they do not have time for bullying.

Not Listening, Noncompliance, Defiance, and Reluctance to Participate

Recently, as I walked across the threshold of a two-year-old classroom, the first word I heard was a child's resounding, "No!" I had not even asked that child to do anything yet! Not listening, noncompliance, defiance, and reluctance to participate are common during early childhood as children try to exert their independence and develop the skills needed to compromise and collaborate with others. But when this opposition becomes frequent, adults must take the time to consider what a child might be communicating with these behaviors.

EXERCISE #5: UNCOVERING THE REASONS FOR NOT LISTENING AND SIMILAR BEHAVIORS

On a piece of paper, list all the reasons why a child would not listen or would be defiant. Here are some ideas:

- Ear infection
- An auditory sensory-processing issue
- Confusion or anxiousness about the next activity
- Activity is developmentally inappropriate or boring

Now think about some tasks or directions that the children you work with often resist completing. Is there something these tasks have in common? Is there anything about these tasks that you can change to make them more attractive to the children? For example, how well do you think it works if I try to get children to wash their hands by saying, "Please come wash your hands"? Not well! Instead, I take out bubbles and blow them as I walk to the sink, and I then ask the children to make some bubbles of their own. Similarly, when a child crawls under a table, how effective do you think it is for me to say, "Get out from under that table"? (Well, I used to say it all the time, but because it never worked, I stopped.) When I see a child under a table, I ask him if he is a bird or a snake. Then I ask him to show me how that animal moves, because I know—and the child does not—that there is not enough room under the table, so he will have to come out to show me. These types of strategies are all about making connections, not giving directions. Children will follow instructions if they are having fun doing so, and leading children is really all about loving them.

FACTORS THAT AFFECT THIS BEHAVIOR

HOME FACTORS

A study by Melinda Leidy and her colleagues shows that positive parenting and family cohesion are associated with social compliance in children ages nine through twelve, though parenting might not play as big a role in the compliance of very young children. Young children are still developing the ability to block out irrelevant information when completing tasks. A study by Deborah Pearson and David Lane indicates that the ability to focus attention is still developing in young children and improves as they age. Furthermore, your classroom may be the first setting in which children have had to follow demands with large groups away from home. The organization and structure of a school setting are quite different than those of a home setting. For example, a classroom is potentially full of distractions, has many directions and rules to remember, and requires children to negotiate learning within groups.

ENVIRONMENTAL FACTORS

If young children are not following your directions, you may need to change how you give the directions. Here are some ideas to consider. First, gain children's attention before giving directions. No matter what instructions you are giving, make a connection first. I might make eye contact; gently touch a child on the arm or shoulder; or use a gesture, song, or attention-getter. Singing is one of my favorite ways to connect. A study from researcher Vinoo Alluri and her colleagues reveals that music engages large-scale networks in the brain. When used purposefully, music is nature's wake-up call. In fact, music lights up the brain more than any other human interaction. Therefore, singing your directions can make connections with children.

Some of you might now be thinking, "Angela, do I look like Beyoncé? If I even try to sing, the windows will crack!" The good news is that you don't have to be Beyoncé. You can choose a simple,

PUSH PAST IT!

familiar song as your go-to tune and change the words depending on what you want the children to do. Some people use "Row, Row, Row, Your Boat," "If You're Happy and You Know It," or "Frère Jacques." Mine is Salt-n-Pepa's "Push It."

> Come wash your hands.
>
> Wash 'em real good!
>
> Come wash your hands.
>
> Do it real good!

Second, good directions include visuals, auditory prompts, and movement. Sing or tell the children specifically what you want them to do. Make it fun! If you spend your whole day trying to control children, you never get the chance to play with them. Add motions or a little dance. Support their understanding with a visual, such as a chart that shows the steps they should take to do what you have asked.

Remember, the word *noncompliance* suggests that a person has mastered the ability to comply, and as we learned in chapter 5, those skills are still under construction in young children. Compliance, in fact, is contingent on how well an adult uses positive strategies to engage with a child. Even though the child ultimately chooses whether to comply, because adults have more-advanced planning skills, you can almost always find an effective technique to persuade a child to do what you are asking. Such positive engagement strategies use self-directed, appealing activities that generate enthusiasm, as pointed out by Jason Downer and his colleagues and by John Fantuzzo, Marlo Perry, and Paul McDermott. For example, if you want a child to get in line, ask him if he wants to hop like a bunny or tiptoe on a tightrope to the line. If a child does not comply, focus not on changing the child but on changing or individualizing the activity.

Now, I know that some of you are wondering, "How will children learn compliance if we don't force them to comply?" Well, research shows that compliance is not something we can teach by force; it is actually a force of nature. Research by Heidi Galinski and Claire Kopp shows that young children gradually move from needing external supports to having internal control as they age and their brains mature. Just as we cannot force a three- or four-year-old to ride a two-wheeled bike before he has the appropriate motor skills, we cannot force a child to comply before he has developed the proper self-regulation skills. Until that time, we provide supports to help the child build skills gradually over time, and we slowly decrease those supports as he grows and develops. Just as it takes six to seven years to build up all the skills it takes to ride a two-wheeled bike, it takes six to seven years for a child to build up the necessary skills to be compliant. If a child has never had the proper experiences, such as exercise, or adult supports, he will not magically ride a bike at age six or seven. The same holds true for complying with rules and instructions.

CASE STUDY #4: WRITING REFUSAL

Many years ago, a preschool teacher I provided consultation for (whom I'll call Olivia) contacted me because she was very concerned about several boys in her classroom. They never engaged in writing activities, and she felt that they might be behind when they entered kindergarten the next year.

"How do you currently organize your writing activities?" I asked. Olivia said she had a writing table, but the boys in question never went there voluntarily. Even when she forced them to sit there, the boys just played instead of writing. Next, I asked what the boys' interests were. Like most boys, Olivia said, they loved superheroes and spent long periods of time at the water table.

Based on Olivia's observations, I suggested that she add sensory elements and superheroes to the writing activities to keep the boys engaged long enough to learn how to write. Olivia decided to create sensory boxes and use sleep masks for a writing activity. The sensory boxes included natural items such as rocks, grass, and leaves. The result was an activity in which the boys put on the masks and concentrated on what they could feel as they touched various objects. Then, once Olivia had them engaged, she encouraged them to talk about their discoveries and then helped them to write those exciting discoveries down. Through observing the boys' interests, Olivia was able to follow the children's lead and guide them toward a learning goal.

OTHER FACTORS

As I mentioned at the start of this chapter, challenging behaviors could signal a physical issue. In particular, noncompliance could be a sign of a hearing, vision, or sensory-processing difficulty. Some children struggle to follow directions in large groups because there are so many distractions. Other children may have difficulty processing words or directions quickly. Remember to stay curious and examine all possible reasons behind a behavior.

Clinginess, Crying, and Tantrums

If your classroom is a hazy blur of crying, screaming, incoherent babbling, snot bubbles, flailing bodies, pounding fists, banging heads, yelling, and small bodies clinging to your leg or waist, you are not alone. As we learned in chapter 5, these behaviors do not mean that children are spoiled or acting out. They are often just going through a normal phase in child development.

EXERCISE #6: UNCOVERING THE REASONS FOR CLINGINESS, CRYING, AND TANTRUMS

On a sheet of paper, list all the possible reasons why a child might cling to you (literally or figuratively), cry, or throw a tantrum. Here are some ideas:

- A new baby in the child's home
- A change in a family member's work schedule
- A new staff member in the classroom
- Sensory overload
- Teething
- Coming down with a cold
- Other physical problems (such as my daughter's torticollis and reflux, mentioned in chapter 2)

FACTORS THAT AFFECT THESE BEHAVIORS

HOME FACTORS

As educators, we should not expect family members to automatically know how to respond to crying or tantrums, especially if they lack knowledge of child development. Even adults in the same family might have different ideas about discipline. Working long hours or going to school on top of working might add even more stress for family members. Robert Fox, Donald Platz, and Kathleen Bentley noted fewer positive parenting practices among mothers who were young, had lower education and income, and had more than one child in the home. So when young children cry or have tantrums, family members may need a great deal of support to get through this phase in development. I suggest starting each year off by talking to family members about tantrums and how to deal with them.

ENVIRONMENTAL FACTORS

If clinginess, crying, or tantrums happen multiple times a day in your classroom, try to think back on what events triggered these episodes, and then adjust those events. That is what lesson planning in early childhood is all about! It is more than just listing which cool activities from Pinterest you will try. It also includes predicting and carefully planning appropriate responses to challenging behaviors. Challenging behaviors are not ruining your lesson plans—they should be a big part of your lesson plans.

So if a child has a downright fit each day at arrival and at circle time—well, at least he is consistent. Instead of trying to get control over children when they cry, we as adults have to get control over our thinking so that we can deal with the crying. Because we are adults and have the capacity to reflect and plan, we must shift our focus toward understanding the child's underlying intentions and then use those observations to intentionally steer him away from challenging behaviors.

During my years a consultant, I often had conversations with caregivers who worried that responding to every cry would result in fragile children wailing incessantly every time they stubbed a toe. Teachers wondered how to balance the needs of one child who may cry frequently with the larger group of children in a classroom. In these cases, you can use lesson planning to help you plan your responses. Most teachers tend to think of lesson planning as paperwork, but in an article for Forbes, Mark Murphy reminds us that writing something down makes you more likely to implement it. Specifically, lesson planning can help you pinpoint times when children are likely to cry, choose strategies and activities to prevent or respond to crying, and make sure all children's needs are met. This technique is particularly helpful if you work with age groups that cry frequently, such as infants, toddlers, and two-year-olds.

Educators and therapists often worry that focusing lessons and activities on social-emotional skills will result in fewer opportunities for academic learning and development. But a quality activity should focus on both academic and social-emotional learning. For example, labeling a child's feelings and asking open-ended questions about them, such as, "What could we do to help you feel better?" can support language and problem-solving skills. Coloring a picture to calm down can help a child develop his fine-motor skills. Counting items in a calm-down box and describing their attributes can boost language and math skills. You do not have to sacrifice academic learning or development in order to address social-emotional challenges.

CASE STUDY #5: "WHAT HAPPENS AT 11:30?"

At one of my workshops, a teacher asked me what to do about a child, whom I'll call Irina, who had frequent tantrums. I began asking the teacher questions about the situation. She stated that Irina would have a tantrum every day around 11:30. Even before I could make any suggestions, the other participants began trying to find the meaning behind the behavior. They asked questions and made comments such as, "Is Irina sleepy?" "Maybe she's hungry," and "What happens at 11:30?" Together, we came up with quite a list of ideas for this teacher to try at 11:30:

- Have a cot ready for Irina to take a nap.
- Give Irina a snack.
- Adapt whatever activity normally occurs at 11:30.
- Have a calming sensory activity, such as adding lavender extract to the water table, ready.
- Put the children in smaller groups.
- Make sure there is not sensory overload.
- Sing Irina's favorite song.
- Give Irina a calming box full of pictures of her family members.
- Hug Irina.
- Have Irina's favorite activity or toy available.
- Arrange for another adult to come into the classroom.

Even taking Irina and a friend for a short walk outside the room at 11:30 could work if that action was planned ahead of time and was not a reaction to a tantrum. In other words, taking a child out of the classroom as a *result* of a tantrum falls into the category of exclusionary discipline, but arranging for that walk *before* a tantrum occurs is a form of individualized planning.

When You Struggle to Find the Meaning behind Challenging Behaviors

Using the information presented so far in this chapter, you will be able to uncover the meanings behind many instances of challenging behavior in your classroom. But when a behavior becomes particularly frequent and intense or when family members and educators are stumped as to what it might mean, it is time to take a more systematic approach. Consider this section as the deep-cleaning treatment that you apply when the situation is really messy.

Like an overturned laundry basket, challenging behaviors can feel like a large, tangled assortment of random words and actions. But you can determine the reason or reasons why students engage in challenging behaviors by using a functional assessment. A *functional assessment*, as explained by Terrance Scott, Peter Alter, and Kathleen McQuillan, is a way of identifying predictable associations between a behavior and the environmental conditions in which it transpires. Put simply, you look for patterns that reveal why a student might be using a challenging behavior.

USING THE MEANING-MAKING MACHINE CHART

Remember the meaning-making machine from our Adult Behavior Laundry List? Appendix D

PUSH PAST IT!

contains a functional-assessment tool called the Meaning-Making Machine Chart (MMMC), which I created to help teachers sort, classify, and group information about challenging behaviors, enabling them to get a clearer picture of the problem. Some particularly challenging behaviors might require you to run the issue through the MMMC multiple times. Additionally, because children, behaviors, and relationships are not static, you should revisit the MMMC (or whatever tool you decide to use) often. In practice, I have found that reflecting on and updating the MMMC every four to six weeks helps educators, caregivers, and parents understand how a problem might grow, change, or dissipate over time.

So how do you use this chart? It does not have to be a linear process. The MMMC begins with section A: Antecedent, which focuses on what happens first chronologically, but most educators start with section B: Behavior because that information is easier to observe. In fact, I have found that starting with section A can actually frustrate teachers and stifle the process because they are so eager to talk about section B.

Here is how each section works:

- Section A describes the *antecedent*, or what happens before the child engages in the challenging behavior. Check any and all conditions that apply to the situation you are analyzing. If none of the options fit the situation, use the space to write a brief description of what happens before the behavior occurs.

- Section B describes the *behavior* itself: what happens, how often it happens, how long it lasts, and how intense it is. You will probably want to use a separate checklist to track frequency in more detail (we will discuss a possible tool in this chapter). Also note any of the child's strengths or interests; we'll discuss why in a moment.

- Section C: Consequences describes the *consequences*, or what happens after the child engages in the challenging behavior. This is not where you describe how you punish the child for the behavior. Instead, you list the responses to the behavior from the other children (if you are in a classroom or group setting) and from all the adults who work with the child.

- The Purpose of Behavior section helps you decide on what you think are the reasons or functions behind the challenging behavior. All functions fit into two categories: to gain something or someone or to avoid something or someone.

- The Note Any Changes in Lifestyle section reminds us to look at lifestyle events that might be affecting the child's behavior.

Remember, challenging behavior is so complex that it often cannot be boiled down to a single factor. These five factors together (antecedent, behavior, consequences, function, and lifestyle events) are all the ingredients needed to lead you to understanding all the possible reasons why a child might be displaying a behavior.

How much time you need to spend on a functional assessment depends on how messy the problem is. Have you ever used a stain remover and moved on too quickly, throwing the garment in the washing machine before the treatment had a chance to set in? Apply the same logic here. Like stubborn stains, some difficult challenges require more time to understand. I find that the MMMC works best when several adults each fill out a copy at the same time and compare notes. You can use the chart by yourself, but with the help of a team, you may be able to figure out what is going on with a child more quickly.

As noted earlier, section B includes a place to record the child's strengths and interests. Why? Isn't the point to figure out what is wrong with the child? For a child to follow your directions—including the ones that will help him change his behavior—you have to make connections with that child. By looking for the interests and strengths of a child in trouble, you find the best ways to make those connections and provide the care that child needs. This logical model helps teachers analyze all the observable variables that might influence human behavior, as Glen Dunlap and Lise Fox point out. Researchers Angel Fettig and Erin Barton explain that these variables can be systematically assembled like puzzle pieces to identify why a child might be demonstrating challenging behaviors and to identify the environmental conditions under which those behaviors might occur. This process teaches you how to find clues that will help you understand the meaning behind a challenging behavior and what message the child is sending.

You might be thinking, "But Angela! There *is* no meaning! The child behaves this way for no reason." I never said that the meaning was easy to find or was even logical. The information from the earlier part of this chapter can give you some ideas. It helps to think like a young child: "Sometimes I hit people because I'm angry. Sometimes I hit people because I'm frustrated. Sometimes I hit people because I have a toothache. And sometimes I hit people because I think it's funny when that little vein pops out of the teacher's forehead!" In all seriousness, the reason behind a challenging behavior may be a genuine medical need or a mental-health issue. But sometimes the reason really is completely illogical.

CASE STUDY #6: THREE-YEAR-OLD LOGIC (OR THE LACK THEREOF)

I worked in one classroom with a three-year-old boy whom I'll call Kiet, who was an only child, by the way. He thought that all the toys in the classroom were his, so he would hit, kick, and push children who played with "his" toys. When teachers would intervene by reprimanding him or removing him from activities, Kiet only acted even more frustrated and confused. In his mind, all the others in the classroom were the ones with the problem: They kept taking his toys!

We can better understand this situation by applying what we have learned about developmentally appropriate behavior. First, three-year-old children are egocentric by nature. Second, the part of the brain that allows us to think logically and control our emotions does not even begin to develop until about age three. Most children cannot consistently self-regulate until about school age, and even then, these skills take two decades to fully mature. So a teacher moving out of little Johnny's line of vision, a playmate holding a blue car when Johnny wants all the blue cars, or a peer brushing up against Johnny at circle time could all be very good reasons (at least in Johnny's mind) for Johnny to embark upon destroying a classroom or attacking his friends. So when teachers say that the behavior has no meaning, they could well be right: the behavior might not make sense from an adult's perspective, or it could be completely irrational.

CASE STUDY #7: CHANGING LOGIC

In another classroom I worked with as a consultant, a preschooler whom I'll call Gina started saying "butts and boo-boo" at circle time because she had a nervous tic and was anxious when sitting in large groups of children. When Gina noticed the other children laughing at her words, she began to say "butts and boo-boo" both when she was anxious and to gain peer attention. This pattern led to frequent disruptions in the classroom.

PUSH PAST IT!

To solve this issue, Gina's teacher and I first stopped overreacting to the challenging behavior, such as by gasping with annoyed or shocked expressions on our faces or by telling Gina to stop doing something that she had no control over. We realized that we were unintentionally rewarding Gina's behavior by giving her attention when she was disruptive. Instead, we told Gina that she could say "butts and boo-boo" all she wanted in the bathroom. We started praising her when she went to the bathroom to say those words. This approach worked so well that if any child wanted to say "butts" or "boo-boo," he or she went to the bathroom to say it. After the novelty wore off, it was an effective strategy.

Gina's story shows us that challenging behavior can start out with a particular meaning, but that the meaning can change because of the response the behavior gets. This is what makes all this so complicated! And it is the reason why you cannot talk about strategies without first talking about the reasons behind a behavior.

USING THE BEHAVIOR CHECKLIST

It is important to track the frequency and intensity of challenging behaviors. How will you know whether a strategy is working and a behavior is getting better unless you know the frequency of the behavior at the start of problem solving? Just as you track your weight at certain intervals when you are on a diet, you track your progress as you help a child adjust his behavior. Appendix C provides a useful checklist to help you more easily track and notice patterns and changes in a child's behavior.

Wrapping Up

To help children eliminate challenging behaviors, we need to spend time reflecting on their meanings. Even good advice can have bad outcomes if we do not take the time to understand the complex, multifaceted factors that could be affecting a situation. All too often, even our colleagues want to rush to giving advice before they have taken time to thoroughly understand a problem. Just as some stains need to soak overnight before you put the garment in the washer, give yourself, family members, and colleagues time to soak in all the potential meanings behind a challenging behavior.

Now that you have found the meanings behind the challenging behaviors you face, you are ready to learn the steps to deal with these challenges. The next leg of our journey involves choosing strategies based on the meanings you have identified.

To see the original version of the MMMC,
visit https://www.gryphonhouse.com/our-authors/author-detail/angela-searcy-edd

CHAPTER 8

Setting Up Your Background Supports

We are almost ready to begin choosing strategies to address challenging behavior (and finally finish the Adult Behavior Laundry List). However, while the techniques you choose will be unique to your situation, anyone who confronts challenging behaviors needs certain background supports in place in order to address those behaviors successfully. As these supports are fairly similar for everyone, we will discuss them first to provide the last layer of the foundation before we move on to specific strategies.

Customize Your Behavior-Review System

Before you begin choosing strategies, you need a way to keep track of them so that you can determine whether they are effective. To that end, your program needs its own behavior-review system in place. You may be saying, "Really, Angela? I already have way too much to do, especially paperwork!" Believe me, I know that feeling. Here is why this additional system is important: While educators are often detail-oriented self-starters when it comes to decisions such as whether an activity is worth getting out the glitter for, they often lack a detailed process or decision-making tree when it comes to dealing with challenging behaviors. Just as with other important teaching-related choices, such as, "Do I really have enough money to buy even more books for my classroom?" or "Should I laminate?" decisions regarding challenging behaviors need clearly defined step-by-step processes and procedures beyond writing up an incident report and informing the child's family members. A standardized system promotes consistency among staff members and across incidents, helping to ensure that children are treated fairly and that behavior expectations are the same for everyone.

COMPONENTS OF A BEHAVIOR-REVIEW SYSTEM

What should be part of a behavior-review system? Each system will be unique to the program that creates it, because different children, adults, locations, and situations have different needs. But there are some common elements to all behavior-review systems.

CLEAR DEFINITION OF CHALLENGING BEHAVIORS

Left to their own devices, not all adults see the same behaviors as challenging. Different staff members might have different tolerance levels for various behaviors. Family members might not see the seriousness of a particular behavior. Administrators might not understand why a certain behavior is problematic. Having clear definitions puts everyone on the same page.

CLEAR THRESHOLD FOR ACTIVATING THE SYSTEM

Sometimes ignoring is the best strategy to eliminate a challenging behavior. In other cases, adults need to address the behavior directly by activating the behavior-review system. So where is the line? Choose a consistent, measurable threshold that all staff members can easily identify, such as, "If an undesirable behavior occurs five times within two days, we will consider it a challenging behavior and begin the process of addressing it." In one program that I worked with, the staff members chose to activate their system after the third incident of a behavior. Without a specific standard to guide them, educators will sometimes wait to ask for help until challenging behaviors have gotten far out of hand. By this time, the behaviors have disrupted the classroom so badly that it is almost impossible to repair the situation.

FLEXIBILITY WITHIN A CLEAR AND ORGANIZED SYSTEM

Situations vary. Sometimes challenging behaviors are temporary (for example, when a child's parent is out of town, there has been a minor change in routine, or a child is testing limits). It may make the situation worse if adults apply long-term strategies to a temporary behavior or short-term strategies to a persistent behavior. Your system should provide easy-to-understand steps to help staff members determine the severity of a problem and how to address each level of severity.

CLEAR UNDERSTANDING OF WHO IS INVOLVED

A teacher will most likely be the person to activate the behavior-review system, but she should not be alone in her efforts. Other teachers, paraprofessionals, administrators, and medical or mental-health professionals can all be included in the team that addresses a challenging behavior. Create specific guidelines for who should be added to the team, under what circumstances they should join, and what roles they will play. Define how an assembled team will work together and who will do what to deal with the behavior.

If at all possible, involve the child's family members in your efforts so that family members can have input. We welcome family members at every step in the system—after all, we all want what is best for their child. However, you might find that family members engage in one part of the process and not another. That is okay. Participating in a behavior-review system can be new and intimidating for family members.

Even if family members decline to participate altogether, you can still move forward in other ways to support teachers in the classroom. For example, if a child's parents do not consent to having her undergo a mental-health evaluation, a mental-health consultant can still do a general observation of the classroom as a whole and suggest supports for the teacher.

CLEAR PROCESS FOR DOCUMENTING AND REPORTING BEHAVIORS

The last thing you want to do is add unnecessary paperwork and meetings on top of everything else you need to do. This system is meant to make your job easier, not harder. So as part of setting up your behavior-review system, establish exactly what forms, reports, or other documents need to be filled out or written and what purposes they will serve. Also determine your reporting protocol: who reports to whom, what information must be part of the report, and when does this happen? For instance, you may decide to have teachers fill out a form for each incident to provide a step-by-step paper trail, or you may choose to record a broader overview of a behavior by having teachers track it for a certain length of time on a single chart. Your reporting protocol might require teachers to discuss the filled-out forms with the behavior team each week and then turn the forms in to their supervisors.

CASE STUDY #1: DESIGNING A BEHAVIOR-REVIEW SYSTEM

In 2004, I worked with a Head Start program in Chicago to design a behavior-review system specifically for that school. Knowing some common pitfalls of other systems, I decided to address them in our design. For example, as a former teacher, I knew that teachers were busy (can I get a witness?) and needed a document that would communicate the new system at a glance, so we organized it as a chart that fit on a single sheet of paper. As a teacher, I had also been inundated with a sea of white forms, so we color-coded forms for easier organization.

It took us one year to design the new system. It took months to pilot the system in one classroom, get feedback on it, and adapt it. It took several more months to introduce the system to the entire staff, get more feedback, and refine the system further. Then it took several additional months for the whole staff to get comfortable using the final system.

Interestingly, with this new system, the administrators noticed that the teachers stopped complaining about challenges and started problem solving about them. It became clear to everyone that what had appeared to be lack of initiative on the part of the teachers was actually lack of clarity and structure from their leadership. The teachers' behavior changed because they finally had a framework and clear guidance for addressing challenging behaviors.

Now, I know what you are wondering: "Was there pushback on filling out all the new forms?" No! Because the teachers had helped make the forms, they had ownership of them, and they used them. The whole process went so well that this program became known in the community for being highly effective in working with children with challenging behaviors. (To see this flow chart, visit https://www.gryphonhouse.com/our-authors/author-detail/angela-searcy-edd)

Inspired by this success, another Head Start program simply took the first program's existing system and tried to implement it wholesale at their site. Guess what happened? It didn't work. And *that*, my friends, is why "nothing ever works" when you are dealing with challenging behaviors! It is not because a particular strategy is not a good idea. It is because you have to adapt the strategy to fit your unique circumstances. Otherwise, it is like using a cookie cutter to carve wood: if you get results at all, they will probably be poor. In the case of the two Head Start sites, the borrowed behavior-review system was never implemented at the second site because there wasn't the same ownership of the system among the site director and staff members.

IMPLEMENT YOUR NEW SYSTEM WITH CAUTION

Designing your own behavior-review system is important, but it is not foolproof. Let me tell you about times in my experience when this process worked and times when it backfired.

- The process worked when administrators piloted the new system with one willing teacher first. If no one is willing, then it might be time for administrators to do some relationship building with staff members. The process backfired when administrators copied the new forms and simply handed them to staff without getting any input.

- The process worked when a pilot classroom was able to try out new forms and give feedback that was then used to adjust the forms. Not all the feedback was used, but enough was that the teachers felt comfortable using the revised forms and found them useful. The process backfired when administrators simply gave teachers new forms and ordered them to use them without ever seeking feedback or customizing the forms to fit the needs of a given program.

- The process worked when administrators looked at the entire behavior-review system and incorporated items they were already using. For example, one site was already using a tool called the *Ages and Stages Questionnaire*, third edition, to screen children for social and emotional delays. Instead of reinventing the wheel, they incorporated this tool into their new process. The process backfired when paperwork in the system was redundant.

- The process worked when administrators reinforced the new system over time, provided support to teachers, and had realistic expectations of how long the system would take to implement. For example, if an administrator learned that there had been an incident of physical aggression in a classroom, she would ask the teacher, "Where are you in the behavior-review process?" This type of conversation occurred repeatedly over a course of months. The process backfired when administrators did not prioritize the importance of the new system, were not consistent in supporting implementation, and had unrealistic expectations about timing.

- The process worked when administrators modeled the behaviors they wanted to see in their staff members. The more the leaders were open and willing to listen, the more the staff members were open and willing to listen. The process backfired when administrators acted as if their role was to give orders instead of provide supports.

Every program is unique, and only you and your colleagues know what will work best for your situation. Furthermore, your final system will only be as good as staff members' willingness to implement it consistently.

General Principles for Implementing Strategies

With your behavior-review system in place, you are almost ready to select particular strategies. Regardless of which ones you choose, the principles in this section will help you implement those strategies successfully.

MATCH

In some ways, you are on a journey to address challenging behavior, and this book is your GPS. But like a GPS, I do not necessarily have up-to-the-minute information about your situation. So keep your wits about you. Do not blindly follow an idea just because it is in this book. As with anything you bring into your classroom, you have to MATCH each of my strategies to your needs and circumstances:

- **Modify** the strategy so that it fits within the culture and context of your program.
- **Adjust** the strategy so that it fits with your background, interests, and strengths.
- **Take into account** the strengths and needs of your administration and teaching teams.
- **Consider** the idea in terms of the strengths and needs of the children and families you serve.
- **Hash out** how this idea fits within the requirements of your curriculum, licensing system, or assessment system.

WERK IT!

When teachers say, "I've tried that idea!" or "That doesn't work," they are not talking about the strategy itself. They are really trying to describe their struggle to implement the strategy. As a consultant, I frequently find that teachers are already implementing excellent ideas but often abandon them before they have given them enough time to work. Or they are not implementing the strategies consistently or as they were intended. The bottom line is this: Strategies in and of themselves don't work. Relationships don't work. People work—or rather, they WERK it:

- Show **willingness** to try a new idea as it was intended and to consistently assess the quality of your implementation.
- **Engage** in the implementation frequently so you can become good at it.
- **Reflect** on the results using objective data (yes, *data*, that four-letter word for observations) with colleagues.
- **Keep the focus** on progress, not perfection, adapting an idea slowly and intentionally over time based on data and the unique needs of your classroom or program.

Unless you MATCH a strategy to your classroom and WERK it, your success will be limited at best.

CASE STUDY #1: VISUAL DISASTER

Many years ago, when I was a teacher, I came home all gung-ho from a workshop on using visual strategies to support children with challenging behaviors. I spent the weekend creating the best visuals on the planet—definitely Pinterest worthy—and putting them on a key ring. When I came to school on Monday, I was actually wishing someone would act up so I could try my new technique. (There is nobody full of more false hope than a teacher armed with a new strategy for challenging behaviors.)

Suddenly, there was my moment! Little "Tammy Tantrum" started her usual cutting up, and I was ready with my key ring. Except then it happened: I choked! I couldn't find the doggone visual I needed. I flipped frantically through the thirty different pieces of card stock on my key ring, trying to find the image I wanted, as my preschoolers stared at me.

Then I fumbled! Before I could pick up my key ring, Tammy had it and was off with my precious pictures. With a big grin on her face, she spiked my key ring directly into the toilet like a professional athlete. Touchdown! As she did her celebration dance, I fished my soggy visuals out of the water.

What did I learn from this experience?

- All visuals need to be laminated for durability. Card stock will not hold up against preschoolers with fast hands.
- Only introduce one or two new concepts at a time to the children. Trying to introduce too many at once will confuse everyone, including you.
- Introduce strategies when children are calm (before something happens), and then reinforce those strategies when children are wound up (after something happens).
- Try to connect new strategies to the children's interests. In this example, if I had made the visuals by including photos of Tammy and her classmates or images of things that they were interested in, such as stickers of their favorite cartoon characters, the children might have been more interested in the visuals.

It was not that the idea of using visuals was bad in and of itself. I was just bad at implementing it! It took me years of practice to perfect my use of this strategy. So if your first attempt at a technique does not go well, keep trying. You cannot expect children (or yourself) to learn something new overnight.

WORK ON ONE BEHAVIOR AT A TIME

Have you ever stuffed all your clothes into one load of laundry? If your washing machine is anything like mine, at least one of three things happened: you had a reenactment of Noah's flood in your laundry room, your washer clunked through the whole cycle as if it was full of marbles and rocks wrapped in chainmail, or your washer went on strike. Regardless, the result was probably not clean clothes.

The same idea applies here. Many of you, I know, would love to be Super Teacher and fix everything. (Most teachers cannot help it—it is in their nature.) But do not try to solve every single problem at one time! I cannot tell you how many times the teachers I have worked with have become overwhelmed by trying to tackle too many challenges at once. Wait until one behavior is resolved before starting to work on another one. And go after the most challenging behaviors first.

KEEP GOOD RECORDS

When you try new ideas, there is a lot of trial and error—mostly error. Successfully changing children's challenging behaviors depends on your ability to continue to perfect strategies over time. And how will you know how to adjust a strategy unless you know what the situation was like to begin with? By comparing records taken before you started a strategy to records taken after you have used the strategy for a while, you can understand where you have been, whether you have had setbacks, and how far you have come. The MMMC and the Behavior Checklist are good places to start, but you may also want to track additional information: how long a behavior lasts, your typical response to the behavior, how a child's bedtime correlates to the number of incidents in a day, and so on.

Good records also help you and the other adults in your program maintain consistency in applying your strategies. Consistency is key to all teaching, but it is especially important when you are dealing with a child who has challenging behaviors. You and your colleagues may be the only adults this child can depend on.

Supporting Yourself and Your Colleagues during This Process

There is a reason we call certain behaviors challenging. They can wear on adults' nerves, stretch their patience thin, and make flipping hamburgers seem like not such a bad career after all. Therefore, educators and caregivers must take care of themselves and each other throughout the process of addressing challenging behavior. Use the tips in this section to help you hang on. After all, if you give up, who will help the child get better?

AVOIDING BURNOUT

FOR TEACHERS

Let's take a moment of silence for all the infant teachers who never get one. I can relate because I was an infant teacher. My classroom usually had six babies in it at a time, and given how much a typical baby cries—let alone six—it was not uncommon for crying to take up the majority of the day. While behavior such as this is normal, it can take an emotional toll on teachers. I cannot deny my love for babies, but I also cannot deny how physically strenuous (you spend most of the day on the floor) and intensely demanding the work can be. These kinds of circumstances, coupled with low pay and being looked upon as glorified babysitters, can leave teachers with undernourished spirits, hungry for self-care and support.

Try repeating some of these phrases to yourself when you are having a hard time:

- Breathe. Reflect. Repeat. You've got this!
- Challenging behaviors are tough, but you are tougher!
- It is not working *yet*. You can't do this *yet*. The power of *yet*!
- This child is behaving the only way she knows how.
- Tomorrow is a new day. Try again.

PUSH PAST IT!

FOR ADMINISTRATORS

When it comes to administrators supporting their staff members, my colleague Pat Husband says it best: "When all the babies are crying, the best thing you can do as a supervisor is not to go hug a baby but to go hug the teachers." Instead of taking over the process of addressing challenging behaviors—a practice that could undermine or disrupt the relationships between caregivers and children—good leaders support their staff members in implementing effective strategies. In a TED Talk, Benjamin Zander points out, "The conductor of an orchestra doesn't make a sound. He depends for his power on his ability to make others powerful." Like a conductor, a good leader directs the work of others. Like a good safety harness, she provides support, adjusts when needed, and lifts others up. Try giving notes such as these to your staff members to offer them some fulfillment so that they, in turn, can fulfill the needs of young children:

- Phone a friend, go for a walk—do something for you tonight!
- You're not alone.
- You've got this because we've got you.

KEEPING YOUR COOL

When a child flies off the handle, it is hard not to fly off right after her. Here are some ideas to help you hang on.

FOR TEACHERS

In a Facebook post, T. D. Jakes Ministries describes starting the process of change by "[getting] your mind out of trouble." Whether or not you are religious, this concept is an important skill for teachers. People often do not realize the concentrated mental dexterity it takes to remember that there really is no malicious intent when a four-year-old is hurling toys in your face, spitting at you, and screaming hysterically because another child looked at her wrong during circle time. But if you do not keep "your mind out of trouble," you can get stuck in unhelpful thoughts, such as, "This child is hopeless." Those thoughts will definitely not improve the situation.

Because I understand this struggle, I love to implement practical reminders to help teachers regain cognitive control. For example, after hearing one of my presentations on children's crying, one of the teachers I work with started to wear a rubber band around her wrist. Then each time she felt sure that several of her students were trying to reenact the movie *Problem Child* in her classroom, she would snap the rubber band against her wrist to help her snap back into reality and stay responsive rather than reactive.

FOR ADMINISTRATORS

Leaders need to foster an environment in which educators, specialists, and support staff:

- look for reasons and strategies instead of looking for people to blame.
- view challenging behaviors as opportunities to teach new skills instead of as troublesome inconveniences.
- view family members with empathy and compassion.

If adults are learning new ways to respond to challenging behaviors, they need constant reminders and support as they internalize those methods. Posting inspiring materials around classrooms at adults' eye levels can help nourish your staff members' minds.

Try posting some of these phrases:

- Calm adults = calm children
- Demonstrate the behavior you want to see.
- All behavior has meaning.
- Label emotions.
- Respond instead of react.
- Misbehavior = What am I missing in this child?
- This is an opportunity to model how to behave.

CHAPTER 9

Strategies for Addressing Challenging Behaviors

This is it: the chapter you have been waiting for. After processing our emotions, discovering how to effectively work with families, learning about developmentally appropriate behavior and the effects of trauma, analyzing the precise challenging behaviors that we face, and putting our background supports in place, we are finally ready to learn specific strategies to help children eliminate challenging behaviors. This chapter begins with strategies that can apply to all kinds of challenging behaviors and then gradually narrows to focus on specific situations or types of behavior.

Choose a Cycle

Remember our Adult Behavior Laundry List? We now have tossed our "clothes" into the washer and are ready to move on to step 5.

ADULT BEHAVIOR LAUNDRY LIST

1. Sort out your feelings.
2. Repair rips in your relationship.
3. Figure out the care instructions.
4. Put behaviors in the meaning-making machine.
5. **Choose a cycle.**
6. Be patient during the trying time.

When you do your laundry, you select different cycles (and sometimes various options within those cycles, depending on how fancy your washer is) according to what types of clothes you are washing and what stains you are trying to treat. Similarly, when you address a challenging behavior, you create a plan by selecting various strategies according to what type of behavior you are facing, the reasons you have uncovered behind that behavior, additional factors affecting the behavior, and more. But how exactly do you use this information to select the most effective strategies for your plan?

Over the years, my methods for dealing with challenging behaviors have progressed from dwelling on angry thoughts such as, "You're going to regret this!" to a multipronged approach that includes identifying associations between behaviors and the environmental conditions in which they transpire, teaching new skills to children, and adapting my responses to behavior. Not every situation requires such a complex plan of attack, but it works well when challenging behaviors become so intense and frequent that they affect the entire classroom environment, interfere with children's social-emotional development and learning, and pose safety risks.

This methodology is drawn from the evidence-based system of interventions for challenging behaviors presented in the book *Prevent-Teach-Reinforce for Young Children: The Early Childhood Model of Individualized Positive Behavior Support* by Glen Dunlap and his colleagues. For my purposes, I have condensed their approach and adapted the language based on my conversations with educators, therapists, and family members. Here are the three main categories of strategies in this process, using my terminology:

1. "Change you" strategies
2. "Change the child" strategies
3. "Change the consequences" strategies

"Change you" strategies are preventions that adults can do before a behavior even starts. "Change the child" strategies involve teaching a child new skills to replace challenging behaviors. "Change the consequences" strategies involve changing the responses from the adults or children who witness the challenging behavior.

Each of these categories contains strategies that can be applied to multiple types of challenging behavior. Use the information on your MMMC and Behavior Checklist to help you choose the strategies that make the most sense in your situation. For best results, select at least one strategy from each category. Your interventions will not be nearly as effective if you put all your efforts into an unbalanced plan.

CHANGE YOU

"Change you" strategies may lead you to speak to a child differently, individualize activities, change the classroom environment, or adjust the daily schedule to minimize the likelihood of a behavior occurring in the first place. Here are some examples of how "change you" strategies might be carried out.

- **Use positive language and tell the child what *to* do instead of what *not* to do.** Instead of saying, "Don't splash the water," say, "Keep the water in the water table."
- **Let the child choose the sequence of activities.** Using a picture die or cards with pictures of activities, let the child decide what to do next. During this activity, you might hear a teacher say, "That's the picture of the art center. That's a great choice."
- **Use a timer to show the length of an activity.** Say, "I'm setting the timer for ten minutes. When you hear it ding, it will be time to put away the blocks."
- **Give a warning before an activity ends.** On the playground, hold up a sign for the child that signals five more minutes of play.
- **Spend more positive time with this child.** Play a game, read a book, tell silly jokes, eat your snacks together, or do something else to repair and strengthen your relationship.
- **Explain rules ahead of time, and use visuals to remind the child of the rules.**
- **Model the rules daily.** If you ask the children to put away the art supplies, help them do it. If you do not want the children to yell indoors, use a soft voice while indoors.
- **Use "first-then" statements.** In a first-then statement, explain what you want the child to do (the "first") and the reward he will receive for complying (the "then"). For instance, say, "First, wash your hands. Then we can have snack."
- **Add the child's interests to an activity.** For example, if the child loves bugs, read a book about bugs and go on a bug hunt outside.
- **Add a sensory element or movement to an activity.** For example, when you are reading a story, give the children streamers that they can wave whenever they hear a phrase repeated in the story.
- **Go to a less stimulating environment.** If you can tell that a child is bothered by the noise of an air-conditioning unit or the music coming from the music center, head over to the library center to read a book.
- **Change the location of an activity.** Instead of having circle time inside, try having it outside, or perhaps keep it inside and adjust the classroom space to allow for more room.
- **Cover tempting items.** If a child continually pulls items off a shelf that is off limits, put a blanket over the shelf so that the child does not see the tempting items.
- **Show the child items that he *can* hit or bite.** Try, for example, using a drum or a basket of teething toys.
- **Limit wait time or make it active.** For example, sing a song or do a fingerplay while waiting for snack. If a child simply cannot wait yet, let that child go first.
- **Act out stories.** If a child struggles to sit still for story time, invite him to act out the story as you read it.
- **Let children color while listening to a story.**
- **Use a puppet to gain a child's attention.** For example, read a story using the puppet as a helper.

- **Let a child stand while learning.**
- **Send home visuals of the steps of a routine.** Family members can use the visuals to help their child practice the routine at home.
- **Add sensory breaks.** If a child starts wiggling at circle time, stop circle time and take a movement break to get the wiggles out. Or if a child looks frustrated during a small-group game, head off a tantrum by leading the group in a quick "shake break" to calm the child down: stand up and shake, shake, shake your head, arms, and shoulders.

CHANGE THE CHILD

"Change the child" strategies teach a child a new skill to replace a challenging behavior instead of removing him from the very place where he would learn those skills. Educators often use books, songs, games, and activities to teach academic skills. Social skills must also be intentionally taught using the same methods.

- **Teach the child a calming technique.** For example, use the "Tucker Turtle Takes Time to Tuck and Think" PowerPoint from the website of the Center on the Social and Emotional Foundations for Early Learning. http://csefel.vanderbilt.edu/resources/strategies.html
- **Teach the child a new skill with a scripted story.** Think of the skill you want the child to display, and with the child's help, create a short story explaining how to use that skill.
- **Teach the child what to do by using a song or a puppet.** For instance, during group time, take out a puppet. Similar to *Sesame Street*, have the puppet demonstrate the "wrong skill"—the challenging behavior—and then teach the puppet the right thing to do.
- **Teach the child to communicate with visuals or sign language.** For example, if a child screams every time he needs help, he is struggling to use his words. Teach him to say, "Help!" Then, for times when he cannot access his words, teach him the word *help* in American Sign Language (ASL). Or make a card with a visual of someone looking upset and needing help, and teach the child to give you that card when he needs help.
- **Teach the child a skill with a game.** For example, help a child learn to understand the emotions of others by matching photos of various facial expressions to cartoon images of emotions with captions ("sad," "mad," and so on). Or make an emotion die with a picture of a different facial expression on each side. Have the child roll the die and explain the emotion he sees. You can find some emotion visuals at http://challengingbehavior.cbcs.usf.edu/docs/SocialEmotionalSkills_feelings_cube.pdf
- **Teach the child dos and don'ts with pictures.** For example, create a book showing examples of what *to* do with a fidget toy on a green background and examples of what *not* to do with a fidget toy on a red background.
- **Teach the child to walk away.** Adapting the song "If You're Happy and You Know It" is useful for this technique. Sing, "If you're angry and you know it, walk away."
- **Teach the child to problem solve with a game.** For example, print out the Solution Kit pictures created by the National Center for Pyramid Model Innovations (available at http://challengingbehavior.cbcs.usf.edu/docs/SocialEmotionalSkills_solution-kit_cue-cards.pdf). Then act out a challenging behavior with puppets, and have the child choose a solution from among the pictures.

CHANGE THE CONSEQUENCES

"Change the consequences" strategies change the responses of the adults or other children who witness a challenging behavior. These are not punishments—they are ways to reinforce what you want the children *to* do. For example, instead of removing a child from the classroom for cursing, you or your coteacher might show him a visual of appropriate ways to express frustration or get attention. Teach other children what you want them to do, such as ignore challenging behavior or get an adult, as appropriate.

- **Give the child attention when he does the right thing.** For example, if a child asks to play with a toy instead of grabbing it from another child, say something like this: "Steven, I heard you ask Mara if you could play with the truck. You're trying hard to be patient and be a good friend."

- **Help the child use American Sign Language (ASL).** For instance, if a child is screaming but will let you gently take his hands, assist him in making the sign for *help*. Then help him. This teaches the child that he can ask for what he needs in a way other than screaming.

- **Let the child choose a positive consequence.** Sometimes we try to reinforce good behavior with a positive consequence that does not actually appeal to the child in question. So offer the child several positive consequences and let him select the one he wants. For instance, he could choose which activity to do first at circle time, he could sit in the teacher's chair, and so on.

- **Ahead of time, offer the child a reward for correct behavior.** For example, tell the child that if he does the right thing during circle time, you will do a silly dance afterwards!

- **Whisper to get a child's attention.** Sometimes a whisper is better than raising your voice. If you whisper, children will come closer to you and become quiet to listen.

- **Use a reward system to track building a new skill.** For example, if a child likes cars, create a visual with a car on a track and title it "On the Road to Good Behavior." Allow the child to move his car forward one space each time he uses the new skill. (Never have him move the car backward—the point of this strategy is to reinforce positive behavior, not to penalize negative behavior.) Moving the car forward is something the child likes and will reinforce the use of the new skill. As the child begins to master using the skill on his own, slowly stop using this strategy.

- **Keep a tally chart for the child of all the right things he is doing.** Make a chart with space to track several positive behaviors. Each time the child demonstrates one of these behaviors, add a tally mark to the appropriate space.

- **With words and visuals, remind the child of what to do.** For instance, make a visual demonstrating what children should do when they want to grab a toy. Then, when a child grabs a toy, show him the visual and verbally explain what he should do instead.

- **Use a social story.** For example, if a child is hitting, show him a social story of what *to* do with his hands. You can find some free social stories at http://challengingbehavior.cbcs.usf.edu/Implementation/Program/strategies.html

- **Give the child movement breaks.**

- **Reward the child for doing something good by letting him go to the office or another room.** Remember, this should be something the child wants to do—not a punishment!

- **Let the child sit on your lap after doing something good**.

Let's look at some fictional scenarios to see how "change you," "change the child," and "change the consequences" can help you address challenging behaviors.

CASE STUDY #1: LILIANA

Liliana drools constantly, and her gums are swollen. She is irritable and frequently rubs and grabs her face and ears. When you research these symptoms, you begin to suspect several possible explanations: Liliana might be teething, have an ear infection, or have an allergy.

Here are some ideas from each category of strategies that could help in this situation:

CHANGE YOU

- From the beginning of the year, remind family members of the importance of regular medical and dental care for their children.
- Keep a basket of chilled teething toys or cold washcloths available in your classroom.
- Avoid bringing materials with strong scents, such as strongly scented cleaners, or possible allergens into the classroom.

CHANGE THE CHILD

- Teach Liliana to use an ASL sign, such as *pain*, or a picture card to communicate when she is not feeling well.
- Teach Liliana—and the other children—how to use the support materials that are already available in your room and any new materials that you add to help her.

CHANGE THE CONSEQUENCE

- Massage Liliana's gums (with gloves on).
- Feed Liliana chilled foods.
- Ask Liliana's family members whether she has had a medical or dental checkup recently.

CASE STUDY #2: KOBE

A different Kobe seems to have come into your classroom this week. He has always been a friendly child, but now he only wants to play by himself and hits other children if they try to come close to him. After carrying out a functional assessment, you believe that Kobe is trying to protect himself and his space with this behavior. You know that his parents recently adopted a new baby, so you suspect that Kobe's behavior may be linked to this major life change.

Here are some ideas from each category of strategies that could help in this situation:

CHANGE YOU

- Show consistent interest in children's and family members' lives. Asking questions can feel awkward if you do not do it until you see a change in behavior.

- Have family members fill out a lifestyle questionnaire at the beginning of the year or when a child first enters your program.
- Encourage family members to communicate with you about life events or lifestyle changes.
- Ask Kobe's family members if there have been any recent lifestyle changes at home.
- Teach the children about personal space. You can use painter's tape, trays, carpet squares, large plastic hoops, or fabric to help the children understand how much room an individual needs.
- Plan for teachers to rotate being in close proximity to Kobe during play to stop challenges before they start.

CHANGE THE CHILD

- Use a story or song to teach Kobe appropriate ways to ask others to give him space. For example, sing, "If you need space and you know it, ask for help!"
- Teach Kobe ASL signs for emotions so that he can express what he is feeling with new, more-appropriate movements.

CHANGE THE CONSEQUENCES

- Teach the other children to give classmates space when they ask for it.
- When Kobe hits, respond with the words and signs that you want him to use when he is upset.

General Strategies for Addressing Common Types of Challenging Behavior

This section provides general strategies to address some of the most common types of challenging behavior. Of course, if you choose to use them, remember to also take into account the reasons you have identified behind a given behavior.

PHYSICAL AGGRESSION

The most frequent question I receive at workshops is, "What do I do when a child hits, kicks, and so on?" These are among the most difficult (and dangerous) behaviors that those who work with children must deal with. These strategies can help you not only protect the people in your classroom but also teach children better ways to express their needs and handle their emotions.

CHANGE YOU

⏱ QUICK IDEAS

- As discussed earlier in this book, create a strong behavior-review system, and make sure that teachers know how to activate it.
- Stay in close proximity to children to catch physical aggression before it starts.
- Provide lots of sensory-play activities, such as water tables, sand boxes, or playdough, in the classroom to calm children.
- Keep "emergency" items, such as finger puppets or tiny containers of bubbles, on your person to distract angry or frustrated children.

- Look for children's unmet needs, such as hunger, illness, or sleep, and do what you can to meet those needs.
- Create bulletin boards for family members that show strategies for expressing emotions in positive ways.

⌕ DETAILED IDEAS

Prevention is the best intervention for physical aggression. Your knowledge about a child's temperament, life situation, and stage of development can help you predict the types of situations that might lead to physical aggression and plan how you can minimize or respond to these situations. For instance, some children are more physically aggressive on Mondays after being off schedule over the weekend. Try making fewer demands on children on Mondays, such as giving more time for transitions and not making a big deal if children are struggling to follow directions.

If biting is a common issue in your classroom, have a "biting bag" in each child's cubby and teach the children how to use them. A biting bag is a ziplock bag with safe items for young children (particularly toddlers and two-year-olds) to bite.

Limit words such as *no* or *don't* when speaking to children, and instead tell children what you *do* want them to do: "Touch softly," "Get your biting bag," and so on. This practice also increases vocabulary. If you say "No," "Don't," or the gentler "No, thank you" all day, children will certainly learn these words. But if you tell the children specifically what *to* do ("Walk," "Talk quietly," and so on), they learn additional words.

Have materials ready and limit wait times. Children are more likely to display physical aggression when they have long wait times with nothing to do. Make wait times active, such as by incorporating songs, actions, or games. You could also create waiting boxes full of things for children to use while waiting, such as clipboards with paper and pencils, books, magnetic drawing toys, and so on.

Particularly with young children, sometimes waiting in line is like waiting to get hit. With two teachers (the typical number of adults in a class of twenty children), you can stagger transitions so that you never have to have all the children in line at the same time. For example, instead cleaning up after free play and then having all the children go to the bathroom, call one or two children at a time during free play to go to the bathroom. Or have all the children clean up and then have one teacher read a story to the group while another teacher takes one or two children at a time to the bathroom.

Children might become physically aggressive to express a sensory challenge. Take a tour of your classroom and see where you can adapt the environment to meet sensory needs. If a child struggles with visual input, you could mute vibrant colors, declutter, or add or limit light. If a child has trouble with auditory input, you could help him mute sounds with earmuffs. If smell is the troublesome sense, try using fewer or unscented cleaners. If touch, bodily awareness, or balance is the issue, you could add or support opportunities for movement, or you could exchange your existing classroom items for ones with more or less texture.

Remember, you have the skills to ask for help when you are upset. A child does not yet have those skills; so when he is physically aggressive, your job is to figure out what he is trying to say.

CHANGE THE CHILD

⏱ QUICK IDEAS

- Each day, use puppets, stories, and songs to teach children what to do when another child is physically aggressive, such as walking or talking it out, taking a breath, or getting a teacher.
- Review the rules daily, and send copies home to family members.
- Model the behavior you wish to see, and use the skills that you want the children to exhibit.
- Use visual instead of verbal prompts to remind children of the rules.
- When you feel upset, model what you want children to say in similar situations.

🔍 DETAILED IDEAS

From the first day of school, start teaching children appropriate ways to deal with feelings. For example, instead of just singing "If You're Happy and You Know It," insert other emotions and strategies for handling them, such as, "If you're mad and you know it, count and breathe," or "If you want to hit a friend, walk away." Create your own variations with the children. Hey, if they can learn pop songs and the corresponding dance moves, they can learn about emotions and how to respond to them. You can begin each day by singing these songs as soon as children walk in the door.

Singing songs is also an easy way to teach and remind children how to use biting bags; try singing, "If you want to bite your friends, get your bag." ("If You're Happy and You Know It" is such a useful tune!) You can also teach the children about the bags by creating a story with pictures.

If a child is an impulsive biter or has immediate sensory or teething needs, try having him wear *chewelry*, or jewelry that he can bite on. Create a song or make a book to teach him how to use chewelry, or simply model by wearing it yourself and chewing on it when you are "mad."

If you are working with preschoolers, set up a peace area and problem-solving buddies so children can support each other when they are frustrated. The peace table should have items to help children learn about and manage feelings, such as a mirror, pictures of emotions, and calming tools such as playdough. Problem-solving buddies help other children go to the peace area to resolve conflicts.

Teach children nine months and older to use ASL signs along with words to support communication. If you worry that this practice will limit children's capacity to speak, you can relax. As Carol Garboden Murray explains in the revised edition of *Simple Signing with Young Children: A Guide for Infant, Toddler, and Preschool Teachers*, "It is typical for babies to stop using [a sign] as soon as they can say [the word], because the word provides a more immediate way of meeting their needs." In the meantime, children may become less frustrated because, even if they cannot verbalize their feelings, they may be able to sign them.

If you know that children might struggle with sharing during free play, start that part of the day by reading the children a story about sharing. Then say, for example, "I know that everyone's excited to see the new pumpkin I added to the science area. It may be hard to share, but I left out a blank piece of paper for everyone to sign up for a turn," or "I know that this will be hard, but I'll help you."

CHANGE THE CONSEQUENCE

⏱ QUICK IDEAS

- Instead of saying, "Use your words," teach children some specific words to help them express themselves: "It looks like you are angry right now."
- Give children space to express their feelings safely.
- Offer positive alternative activities to replace physical aggression, such as "building" with a child-safe hammer, going for a walk, dancing out feelings, blowing on a pinwheel, breathing like a dragon, popping bubble wrap, biting a teething toy, and so on.
- If all else fails, focus on keeping everyone safe until the child calms down.

🔍 DETAILED IDEAS

Instead of saying, "Don't bite," get an item from a child's biting bag and tell her, "Bite here," or "Bite this."

Say, "I can tell you are [insert whatever emotion the child is feeling]. Let's sing a song about it." Then insert the applicable feeling and a coping strategy: "If you're angry and you know it, walk away."

IMPORTANT NOTE

Never move a child who is physically aggressive and does not want to be moved. You could escalate the situation, endanger yourself or other children, and hurt the child who is struggling. Remove the other children from the area to keep them safe. One adult should stay near the child who is struggling to make sure he is also safe.

Observe each child's cues so you can learn to recognize when he is in distress or what might trigger him to resort to physical aggression. If you cannot find the trigger, keep observing, or have another person observe during the times when the child is most likely to become physically aggressive. (You may say, "But there isn't a pattern, Angela!" There is always a pattern. Keep looking.)

Respond to physical aggression with phrases such as, "What are you feeling right now?" or "What will make this situation better?" If the child cannot answer because he is so upset, label or narrate what you see him feeling. Narrating often helps me to calm down as well. This strategy may not be realistic in every situation, such as when danger is imminent, but when you provide words for what a child is feeling, he is more likely to say those words himself the next time he feels that way.

After incidents of physical aggression occur, process them with the other children so that they are not afraid. Say, "That was really scary. Tell me about what you're feeling. I'm here with you." If you do not process these events as a class, the children will process them with their family members, and you might end up with some angry family members on your hands. It is not the event itself that scares children the most. It is not processing it that makes it really scary.

Reflect on how to prevent the situation from occurring again. Consider what you might have missed and how you can spot it next time before the child resorts to physical aggression. For example, you might realize that Juan pushed Luisa to get your attention, so you keep an eye on him and praise him the next time you see him doing the right thing.

VERBAL AGGRESSION

The early childhood period is a critical time for language development. But it is understandable to be shocked when you hear children cursing or saying unkind things to each other in your classroom. Try these strategies to calm yourself and to help children use appropriate words.

CHANGE YOU

Q DETAILED IDEAS

Children sometimes resort to verbal aggression to express frustration or displeasure over having to perform an activity they do not like. If you think this is likely to happen in your classroom, have alternative activities ready.

Sometimes children respond with verbal aggression after being told "no" or "don't." They may be trying to express how much they dislike your disapproval, or they might feel upset, hurt, frustrated, or even confused when they hear these words. Limit your use of "no" and "don't" when you speak to children, and tell them what you *do* want them to do: "Sit down," "Keep the blocks in the block center," and so on.

CHANGE THE CHILD

Ⓞ QUICK IDEAS

- Use puppets and songs to teach children the right words to say during a conflict.
- Model positive language.
- Create a list of kind words that children can say, and post it in the classroom. When a child says one of the words, put a star next to that word.
- Have a "compliment circle" as part of circle time, during which you invite children to give each other compliments.
- Have a child be a kind-word detective and high-five other children who are using kind words.
- Teach children to follow Vivian Paley's rule: "You can't say, 'You can't play'" (from her book of the same name).

Q DETAILED IDEAS

Start building a strong emotional vocabulary with the children from the first day of school. Teach them lots of novel words to express what they might be feeling. Teaching them to "use their words" is often about setting the stage for positive social and emotional expression and giving children words to say when they cannot think of words on their own.

Teach children to "tootle." Tootling is the opposite of tattling: children tell on peers whom they see doing right things. For example, a child can describe the good thing to you, you can write it on a sticky note, and the child can put the note in the applicable person's cubby. Or you can toot a horn and have the child tell everyone the tootle.

CHANGE THE CONSEQUENCE

Ⓞ QUICK IDEAS

- Focus less on the words a child says and more on the emotion he is trying to express, and give him the right word for it.

- Praise children for using their words, and explain the right ones to say.
- Let children say angry words on a toy "angry phone" or into an "angry-word bag."
- Write down angry words for children, and let the children ball them up and throw them away.
- When children want to tattle on friends, have them use a toy "tattle phone." Put paper and pencils near the tattle phone so the children can "write" their tattles down.

Q DETAILED IDEAS

Try to keep a neutral face when children use inappropriate words, and then calmly tell them which words to use instead. Responses such as, "No" or "Those aren't nice words" are not very helpful because children do not automatically know what else to say or what "nice words" are. Instead, teach children alternative words: "Here is a better word to say," or "What you mean is . . ."

BULLYING AND EXCLUSION

Children are not automatically friends just because we put them in a room together and call them friends. As educators, we have to set up an environment that not only helps children get to know each other but also supports the development of friendships.

CHANGE YOU

Q QUICK IDEAS

- Help children's family members set up playdates outside of school to build community.
- Before taking children outside or before the beginning of free play, ask them, "Who will you play with today?" and "How can we make sure everyone is included?"
- Set up transition or circle-time buddies. Pair children who do well during those times with children who struggle.
- Pair children to create paintings together.
- Instead of having children transition to a center, have them transition to a friend so that they play with different friends in different areas of the room.

CHANGE THE CHILD

Q QUICK IDEAS

- Help the children make and eat snacks with partners.
- Have children build "friend ships" in the block area: ships out of blocks, with a friend.
- Have a "mix-it-up day." Put each child's name in a box, and randomly have children pick the name of someone to play with.
- Read books about friendship with the children.
- Assign some children classroom jobs as peacemakers. With the help of an adult, peacemakers help other children solve bullying and exclusion problems.

Q DETAILED IDEAS

Assign some children to be friendship detectives. These children walk around the room making sure that everyone has a friend to play with. If a detective finds someone without a friend, the detective plays with that child.

Take a photo of each child, and put the photos on blocks with contact paper. Children can then "build friendship" by using these blocks. As children build, talk with them about their friends on the blocks, referring to each person by name.

Take photos of all the children, blow the photos up to 8 ½" x 11" size, laminate them, and cut them up to create friendship puzzles. As children put together the puzzles, talk about their friends and describe attributes or good qualities of those friends.

Take photos of all the children, cut out parts of the faces (such as mouths, eyes, and noses), and write the applicable person's name on the back of each piece. Then hold up one piece at a time and ask the children, for example, "Whose smile is this?" What a great way for children to learn names and literacy!

Each day, set up a friendship table or spread out a friendship blanket on the floor. Place a highly preferred item or toy in this area. Tell the children that to play there, they must invite a new friend—someone they have not yet played with that day—to play with them.

CHANGE THE CONSEQUENCE

⏱ QUICK IDEAS

- Have the child who was bullying or excluding help the child who was bullied or excluded.
- Use visuals to remind children of how to play together appropriately.

🔍 DETAILED IDEAS

If you are working with preschoolers, set up a peace area, and assign some children to be problem-solving buddies. The peace table should have items to help children learn about and manage feelings, such as a mirror, pictures of emotions, and calming tools such as playdough. Problem-solving buddies help other children go to the peace area to resolve conflicts.

NOT LISTENING, NONCOMPLIANCE, DEFIANCE, AND RELUCTANCE TO PARTICIPATE

As young children go about the task of developing independence, they often resort to frustrating tactics to avoid complying with adult requests. The following strategies can help—often without the child even realizing that he is actually doing what you want.

CHANGE YOU

⏱ QUICK IDEAS

- Let children choose their own activities.
- Sing your directions.
- Give directions in a child's home language.
- If an activity has multiple steps that do not need to occur in a certain order, let children choose the order of the steps.
- Always turn off any background music before giving a direction. Children cannot tune out music the way you can.
- Have alternate activities ready in case children do not like an activity.

- Add children's interests to a task (as in Case Study #4: Writing Refusal in chapter 7).
- Add movement to a task. For example, say, "Jump twice to the number two," or "Clap when you see the letter *A*."
- Add a sensory component to a task. For instance, you could put puzzle pieces in the sand table and have children dig them up to put the puzzle together.
- Put pictures of tasks on a large die, and have children roll the die to determine which task they will do.
- Use fewer words when giving directions. You could also use both words and pictures to explain what you want the children to do.
- When giving directions, be specific: "Ari, you clean up the blue blocks. Genji, you clean up the scarves."

DETAILED IDEAS

Did you know that play makes learning more permanent? If you make directions fun to follow, especially for regular routines, children will learn the directions better and be more likely to comply. This happens because when children engage in playful interactions, a chemical called *dopamine* is released in the brain. Dopamine activates the reward centers in the midbrain and prompts those structures to pay particular attention to all features of that experience so it can be repeated. When children repeat the experience, the neurons involved learn to activate together, gradually establishing a neural network so that the brain can reliably access the relevant information over time. To create fun-to-follow directions, try something like this: instead of saying, "Let's go to the bathroom," blow a few soap bubbles and ask, "Can you follow these bubbles to the bathroom?"

Sometimes children do not want to transition to a new activity because they have to take apart their work, such as a block tower or a puzzle. Try having children start puzzles on trays so that you can move them when needed and the children can finish later. If you can, save block towers, or take photos of them so that the children can show everyone their creations even if the structures are no longer standing.

CHANGE THE CHILD

QUICK IDEAS

- Make a picture book of directions for different times of the day, and send it home with the children.
- If a child struggles with listening during transitions, give him a transition buddy. The transition buddy is usually a child who always follows directions.

CHANGE THE CONSEQUENCE

QUICK IDEAS

- Have a child roll a die. Whatever number he rolls is the number of times he must do something that you want him to do. For instance, if he rolls a three, he must put away three toys.
- Give the child a buddy to do the activity or task with.
- Sing songs from a child's culture to get his attention.
- Do the task with the child.

DETAILED IDEAS

Instead of being directive, be reflective. Prompt children to think about their actions by asking open-ended questions such as the following:

- "What do you think you should do first?"
- "How can you move so you are safe?"
- "What do you notice when you . . . ?"
- "What is the rule about . . . ?"
- "What is next on our schedule?"
- "What should you be doing right now?"
- "What do you notice your friends doing?"

Beat the clock! Turn tasks such as cleaning up into games in which children try to beat their best times for completing the tasks. You can even turn these games into math activities by talking with the children about the differences between their times each day.

Use cleanup or getting in line to problem solve and brainstorm. Ask questions such as, "How could we make sure the toys are put away in the right places?" or "How could we make a good line?"

Stop threatening children. Change "If you don't . . ." statements to "What could we do to . . . ?" statements. Instead of saying, "If you don't hurry, we aren't going to make it outside in enough time to play," say, "What could we do so we can make it outside on time?"

CLINGINESS, CRYING, AND TANTRUMS

Few things can wear on your nerves like children who monopolize your time, can't tolerate your attention being elsewhere, cry frequently, and are clingy and seeking attachment. When these behaviors appear in your classroom, try these strategies to avoid breaking down yourself.

CHANGE YOU

QUICK IDEAS

- Children exhibit a wide range of emotions. Be prepared for them to show both positive and negative feelings in your classroom.
- Set up the classroom with a designated calming corner and calming baskets or caddies placed around the room (we will discuss this in a moment). You can even make calming backpacks for times when a child has a tantrum outside the classroom.

DETAILED IDEAS

As you have probably experienced, no child in the history of calming down has ever calmed down simply by hearing an adult say, "Calm down." You have to go beyond that. One particularly useful technique involves creating an individualized basket of calming tools, such as songs, toys, photos, pinwheels for deep breathing, stuffed animals, bubbles, toy phones to "call" family members, family pictures, and so on, for each child, or at least for the ones who cry frequently. Have these items ready in baskets or caddies to help distract children from starting to cry in the first place or to redirect crying. During my teaching years, I would keep calming tools in my pockets or smock for quick access.

At the same time, remember that you cannot just shove a calming toy in a child's face when he cries and expect him to snap out of it. You have to introduce calming baskets when children are already calm, such as during circle time; model daily how to use those tools; and let children practice using them. If a child first sees a calming basket while he is in the midst of a fit, the object will probably have little effect on him.

CHANGE THE CHILD

🕑 QUICK IDEAS

- Each day, teach children coping skills for strong emotions.
- Rather than labeling strong or negative emotions as "bad," explain how all emotions are needed and necessary.
- Name all emotions, positive and negative, that you see in your classroom.
- Draw attention to children or adults who are using healthy coping skills to deal with negative emotions.

CHANGE THE CONSEQUENCE

🕑 QUICK IDEAS

- Use the list of cool-down strategies that you made in chapter 3 to help you keep it together and PUSH PAST It.
- Know the individual needs of each child. For some children, the best response to a tantrum is being silent and pretending not to look at them.
- Narrate the feelings that the child is experiencing.
- Lower yourself to the child's eye level, and look for the reasons behind his behavior. For example, he might want attention; he might be testing limits; or he might be sleepy, hurt, hungry, confused, frustrated, or bored.
- Sometimes a gentle touch can help a child calm down, but know the child—sometimes a touch can make things worse.
- Give children space, such as a designated calming area in the classroom, to express their feelings safely.
- Say things such as, "It's okay to be sad. You can hug this teddy bear until you feel better. I'm right here if you need me."

🔍 DETAILED IDEAS

Our goal as adults is not to eliminate crying or the expression of negative emotions. Our goal is to understand the message a child is trying to convey when he cries and to offer alternatives when appropriate. Each time you ignore, miss, or silence a message, the child will feel the need to intensify his behavior to get the message across. It is your job to stay calm, not start crying yourself, and consistently teach exactly what you want the child to do when he is upset. As you will recall from the discussion about "other regulation," Elena Bodrova and Deborah Leong assert that the more you respond to a child's cries by keeping calm and providing comfort, the more he learns to regulate his emotions.

Some comments are less than helpful during episodes of intense negative emotion. Disliking ("I don't like it when you . . ."), dismissing ("You're okay," "There's nothing to be scared of," or "All this for that little scratch?"), or devaluing negative emotions ("Big boys and girls don't cry") can teach children that their experiences or feelings are invalid.

A child with frequent clinginess, crying, or tantrums may have an attachment issue. To alleviate the problem, stay close to the child. This situation may be frustrating, but it is also a precious time. As anyone who works with tweens or teens can tell you, this period of seeking attachment is a brief one in child development.

Even if you try all these tools and children still cry, it does not mean that you are ineffective or that the strategies do not work. Keep in mind that crying is a developmentally appropriate behavior for young children, and make sure to have a good support system in place for yourself.

Time-of-Day Challenges

Sometimes a particular time of day or part of a schedule seems to trigger challenging behaviors. Let's explore some strategies to address these time-specific difficulties.

ARRIVAL

⏱ QUICK IDEAS

- Have family members put small photos of you and of favorite toys from your classroom on their key rings so that children have visuals of where they are going each day.
- Have calming baskets near the drop-off area. If a certain child has an especially hard time during drop-off, create an arrival basket just for him with his favorite calming items.
- Create a classroom job called the greeter. This child greets other children as they arrive and welcomes them to the classroom.
- Make a welcome mat with pictures of possible greetings (a high-five, a hug, and so on). As each child arrives, have him hop on which greeting he wants from you, and give him that greeting.

CIRCLE TIME

⏱ QUICK IDEAS

- If a certain child struggles during circle time, allow him to be your helper. Many children may want this job, so have different jobs ready for them to do.
- Have other adults sit near children who struggle.
- Let children color while they listen to a story.
- Shorten circle time.
- Add movement or additional songs to circle time.
- Let children pick the order of circle-time activities. For children who cannot speak, use a visual agenda and have them point to which activity they want next.
- Have circle time in two small groups instead of in one big group.
- Make a visual of where in the circle each child should sit.

- Make visuals of each step in the circle-time routine, post them on the wall at child level, and send them home with children.
- Redirect children with a visual instead of verbally.
- Give several children jobs as circle-time buddies to support children who struggle.

🔍 DETAILED IDEAS

To support all children, try adding props to circle time. Yes, I know: the first time you use them, all the children will either chew on them or bang each other on the head with them. Welcome to early childhood! Remember, anytime you bring new materials into your classroom, you need to teach the children how to use them correctly. Then, if you implement the idea long enough, you will see the novelty wear off.

A fidget can be a useful tool for an individual child who has difficulty sitting still at circle time. Again, you need to teach all the children what the fidget is for and explain why not everybody gets one. Of course, the rest of the class will still want fidgets—they are small children, after all—but eventually they will get used to the situation.

Instead of telling all children to sit "crisscross applesauce," ask them, "How can you sit so everyone can see?" or "How can you sit so you are safe?" It may not be wise to force all children to sit the same way. Some children, for instance, have low muscle tone and cannot sit without support, so let these children choose where they want to be during circle time, such as sitting on the floor, sitting in a chair, or standing near you.

MEALTIMES (INCLUDING SNACK)

⏱ QUICK IDEAS

- Make visuals of each step in the mealtime routine, post them at child level, and send them home with the children.
- Similarly, create a book with these visuals and put it in the dramatic-play area so children can "practice" the routine.
- Go over the steps of the routine ahead of time.
- Give children classroom jobs to support mealtimes.
- Sing directions.
- Make all wait times active: sing, play I Spy, do fingerplays, and so on.

FREE PLAY

⏱ QUICK IDEAS

- Give children jobs as "problem solvers of the day" during free play. These children circulate through the room and help other children resolve conflicts.
- Teach children about giving others personal space. You can use painter's tape, trays, carpet squares, large plastic hoops, or fabric as visuals to help the children understand.
- Ask children, "Who will you play with today?"

- Have calming baskets in each area.
- Have all adults move around to each center, playing with children as they go.
- Place timers of all types (sand, egg, digital, and so on) in every area to encourage sharing.
- Before free play, use puppets to demonstrate how children should behave and resolve play challenges during free play.
- Create a story about free play with words and pictures explaining the expectations. Keep one copy in each center, and send copies home to family members.
- During circle time, role-play potential free-play challenges with children so they can practice cooperative skills.

Q DETAILED IDEAS

In each area, post several items at child level:

- Rules for that area in words and pictures
- Pictures of how to use that area's materials
- Descriptions and pictures of solutions for play challenges, such as getting a teacher or using a timer
- A photo of what that area looks like when it is clean (to give children a reference when you ask them to clean up)

Try making a Fun Friend Wall to encourage appropriate behavior during free play. Put children's names on index cards and laminate them, then post them on the designated area of the wall. Make a Fun Friend badge that you can stick onto a card. At the end of free play, pick one child who behaved well and put the Fun Friend badge on his card. That child then gets to pick his free-play area first the next day.

NAP TIME

QUICK IDEAS

- During the first few weeks of school (and as needed thereafter), talk about nap time with a "nap puppet" at circle time.
- Create a book of the nap-time routine. Keep a copy in the room, and send copies home. Read it to the children each day before nap time.
- Start nap music toward the end of lunch. Play the same songs each day so that the children associate those songs with sleep.
- Have children who fight sleep or do not sleep at all serve as your helpers so that they are last to lie down.
- Make sure beds or cots are in the same location each day, and be intentional about where you place children.
- Let children listen to books on tape with headphones during nap time.
- Spray "sweet-dream spray" (water with lavender or vanilla extract—make sure to check whether any children have allergies first!) near a child's cot to give him the "magic" needed to go to sleep. Remember to spray just once or twice in the air, not on the children. A little spray goes a long way.

- Put the label "Sleep Fairy Dust" on an empty bottle. Pretend to be invisible and sprinkle the "dust" on children to help them go to sleep. You could also give this job to a child.
- Have the children play "possum" and lie as still as they can. At the end of nap time, give a prize to whoever was the most still.
- Make a "Magic Sleep Wand." Tell the children that when you hold the wand over them, they are sent to sleep by "magic."
- Put decals on the ceiling for children to look at during nap time if they cannot sleep.
- At the end of nap time, give a prize to the child who fell asleep first.
- If a child is quiet during nap time, give him a turn to choose some music during the next day.
- Remember, as long as a child is quiet and not bothering anyone else, it is okay if he does not sleep during nap time.

🔍 DETAILED IDEAS

For children who do not sleep, prepare nap baggies or busy boxes with quiet activities they can do after the other children fall asleep. You can also allow them to use small flashlights to read—these flashlights provide strong reinforcements to stay quiet.

Try making a Super Napper box as an incentive. Write each child's name on a wooden craft stick. If a child is quiet during nap time, put his stick in the Super Napper box. Pick one name out of the box after nap time each day, and give a reward to that child. This way, children get reinforcement for being quiet or going to sleep, but it is still a surprise who wins. By the end of the year, you can pick a name once a week instead of every day.

DEPARTURE

⏱ QUICK IDEAS

- Post visuals and descriptions of the steps in the departure routine at child level.
- Make laminated copies of a small photo of the teachers. If a child is sad to leave, he can take a copy with him.
- Talk to children about their favorite people at home to prepare them to leave.
- Have calming baskets near the pick-up area for children who have a hard time leaving.
- Create a classroom job called the departure buddy. This is a child who tends to stay later and helps his classmates pack up to leave.
- Similar to what you did at arrival time, have each child hop on the part of your welcome mat that shows the way he wants to say goodbye to you (a high-five, a hug, and so on), and give the child that farewell.

CHAPTER 10

Successfully Implementing Strategies

Take a deep breath. We have come a long way, but we are not done yet. Now that we have chosen some strategies and created a challenging-behavior plan, we are finally ready to address the last step on the Adult Behavior Laundry List.

ADULT BEHAVIOR LAUNDRY LIST

1. Sort out your feelings.
2. Repair rips in your relationship.
3. Figure out the care instructions.
4. Put behaviors in the meaning-making machine.
5. Choose a cycle.
6. **Be patient during the trying time.**

Be Patient during the Trying Time

When you take your clean clothes out of the washing machine, are they ready to wear? Not yet. But similar to putting on wet, cold garments straight out of the washer, many professional-development workshops simply end after giving potential solutions to behavior challenges—without providing any counsel for implementing those solutions. However, researcher Bradley Ermeling points out that even veteran teachers need concrete guidance in the first phases of using a new strategy. In their article "The Coaching of Teaching," Bruce Joyce and Beverly Showers get even more specific, explaining that it can take hours of studying the theory behind a strategy, ten to twenty observations of someone else using the strategy, and ten to fifteen opportunities to practice the strategy before a teacher is ready to actually implement the idea with her students.

This section of the book is all about the implementation piece that so often gets left out in discussions about strategies. I call this part of the process the *trying* time because it mirrors the experience of *drying* clothes. Just as drying clothes takes time, so does trying out new strategies. In fact, you must try any given strategy repeatedly over multiple weeks before you will begin to see any improvement, as Bruce Joyce and Beverly Showers state in their book *Student Achievement through Staff Development.* The exact amount of time required depends on a number of factors:

- How consistently you apply the strategy
- Whether you implement the strategy as it was intended
- How good you are at using the strategy
- Whether and how effectively you filter out what is not working

We will discuss more about timing later in this chapter. For now, let's look at what you will actually be doing during the trying time.

The 5R Cycle

Trying time is a continuous cycle of five steps:

1. Respond
2. Record
3. Reflect
4. Revise
5. Repeat

These steps explain what you should do and what you should expect at each phase of implementation for a challenging-behavior plan. Let's look at each step in detail.

RESPOND

This step is when you respond to challenging behavior by starting to use your plan. This is also the level at which many teachers, therapists, and family members abandon great ideas before giving

PUSH PAST IT!

them enough time to work. Why? If you have ever tried a new idea from a workshop, you know the answer: because behavior often gets *worse* at this stage. This happens because as adults introduce a plan to support a child with challenging behavior (whom I will call the "target child" in this part of the book), those strategies can generate "static"—additional challenges that arise as all the children try to understand and respond to the new strategies. In other words, responding to behavior problems with new strategies often brings about new problems!

Remember, this phenomenon is normal; it does not mean that you have failed or that the plan does not work. If strategies are new to you, you need time to get good at implementing them. Even if you have tried them before, they might be new to this set of circumstances or this group of students. You, the target child, and the other children all need time to adjust to the new plan. If you have introduced a new material (such as a fidget) as part of the plan, all the children will want that material whether or not they need it—while, ironically, the target child may not respond to the material right away.

Regardless of which strategies you have included in your plan, you have to give them sufficient time to work. Unfortunately, as part of that process, things typically get worse before they get better. The Respond phase lasts four to six weeks, and during that time, you might be tempted to abandon the plan as the new strategies begin to wreak havoc on your classroom. But don't give up! It takes take that long for children to process and get used to new ideas and for adults to practice using them. Even though there may be a rough road ahead, remember to PUSH PAST It! You can do this! And keep in mind that not trying any plan will be an even rougher road than this one.

If you are an administrator, remember that your staff members need lots of support during this step. You might want to check in with them more often, offer extra break time, or provide more time for teams to reflect together. You could also have volunteers clean toys or help with bulletin boards to free up time for staff members to concentrate on more complex work. Even simple tools such as pep talks and "take what you need" boards can make all the difference.

RECORD

The Record step happens simultaneously with the Respond step. During those four to six weeks, you observe and record the responses of the target child and the adults in your classroom to the challenging-behavior plan. Sounds easy, right? Wrong! As some of you might already be thinking, if a cup has just gone flying across the room, who has time to write, "Becky is still throwing things"? However, this step is important because you cannot measure progress if you do not know where you started. Additionally, challenging behaviors generally do not abruptly stop. Progress occurs gradually, and unless you are keeping records, it can be easy to miss small gains.

Bad news: You do have to record consistently. Good news: If you are intentional about when you record, it does not have to take up all your time. For example, you do not have to grab your tracking sheet every single time the target child cries. Pick one time of day when the child tends to cry, and at that time, record data for two minutes. Yes! Even two minutes a day can help you find patterns and make sense of the target child's responses to your plan.

Administrators can assist in this step by noticing and pointing out small gains to their staff members. Even if staff members are recording data as they should, they are so close to the situation that they may not be able to easily see the progress they are making. Speaking of recording data, administrators can help with this key procedure. Anyone can record data—it does not have to be the adults who work directly with the child. Administrators can greatly ease the burden on staff members by stepping into a classroom for two minutes to take these important notes.

REFLECT

The Reflect step happens in weekly group meetings. At each gathering, you and your colleagues analyze what you know about the situation, including all forms and information from the last meeting and created since then, and reflect on what about your plan is and is not working.

Start each meeting by having everyone use PUSH PAST It to sort out any new emotions she might be feeling about the target child or the situation. Then you will be ready to problem solve. Each meeting should have an agenda to keep the discussion on track so that it does not turn into a venting session. Try including some or all of these questions on the agenda:

- What are some successes you have noticed this week? (Always start with positives.)
- How is the child responding to the plan?
- What is the frequency of the behavior now? compared to last week? compared to when we started?
- Do we need to individualize the plan more? If so, what should we change?
- How are the other children in the classroom responding to the plan?
- Are the adults all using the plan the same way? If not, what should they be doing?
- Are the adults all using the plan with the same frequency? If not, how often should they use it?
- Do the adults need more information about the theories behind the strategies in the plan?
- Do the adults need more examples of how to implement certain strategies?
- Do the adults need more emotional support?
- Do the adults need more materials?
- Should we add a new strategy?
- Do we have too many strategies in the plan? If so, which one or ones should we eliminate?
- What are other staff members noticing about the behavior?
- What are family members noticing about the behavior?
- Have there been any recent lifestyle changes for this child or family?

Even brief reflections such as, "I tried this strategy for five minutes at circle time," can be helpful during these meetings. On the other hand, if the discussion starts to stray, team members can help each other with statements such as, "I think we've gone off track," "We need to make sure we have time for all the questions," or "What does that have to do with question number four?" If meetings frequently become chaotic or your team consistently cannot get through most of the questions, the team members are probably venting too much and not reflecting enough. In this case, it may help to meet more often—up to three or four times per week, if needed.

REVISE

This step should not occur until at least four weeks into the implementation process. It takes this long for everyone to get used to the new plan, for the novelty to wear off for the other children, for adults to get better at applying the strategies, and for the target child to begin understanding the purpose of the plan. After the first four weeks or so, you and your colleagues can begin to review and revise the plan based on your observations.

Revising does *not* mean that you make a new plan at this point. It means that you adjust what you are currently doing. Here are some possibilities for revisions:

- Add a new strategy.
- Eliminate a strategy.
- Add opportunities for teachers to observe other teachers using a particular strategy.
- Give family members additional resources.
- Find out whether a strategy used at school could be used at home.
- Come to terms with the disappointment of realizing that the target child's family cannot implement any new strategies at home.

Your team as a whole should decide what to change about the plan. However, everyone needs to understand the capacities of the people who will be implementing the plan. Some strategies might be challenging to implement because a team member lacks the necessary knowledge or experience. As a result, some strategies might work better than others.

Administrators may be tempted to mandate certain elements as part of a challenging-behavior plan. Don't do it! In my practice as a consultant, I never write or even revise someone else's plan for addressing challenging behaviors. Someone who will help implement the plan must write or type the necessary information because, even though I might be a facilitator or a supporter of the plan, it is not *my* plan. I have learned that if I create or alter a plan for others to carry out, those people perceive the plan as mine. Because they do not have ownership in the plan, they will not implement it successfully, if at all. Therefore, only the people who will actually execute a plan (not their principal or director) should make any final decisions on or record any adjustments to that plan.

REPEAT

Behavior change is not a one-and-done event. (Otherwise, everyone would have six-pack abs!) It is a continuous cycle. It can take several rounds and multiple revisions of the plan to help the target child eliminate the challenging behavior—especially if you have to start over because of a change in the child's life or a change in the school schedule that triggers new behaviors or revives old ones. Thankfully, in these cases you have the old plan as a starting point.

On the other hand, if the cycle works the first time and the child eliminates the challenging behavior, pause for a moment and acknowledge your success. This process is one of the hardest things you will ever attempt as an educator, and you made it through! Well done! Then, with this experience to motivate you, start the cycle again with the next challenging behavior.

CELEBRATE THE SMALL VICTORIES

I will never forget discussing data about a child with one of my consultants—mostly because my husband, Reginald, overheard us:

CONSULTANT: We had six [expletives] last week, but this week the teacher was only called an [expletive] twice!

ME: *Yes*! It's working!

REGINALD: (*Horrified.*) Are these the little, sweet children at the child care?

I had to explain that children do not just stop a behavior. The change is gradual, and those small wins help everyone to keep going!

Conclusion

Thank you for the opportunity to share my ideas with you. We have come to the end of our journey together, but your personal journey is by no means over. Ideally, this book has helped you write your own narrative, gain cognitive control of your emotions, step into different perspectives, and move beyond hurting to helping and healing. I hope that you continue to explore your relationship with emotions, question yourself, and engage in regular self-reflection.

The ultimate goal of this book is to leave you with an increased ability to love, accept, get along with, and help children, their family members, and your colleagues. People are more than their worst moments. The next time someone describes a person as "bad," "crazy," or "angry," PUSH PAST that one-dimensional label and learn more about that person. The next time someone behaves badly, respond with curiosity and compassion, keeping in mind that behind every person's behavior is a complicated story as multifaceted as your own. Take what you have learned on this journey and use it to lead the children you care for on their own journeys.

Appendix A: PUSH PAST It Handout

P	Pick out positives.			

U	Understand everyone's perspective.			

S	Seek neutral support.			

H	Home in on everyone's intentions.			

P	Pay attention to your own behavior.			

A	Ask questions.			

S	Step back.			

T	Take care of yourself.			

I

T

Appendix B: Relationship-Repair Planning Sheet

Use this chart to help you plan your relationship-repairing time with a child (2 consecutive minutes per day for 2 weeks). Fill in each box with the positive interaction(s) you will have with the child that day. Try to plan a variety of activities; some ideas are listed below.

- Point out what child is doing right
- Talk with child and call him/her by name
- Make eye contact
- Play with child
- Ask child to help you
- Read to child
- Hug child

- Let child choose which activity to do first
- Let child tell you about his/her interests
- Tell a joke and laugh with child
- Sit with child at lunch or snack
- Let child choose an activity that you can do together
- Invent your own positive interaction

WEEK 1				
Day 1	Day 2	Day 3	Day 4	Day 5

WEEK 2				
Day 1	Day 2	Day 3	Day 4	Day 5

Appendix C: Behavior Checklist

Complete each table by circling "A lot," "Some," or "None" to indicate how much challenging behavior the child displayed during that activity on each day. Circle the smiley face if the child usually enjoys the activity. Use the spaces at the side of each table to describe the challenging behavior and add any comments.

WEEK ONE

ARRIVAL / DEPARTURE ☺

Day	Level of Challenging Behavior		
Monday	A lot	Some	None
Tuesday	A lot	Some	None
Wednesday	A lot	Some	None
Thursday	A lot	Some	None
Friday	A lot	Some	None

Description of challenging behavior:
_____

Comments:
_____

MEALS / SNACKS ☺

Day	Level of Challenging Behavior		
Monday	A lot	Some	None
Tuesday	A lot	Some	None
Wednesday	A lot	Some	None
Thursday	A lot	Some	None
Friday	A lot	Some	None

Description of challenging behavior:
_____

Comments:
_____

BATHROOM ☺

Day	Level of Challenging Behavior		
Monday	A lot	Some	None
Tuesday	A lot	Some	None
Wednesday	A lot	Some	None
Thursday	A lot	Some	None
Friday	A lot	Some	None

Description of challenging behavior:
_____

Comments:
_____

CIRCLE TIME ☺

Day	Level of Challenging Behavior		
Monday	A lot	Some	None
Tuesday	A lot	Some	None
Wednesday	A lot	Some	None
Thursday	A lot	Some	None
Friday	A lot	Some	None

Description of challenging behavior:
_____

Comments:
_____

FREE PLAY ☺

Day	Level of Challenging Behavior		
Monday	A lot	Some	None
Tuesday	A lot	Some	None
Wednesday	A lot	Some	None
Thursday	A lot	Some	None
Friday	A lot	Some	None

Description of challenging behavior:
_____

Comments:
_____

SMALL-GROUP ACTIVITIES ☺

Day	Level of Challenging Behavior		
Monday	A lot	Some	None
Tuesday	A lot	Some	None
Wednesday	A lot	Some	None
Thursday	A lot	Some	None
Friday	A lot	Some	None

Description of challenging behavior:
_____
_____

Comments:
_____
_____

NAP TIME ☺

Day	Level of Challenging Behavior		
Monday	A lot	Some	None
Tuesday	A lot	Some	None
Wednesday	A lot	Some	None
Thursday	A lot	Some	None
Friday	A lot	Some	None

Description of challenging behavior:
_____
_____

Comments:
_____
_____

TRANSITIONS ☺

Day	Level of Challenging Behavior		
Monday	A lot	Some	None
Tuesday	A lot	Some	None
Wednesday	A lot	Some	None
Thursday	A lot	Some	None
Friday	A lot	Some	None

Description of challenging behavior:
_____
_____

Comments:
_____
_____

OTHER _____ ☺

Day	Level of Challenging Behavior		
Monday	A lot	Some	None
Tuesday	A lot	Some	None
Wednesday	A lot	Some	None
Thursday	A lot	Some	None
Friday	A lot	Some	None

Description of challenging behavior:
_____
_____

Comments:
_____
_____

PUSH PAST IT!

Complete each table by circling "A lot," "Some," or "None" to indicate how much challenging behavior the child displayed during that activity on each day. Circle the smiley face if the child usually enjoys the activity. Use the spaces at the side of each table to describe the challenging behavior and add any comments.

WEEK TWO

ARRIVAL / DEPARTURE ☺

Day	Level of Challenging Behavior		
Monday	A lot	Some	None
Tuesday	A lot	Some	None
Wednesday	A lot	Some	None
Thursday	A lot	Some	None
Friday	A lot	Some	None

Description of challenging behavior: _____

_____

Comments: _____

_____

MEALS / SNACKS ☺

Day	Level of Challenging Behavior		
Monday	A lot	Some	None
Tuesday	A lot	Some	None
Wednesday	A lot	Some	None
Thursday	A lot	Some	None
Friday	A lot	Some	None

Description of challenging behavior: _____

_____

Comments: _____

_____

BATHROOM ☺

Day	Level of Challenging Behavior		
Monday	A lot	Some	None
Tuesday	A lot	Some	None
Wednesday	A lot	Some	None
Thursday	A lot	Some	None
Friday	A lot	Some	None

Description of challenging behavior: _____

_____

Comments: _____

_____

CIRCLE TIME ☺

Day	Level of Challenging Behavior		
Monday	A lot	Some	None
Tuesday	A lot	Some	None
Wednesday	A lot	Some	None
Thursday	A lot	Some	None
Friday	A lot	Some	None

Description of challenging behavior: _____

_____

Comments: _____

_____

FREE PLAY ☺

Day	Level of Challenging Behavior		
Monday	A lot	Some	None
Tuesday	A lot	Some	None
Wednesday	A lot	Some	None
Thursday	A lot	Some	None
Friday	A lot	Some	None

Description of challenging behavior: _____

_____

Comments: _____

_____

SMALL-GROUP ACTIVITIES ☺

Day	Level of Challenging Behavior		
Monday	A lot	Some	None
Tuesday	A lot	Some	None
Wednesday	A lot	Some	None
Thursday	A lot	Some	None
Friday	A lot	Some	None

Description of challenging behavior:
_____

_____

Comments:
_____

_____

NAP TIME ☺

Day	Level of Challenging Behavior		
Monday	A lot	Some	None
Tuesday	A lot	Some	None
Wednesday	A lot	Some	None
Thursday	A lot	Some	None
Friday	A lot	Some	None

Description of challenging behavior:
_____

_____

Comments:
_____

_____

TRANSITIONS ☺

Day	Level of Challenging Behavior		
Monday	A lot	Some	None
Tuesday	A lot	Some	None
Wednesday	A lot	Some	None
Thursday	A lot	Some	None
Friday	A lot	Some	None

Description of challenging behavior:
_____

_____

Comments:
_____

_____

OTHER _____ ☺

Day	Level of Challenging Behavior		
Monday	A lot	Some	None
Tuesday	A lot	Some	None
Wednesday	A lot	Some	None
Thursday	A lot	Some	None
Friday	A lot	Some	None

Description of challenging behavior:
_____

_____

Comments:
_____

_____

Appendix D: Meaning-Making Machine Chart (MMMC)

Child's Name _____ Observer(s) _____ Date: ___/___/___ Time:_____

A: ANTECEDENT
What happened *before*?

Describe:

```

```

— or —

Check all that apply:

- [ ] Difficult activity
- [ ] Child did not like activity
- [ ] Changed or ended activity
- [ ] Moved from one activity or place to another
- [ ] Another child moved into area/personal space
- [ ] Unstructured activity
- [ ] Uncomfortable environment (too cold, hot, loud, etc.)
- [ ] Sitting down for more than 15 minutes
- [ ] Told or asked to do something

- [ ] Told "No," "Don't," or "Stop"
- [ ] Attention given to others
- [ ] Touched by someone
- [ ] Someone took away object
- [ ] Other student had object child wanted
- [ ] Child wanted to play with others
- [ ] Child(ren) refused to play with child
- [ ] Another child upset child

B: BEHAVIOR
Prioritize and pick behaviors or time of day that is MOST challenging or concerning.

Describe:

```

```

* How often? _____ / week   * How long? _____ / week

* Intensity: 1   2   3   4   5

(Circle)   *minor*   *severe*

Interests/Strengths of child

```

```

C: CONSEQUENCES
What happened *after*?

Describe:

[   ]

or

Check all that apply:

☐ Given attention (hug, time one on one with another adult, other children laugh)

☐ Given help

☐ Child was comforted

☐ Child was offered reward for correct behavior

☐ Ignored by adults

☐ Ignored by other children

☐ Teacher talked to the child about behavior

☐ Child needed to sit

☐ Child was told rules

☐ Child did not have to do what was asked

☐ Child did not have to do what was asked until later

☐ Child was moved to another activity

☐ Removed from activity/area

☐ Child sent to another room

How did the adults react?

[   ]

How did the other children react?

[   ]

PURPOSE OF BEHAVIOR
Describe:

[   ]

or

Check all that apply:

To get or obtain:

☐ Activity   ☐ Stimulation

☐ Help   ☐ Person

☐ Place   ☐ Attention

☐ Object   ☐ Other: _____

☐ Food

To avoid:

☐ Activity   ☐ Stimulation

☐ Help   ☐ Person

☐ Place   ☐ Attention

☐ Object   ☐ Other: _____

☐ Food

NOTE ANY CHANGES IN LIFESTYLE

- Absence of person
- Recent illness (or family member illness)
- New baby/family member
- Other (specify):
- Change in routine
- Absence of activities or toy
- Unexpected loss of object
- Absence of sleep
- No dental exam recently
- No water/refusal of certain foods
- Constipation/diarrhea
- No vision screen/ test recently
- Caregiver in school/ working longer hours

CHANGE YOU		CHANGE THE CHILD	CHANGE THE CONSEQUENCES
Check all that you will apply:			Check all that you will apply:

CHANGE YOU		CHANGE THE CHILD	CHANGE THE CONSEQUENCES
☐ Use positive language. Tell the child what to do. ☐ Use visuals to show the child the sequence of activities or routines. ☐ Let the child choose the sequence of activities with dice or visuals. ☐ Use a timer to show the length of an activity. ☐ Spend more positive time with this child. ☐ Act out rules daily. ☐ Use *first and then* language. ☐ Add the child's interest to an activity. ☐ Add sensory or movement to an activity. ☐ Show the child when an activity is ending, or give a warning. ☐ Go to a less stimulating environment. ☐ Cover distracting items with a blanket.	☐ Show the child items it is okay to hit or bite. ☐ Change the location of an activity. ☐ Limit wait time or make wait time active. ☐ Let the child always go first. ☐ Explain rules and expectations ahead of time. ☐ Use visuals with words to enhance comprehension of expectations. ☐ Act out stories. ☐ Let children color while listening to a story. ☐ Use a puppet to gain the child's attention. ☐ Let the child stand while learning. ☐ Send home a visual of a routine with steps. ☐ Add sensory breaks.	• Teach calming breathing or the Tucker the Turtle technique. • Teach the child a new skill with a scripted story. • Teach the child what to do using a puppet or song. • Teach the child to communicate with signs or visuals. • Teach the child with a game, such as How to Deal with Disappointment BINGO. • Teach the child cause and effect with toys. • Teach sharing with a sharing center or buddy pictures. • Teach the child to walk away. • Teach the child to problem solve with an ignoring shield or solution kit.	☐ Give the child attention after doing the right thing. ☐ Use the *help* sign (hand over hand) with the child before giving help. ☐ Let the child choose a positive consequence. ☐ Give the child a reward for correct behavior. ☐ Give the child comfort after doing the right thing. ☐ Whisper to get a child's attention. ☐ Use a reward system to track new skills. ☐ Show the child a tally of all the right things he or she is doing. ☐ Remind the child with words or visuals of what to do. ☐ Show the child a social story. ☐ Give the child movement breaks. ☐ Reward the child with going to another room or the office after doing something positive. ☐ Let the child sit in your lap after doing something positive.

References and Resources

Abercrombie, M. L. J. 1989. *The Anatomy of Judgement: An Investigation into the Processes of Perception and Reasoning.* London, UK: Free Association.

Adams, Jennifer. 2008. "Preschool Aggression within the Social Context: A Study of Families, Teachers, and the Classroom Environment." Doctoral diss. Tallahassee, FL: Florida State University.

Administration for Children and Families and US Department of Health and Human Services. 2006. *Depression in the Lives of Early Head Start Families: Research to Practice Brief.* Washington, DC: Administration for Children and Families. https://www.acf.hhs.gov/sites/default/files/opre/research_brief_depression.pdf

Allen, K. Eileen, et al. 1964. "Effects of Social Reinforcement on Isolate Behavior of a Nursery School Child." *Child Development* 35(2): 511–518.

Alluri, Vinoo, et al. 2012. "Large-Scale Brain Networks Emerge from Dynamic Processing of Musical Timbre, Key, and Rhythm." *NeuroImage* 59(4): 3677–3689.

Almeida, David, et al. 2005. "Do Daily Stress Processes Account for Socioeconomic Health Disparities?" Special issue, *The Journals of Gerontology: Series B* 60(2): S34–S39.

American Academy of Child and Adolescent Psychiatry. 2017. "Lying and Children." American Academy of Child and Adolescent Psychiatry. https://www.aacap.org/AACAP/Families_and_Youth/Facts_for_Families/FFF-Guide/Children-And-Lying-044.aspx

American Academy of Pediatrics. 2018. "Discipline." American Academy of Pediatrics. https://www.aap.org/en-us/about-the-aap/aap-press-room/aap-press-room-media-center/Pages/Discipline.aspx

American Academy of Pediatrics. 2018. "Preschool." HealthyChildren.org. https://www.healthychildren.org/English/ages-stages/preschool/Pages/default.aspx

American Counseling Association's Traumatology Interest Network. n.d. "Disaster and Trauma Responses of Children." American Counseling Association. https://www.counseling.org/docs/trauma-disaster/fact-sheet-3---disaster-and-trauma-responses-of-children.pdf

American Psychiatric Association. 2013a. *Diagnostic and Statistical Manual of Mental Disorders.* 5th ed. Washington, DC: American Psychiatric Association Publishing.

American Psychological Association. 2018. "Bullying." American Psychological Association. https://www.apa.org/topics/bullying/

Anand, Kanwaljeet, and Paul Hickey. 1987. "Pain and Its Effects in the Human Neonate and Fetus." *New England Journal of Medicine* 317(21): 1321–1329.

Anand, Kanwaljeet, and Paul Hickey. 1992. "Halothane-Morphine Compared with High-Dose Sufentanil for Anesthesia and Post-Operative Analgesia in Neonatal Cardiac Surgery." *New England Journal of Medicine* 326(1): 1–9.

Archer, Deborah. 2009. "Introduction: Challenging the School-to-Prison Pipeline." *New York Law School Law Review* 54: 867–872. https://digitalcommons.nyls.edu/cgi/viewcontent.cgi?article=1360&context=fac_articles_chapters

Arcia, Emily. 2006. "Achievement and Enrollment Status of Suspended Students: Outcomes in a Large, Multicultural School District." *Education and Urban Society* 38(3): 359–369.

Arnold, David, Lorette McWilliams, and Elizabeth Arnold. 1998. "Teacher Discipline and Child Misbehavior in Day Care: Untangling Causality with Correlational Data." *Developmental Psychology* 34(2): 276–287.

Balfanz, Robert, et al. 2013. *Building a Grad Nation: Progress and Challenge in Ending the High School Dropout Epidemic—2013 Annual Update.* Washington, DC: Civic Enterprises, the Everyone Graduates Center at Johns Hopkins University School of Education, America's Promise Alliance, and the Alliance for Excellent Education. http://www.civicenterprises.net/MediaLibrary/Docs/Building-A-Grad-Nation-Report-2013_Full_v1.pdf

Balfanz, Robert, Vaughan Byrnes, and Joanna Fox. 2014. "Sent Home and Put Off-Track: The Antecedents, Disproportionalities, and Consequences of Being Suspended in the Ninth Grade." *Journal of Applied Research on Children: Informing Policy for Children at Risk* 5(2): 1–19.

Barker, Jane, et al. 2014. "Less-Structured Time in Children's Daily Lives Predicts Self-Directed Executive Functioning." *Frontiers in Psychology* 5: 593. http://doi.org/10.3389/fpsyg.2014.00593

Barth, Joan, et al. 2004. "Classroom Environment Influences on Aggression, Peer Relations, and Academic Focus." *Journal of School Psychology* 42(2): 115–133.

Barth, Richard, et al. 2007. *Developmental Status and Early Intervention Service Needs of Maltreated Children.* Washington, DC: US Department of Health and Human Services, Office of the Assistant Secretary for Planning and Evaluation. https://aspe.hhs.gov/system/files/pdf/75351/report.pdf

Baum, Graham, et al. 2017. "Modular Segregation of Structural Brain Networks Supports the Development of Executive Function in Youth." *Current Biology* 27(11): 1561–1572.

Baumeister, Roy, et al. 2001. "Bad Is Stronger Than Good." *Review of General Psychology* 5(4): 323–370.

Björkqvist, Kaj, Karin Österman, and Ari Kaukiainen. 1992. "The Development of Direct and Indirect Aggressive Strategies in Males and Females." In *Of Mice and Women: Aspects of Female Aggression.* San Diego, CA: Academic Press.

Bodrova, Elena, and Deborah Leong. 2006. "Self-Regulation as a Key to School Readiness: How Early Childhood Teachers Can Promote This Critical Competency." In *Critical Issues in Early Childhood Professional Development.* Baltimore, MD: Brookes Publishing.

Boffey, Philip. 1987. "Infants' Sense of Pain Is Recognized, Finally." *The New York Times,* November 24. https://www.nytimes.com/1987/11/24/science/infants-sense-of-pain-is-recognized-finally.html

Brantlinger, Ellen. 1991. "Social Class Distinctions in Adolescents' Reports of Problems and Punishment in School." *Behavioral Disorders* 17(1): 36–46.

Brazy, Jane. 1988. "Effect of Crying on Cerebral Blood Volume and Cytochrome *aa3*." *Journal of Pediatrics* 112(3): 457–461.

Bulotsky-Shearer, Rebecca, John Fantuzzo, and Paul McDermott. 2008. "An Investigation of Classroom Situational Dimensions of Emotional and Behavioral Adjustment and Cognitive and Social Outcomes for Head Start Children." *Developmental Psychology* 44(1): 139–154.

Burk, Linnea, et al. 2008. "Identification of Early Child and Family Risk Factors for Aggressive Victim Status in First Grade." *Journal of Abnormal Child Psychology* 36(4): 513–526.

Burke, Arthur, and Vicki Nishioka. 2014. *Suspension and Expulsion Patterns in Six Oregon School Districts (REL 2014-028)*. Washington, DC: US Department of Education, Institute of Education Sciences, National Center for Education Evaluation and Regional Assistance, Regional Educational Laboratory Northwest. https://ies.ed.gov/ncee/edlabs/regions/northwest/pdf/REL_2014028.pdf

Butler, Stephen, Mark Suskind, and Saul Schanberg. 1978. "Maternal Behavior as a Regulator of Polyamine Biosynthesis in Brain and Heart of the Developing Rat Pup." *Science* 199(4327): 445–447.

Buyse, Evelien, et al. 2008. "Classroom Problem Behavior and Teacher-Child Relationships in Kindergarten: The Moderating Role of Classroom Climate." *Journal of School Psychology* 46(4): 367–391.

Byington, Carrie, et al. 2015. "Community Surveillance of Respiratory Viruses among Families in the Utah Better Identification of Germs-Longitudinal Viral Epidemiology (BIG-LoVE) Study." *Clinical Infectious Diseases* 61(8): 1217–1224.

Cacioppo, John, and Wendi Gardner. 1999. "Emotion." *Annual Review of Psychology* 50: 191–214.

Caine, Geoffrey, and Renate Caine. 2006. "Meaningful Learning and the Executive Functions of the Brain." *New Directions for Adult and Continuing Education* 2006(110): 53–61.

Caine, Renate, and Geoffrey Caine. 1991. *Making Connections: Teaching and the Human Brain*. Wheaton, MD: Association for Supervision and Curriculum Development.

Caine, Renate, et al. 2005. *12 Brain/Mind Learning Principles in Action: The Fieldbook for Making Connections, Teaching, and the Human Brain*. Thousand Oaks, CA: Corwin Press.

Campbell, Susan, and Linda Ewing. 1990. "Follow-Up of Hard-to-Manage Preschoolers: Adjustment at Age 9 and Predictors of Continuing Symptoms." *Child Psychology and Psychiatry and Allied Disciplines* 31(6): 871–889.

Campbell, Susan, et al. 2006. "Trajectories of Aggression from Toddlerhood to Age 9 Predict Academic and Social Functioning through Age 12." *Journal of Child Psychology and Psychiatry* 47(8): 791–800.

Carlson, John, et al. 2012. "Implementing a Statewide Early Childhood Mental Health Consultation Approach to Preventing Childcare Expulsion." *Infant Mental Health Journal* 33(3): 265–273.

Carpenter, Erika, and Douglas Nangle. 2002. "The COMPASS Program: Addressing Aggression in the Classroom." *Head Start Bulletin* 73: 27–28. https://files.eric.ed.gov/fulltext/ED465154.pdf#page=31

Carr, Edward. 1977. "The Motivation of Self-Injurious Behavior: A Review of Some Hypotheses." *Psychological Bulletin* 84(4): 800–816.

Carr, Edward, and V. Mark Durand. 1985. "Reducing Behavior Problems through Functional Communication Training." *Journal of Applied Behavior Analysis* 18(2): 111–126.

Carta, Judith, and Charles Greenwood. 1985. "Eco-Behavioral Assessment: A Methodology for Expanding the Evaluation of Early Intervention Programs." *Topics in Early Childhood Special Education* 5(2): 88–104.

Caulfield, Joan, Sue Kidd, and Thel Kocher. 2000. "Brain-Based Instruction in Action." *Educational Leadership* 58(3): 62–65.

Center on the Developing Child. 2018. "Key Concepts: Toxic Stress." Center on the Developing Child at Harvard University. https://developingchild.harvard.edu/science/key-concepts/toxic-stress/

Center on the Social and Emotional Foundations for Early Learning. n.d. "Resources: Practical Strategies for Teachers/Caregivers." Center on the Social and Emotional Foundations for Early Learning. http://csefel.vanderbilt.edu/resources/strategies.html

Centers for Disease Control and Prevention. 2017a. "Important Milestones: Your Child by Three Years." Centers for Disease Control and Prevention. https://www.cdc.gov/ncbddd/actearly/milestones/milestones-3yr.html

Centers for Disease Control and Prevention. 2017b. "Middle Childhood (6–8 Years of Age)." Centers for Disease Control and Prevention. https://www.cdc.gov/ncbddd/childdevelopment/positiveparenting/middle.html

Chatham, Christopher, Michael Frank, and Yuko Munakata. 2009. "Pupillometric and Behavioral Markers of a Developmental Shift in the Temporal Dynamics of Cognitive Control." *Proceedings of the National Academy of Sciences* 106(14): 5529–5533.

Clear, James. 2018. *Atomic Habits: An Easy and Proven Way to Build Good Habits and Break Bad Ones.* New York, NY: Avery.

Coe, Christopher, et al. 1985. "Endocrine and Immune Responses to Separation and Maternal Loss in Nonhuman Primates." In *The Psychobiology of Attachment and Separation.* Orlando, FL: Academic Press.

Coley, Rebekah, et al. 2018. "Locating Economic Risks for Adolescent Mental and Behavioral Health: Poverty and Affluence in Families, Neighborhoods, and Schools." *Child Development* 89(2): 360–369.

Committee for Children. 2018. *Recent Trends in State Legislative Exclusionary Discipline Reform.* Seattle, WA: Committee for Children. https://www.cfchildren.org/wp-content/uploads/policy-advocacy/exclusionary-policy-brief.pdf

Conroy, Maureen, et al. 2005. "A Descriptive Analysis of Positive Behavioral Intervention Research with Young Children with Challenging Behavior." *Topics in Early Childhood Special Education* 25(3): 157–166.

Cowen, Emory, et al. 1997. "Follow-Up Study of Young Stress-Affected and Stress-Resilient Urban Children." *Development and Psychopathology* 9(3): 565–577.

Craig, Holly, and Julie Washington. 1993. "Access Behaviors of Children with Specific Language Impairment." *Journal of Speech, Language, and Hearing Research* 36(2): 322–337.

Crenshaw, Kimberlé, Priscilla Ocen, and Jyoti Nanda. 2015. *Black Girls Matter: Pushed Out, Overpoliced, and Underprotected.* New York, NY: African American Policy Forum and Center for Intersectionality and Social Policy Studies. https://www.law.columbia.edu/sites/default/files/legacy/files/public_affairs/2015/february_2015/black_girls_matter_report_2.4.15.pdf

Crosser, Sandra. 1996. "Do You Know How I Feel? Empathy and the Young Child." *Early Childhood News* 8(2): 21–23.

Curby, Timothy, Sara Rimm-Kaufman, and Tashia Abry. 2013. "Do Emotional Support and Classroom Organization Earlier in the Year Set the Stage for Higher Quality Instruction?" *Journal of School Psychology 51*(5): 557–569.

Cutler, Ann, and Linda Gilkerson. 2002. *Unmet Needs Project: A Research, Coalition Building, and Policy Initiative on the Unmet Needs of Infants, Toddlers, and Families.* Chicago, IL: University of Illinois at Chicago and Erikson Institute. https://www.erikson.edu/wp-content/uploads/2017/10/unmetneedsreport1.pdf

DeGruy, Joy. 2005. *Post-Traumatic Slave Syndrome: America's Legacy of Enduring Injury and Healing.* Portland, OR: Joy DeGruy Publications.

Delplanque, Sylvain, et al. 2005. "Event-Related P3a and P3b in Response to Unpredictable Emotional Stimuli." *Biological Psychology* 68(2): 107–120.

Deming, David. 2009. "Early Childhood Intervention and Life-Cycle Skill Development: Evidence from Head Start." *American Economic Journal: Applied Economics* 1(3): 111–134.

Demirkaya, Pervin, and Hatice Bakkaloglu. 2015. "Examining the Student-Teacher Relationships of Children Both with and without Special Needs in Preschool Classrooms." *Educational Sciences: Theory and Practice* 15(1): 159–175.

Dennis, Maureen. 1988. "Language and the Young Damaged Brain." In *Clinical Neuropsychology and Brain Function: Research, Measurement, and Practice.* Washington, DC: American Psychological Association.

Dennison, Paul, and Gail Dennison. 1986. *Brain Gym: Simple Activities for Whole-Brain Learning.* Glendale, CA: Edu-Kinesthetics.

DeRidder, Lawrence. 1990. "The Impact of School Suspensions and Expulsions on Dropping Out." *Educational Horizons* 68(3): 153–157.

de Villiers, Jill, and Peter de Villiers. 2014. "The Role of Language in Theory of Mind Development." *Topics in Language Disorders* 34(4): 313–328.

DiLalla, Lisabeth, and Paula Mullineaux. 2008. "The Effect of Classroom Environment on Problem Behaviors: A Twin Study." *Journal of School Psychology* 46(2): 107–128.

Dishion, Thomas, Doran French, and Gerald Patterson. 1995. "The Development and Ecology of Antisocial Behavior." In *Developmental Psychopathology, Vol. 2: Risk, Disorder, and Adaptation.* Oxford, UK: John Wiley and Sons.

Ditto, Peter, David Pizarro, and David Tannenbaum. 2009. "Motivated Moral Reasoning." In *Moral Judgment and Decision Making.* London, UK: Academic Press.

Dodge, Kenneth. 1980. "Social Cognition and Children's Aggressive Behavior." *Child Development* 51(1): 162–170.

Dodge, Kenneth. 1993. "The Future of Research on the Treatment of Conduct Disorder." *Development and Psychopathology* 5(1–2): 311–319.

Domínguez, Ximena, et al. 2011. "The Role of Context in Preschool Learning: A Multilevel Examination of the Contribution of Context-Specific Problem Behaviors and Classroom Process Quality to Low-Income Children's Approaches to Learning." *Journal of School Psychology* 49(2): 175–195.

Domonell, Kristen. 2017. "This Is Your Body on Fear." Right as Rain by UW Medicine. https://rightasrain.uwmedicine.org/well/health/your-body-fear-anxiety

Dong, Guangheng, et al. 2011. "Early Negativity Bias Occurring prior to Experiencing of Emotion: An ERP Study." *Journal of Psychophysiology* 25(1): 9–17.

Downer, Jason, et al. 2010. "The Individualized Classroom Assessment Scoring System (inCLASS): Preliminary Reliability and Validity of a System for Observing Preschoolers' Competence in Classroom Interactions." *Early Childhood Research Quarterly* 25(1): 1–16.

Dunlap, Glen, and Lise Fox. 2011. "Function-Based Interventions for Children with Challenging Behavior." *Journal of Early Intervention* 33(4): 333–343.

Dunlap, Glen, et al. 2010. *Prevent-Teach-Reinforce: The School-Based Model of Individualized Positive Behavior Support.* Baltimore, MD: Brookes Publishing.

Dunlap, Glen, and Lee Kern. 1996. "Modifying Instructional Activities to Promote Desirable Behavior: A Conceptual and Practical Framework." *School Psychology Quarterly* 11(4): 297–312.

Dunlap, Glen, et al. 2006. "Prevention and Intervention with Young Children's challenging behavior: Perspectives regarding Current Knowledge." *Behavioral Disorders* 32(1): 29–45.

Dunn, Judy, and Shirley McGuire. 1992. "Sibling and Peer Relationships in Childhood." *The Journal of Child Psychology and Psychiatry* 33(1): 67–105.

Eamon, Mary. 1994. "Poverty and Placement Outcomes of Intensive Family Preservation Services." *Child and Adolescent Social Work Journal* 11(5): 349–361.

Early Development and Learning Lab. 2018. "What Is Temperament?" University of Nebraska–Lincoln. https://cehs.unl.edu/cyaf/edl/what-temperament/

Early Head Start Research and Evaluation Project. 2006. *Research to Practice: Depression in The Lives of Early Head Start Families.* Washington, DC: Administration for Children and Families. https://www.acf.hhs.gov/sites/default/files/opre/research_brief_depression.pdf

Ekstrom, Ruth, et al. 1986. "Who Drops Out of High School and Why? Findings from a National Study." *Teachers College Record* 87(3): 356–373.

Elliot, Andrew, and Martin Covington. 2001. "Approach and Avoidance Motivation." *Educational Psychology Review* 13(2): 73–92.

Ermeling, Bradley. 2010. "Tracing the Effects of Teacher Inquiry on Classroom Practice." *Teaching and Teacher Education* 26(3): 377–388.

Fabelo, Tony, et al. 2011. *Breaking Schools' Rules: A Statewide Study of How School Discipline Relates to Students' Success and Juvenile Justice Involvement.* New York, NY: Council of State Governments Justice Center. https://csgjusticecenter.org/wp-content/uploads/2012/08/Breaking_Schools_Rules_Report_Final.pdf

Fabes, Richard, et al. 2001. "Parental Coping with Children's Negative Emotions: Relations with Children's Emotional and Social Responding." *Child Development* 72(3): 907–920.

Fantuzzo, John, et al. 2005. "An Investigation of Preschool Classroom Behavioral Adjustment Problems and Social-Emotional School Readiness Competencies." *Early Childhood Research Quarterly* 20(3): 259–275.

Fantuzzo, John, Marlo Perry, and Paul McDermott. 2004. "Preschool Approaches to Learning and Their Relationship to Other Relevant Classroom Competencies for Low-Income Children." *School Psychology Quarterly* 19(3): 212–230.

Felitti, Vincent, et al. 1998. "Relationship of Childhood Abuse and Household Dysfunction to Many of the Leading Causes of Death in Adults: The Adverse Childhood Experiences (ACE) Study." *American Journal of Preventive Medicine* 14(4): 245–258.

Fettig, Angel, and Erin Barton. 2014. "Parent Implementation of Function-Based Intervention to Reduce Children's challenging behavior: A Literature Review." *Topics in Early Childhood Special Education* 34(1): 49–61.

Fettig, Angel, and Michaelene Ostrosky. 2011. "Collaborating with Parents in Reducing Children's Challenging Behaviors: Linking Functional Assessment to Intervention." *Child Development Research* 2011: 1–10.

Fox, Lise, and Barbara Smith. 2007. *Issue Brief: Promoting Social, Emotional, and Behavioral Outcomes of Young Children Served under IDEA*. Tampa, FL: Technical Assistance Center on Social Emotional Intervention for Young Children. https://files.eric.ed.gov/fulltext/ED526382.pdf

Fox, Robert, Donald Platz, and Kathleen Bentley. 1995. "Maternal Factors Related to Parenting Practices, Developmental Expectations, and Perceptions of Child Behavior Problems." *The Journal of Genetic Psychology* 156(4): 431–441.

Fraiberg, Selma. 1980. *Clinical Studies in Infant Mental Health: The First Year of Life.* New York, NY: Basic Books.

Fraiberg, Selma, Edna Adelson, and Vivian Shapiro. 1975. "Ghosts in the Nursery: A Psychoanalytic Approach to the Problems of Impaired Infant-Mother Relationships." *Journal of the American Academy of Child and Adolescent Psychiatry* 14(3): 387–421.

Frick, Paul. 2016. "Current Research on Conduct Disorder in Children and Adolescents." *South African Journal of Psychology* 46(2): 160–174.

Frick, Paul, et al. 1994. "*DSM-IV* Field Trials for the Disruptive Behavior Disorders: Symptom Utility Estimates." *Journal of the American Academy of Child and Adolescent Psychiatry* 33(4): 529–539.

Fuhs, Mary, Dale Farran, and Kimberly Nesbitt. 2013. "Preschool Classroom Processes as Predictors of Children's Cognitive Self-Regulation Skills Development." *School Psychology Quarterly* 28(4): 347–359.

Fuligni, Allison, et al. 2012. "Activity Settings and Daily Routines in Preschool Classrooms: Diverse Experiences in Early Learning Settings for Low-Income Children." *Early Childhood Research Quarterly* 27(2): 198–209.

Garner, Pamela, et al. 2014. "Associations of Preschool Type and Teacher-Child Relational Quality with Young Children's Social-Emotional Competence." *Early Education and Development* 25(3): 399–420.

Gerdes, Marsha, and Natalie Renew. 2016. *Incidence of Expulsion and Suspensions in Philadelphia 2016: Summary of Survey Findings*. Philadelphia, PA: Children's Hospital of Philadelphia PolicyLab.

Gersch, Irvine, and Anna Nolan. 1994. "Exclusions: What the Children Think." *Educational Psychology in Practice* 10(1): 35–45.

Gershoff, Elizabeth. 2002. "Corporal Punishment by Parents and Associated Child Behaviors and Experiences: A Meta-Analytic and Theoretical Review." *Psychological Bulletin* 128(4): 539–579.

Gershoff, Elizabeth, and Andrew Grogan-Kaylor. 2016. "Spanking and Child Outcomes: Old Controversies and New Meta-Analyses." *Journal of Family Psychology* 30(4): 453–469.

Gilliam, Walter. 2005. *Prekindergarteners Left Behind: Expulsion Rates in State Prekindergarten Programs.* New York, NY: Foundation for Child Development. https://medicine.yale.edu/childstudy/zigler/publications/National%20Prek%20Study_expulsion%20brief_34775_5379_v1.pdf

Gilliam, Walter, et al. 2016. *Do Early Educators' Implicit Biases Regarding Sex and Race Relate to Behavior Expectations and Recommendations of Preschool Expulsions and Suspensions?* New Haven, CT: Yale Child Study Center. https://medicine.yale.edu/childstudy/zigler/publications/Preschool%20Implicit%20Bias%20Policy%20Brief_final_9_26_276766_5379_v1.pdf

Glasgow, Neal, and Cathy Hicks. 2009. *What Successful Teachers Do: 101 Research-Based Classroom Strategies for New and Veteran Teachers.* Thousand Oaks, CA: Corwin Press.

Glenwright, Melanie, and Penny Pexman. 2010. "Development of Children's Ability to Distinguish Sarcasm and Verbal Irony." *Journal of Child Language* 37(2): 429–451.

Goodenough, Florence. 1931. *Anger in Young Children.* Minneapolis, MN: University of Minnesota Press.

Gottman, John, and Robert Levenson. 1999. "What Predicts Change in Marital Interaction Over Time? A Study of Alternative Models." *Family Process* 38(2): 143–158.

Government of Western Australia Department of Health. "Child Development 3–4 Years." Healthy WA. https://healthywa.wa.gov.au/Articles/A_E/Child-development-3-4-years

Gralinski, J. Heidi, and Claire Kopp. 1993. "Everyday Rules for Behavior: Mothers' Requests to Young Children." *Developmental Psychology* 29(3): 573–584.

Gray, Jeremy. 2004. "Integration of Emotion and Cognitive Control." *Current Directions in Psychological Science* 13(2): 46–48.

Gulamhussein, Allison. 2013. *Teaching the Teachers: Teaching Effective Professional Development in an Era of High-Stakes Accountability.* Alexandria, VA: Center for Public Education. http://www.centerforpubliceducation.org/system/files/Professional%20Development.pdf

Haapasalo, Jaana, and Richard Tremblay. 1994. "Physically Aggressive Boys from Ages 6 to 12: Family Background, Parenting Behavior, and Prediction of Delinquency." *Journal of Consulting and Clinical Psychology* 62(5): 1044–1052.

Halberstadt, Amy, et al. 2018. "Preservice Teachers' Racialized Emotion Recognition, Anger Bias, and Hostility Attributions." *Contemporary Educational Psychology* 54: 125–138.

Hall, Edward. 1976. *Beyond Culture.* Garden City, NY: Anchor Books.

Halpern, Ricardo, and Renato Coelho. 2016. "Excessive Crying in Infants." *Jornal de Pediatria* 92(3): S40–S45, supplement 1.

Hannaford, Carla. 1995. *Smart Moves: Why Learning Is Not All in Your Head*. Arlington, VA: Great Ocean Publishers.

Harrison, Helen. 1987. "Why Infant Surgery without Anesthesia Went Unchallenged." *The New York Times,* December 17. https://www.nytimes.com/1987/12/17/opinion/l-why-infant-surgery-without-anesthesia-went-unchallenged-832387.html

Haynes, Stephen, and William O'Brien. 1990. "Functional Analysis in Behavior Therapy." *Clinical Psychology Review* 10(6): 649–668.

Hemmeter, Mary Louise, Robert Corso, and Gregory Cheatham. 2006. "Issues in Addressing Challenging Behaviors in Young Children: A National Survey of Early Childhood Educators." Paper presented at the Conference on Research Innovations in Early Intervention, San Diego, CA.

Hemmeter, Mary Louise, et al. 2007. "A Program-Wide Model of Positive Behavior Support in Early Childhood Settings." *Journal of Early Intervention* 29(4): 337–355.

Hong, Ji, Rebecca Tillman, and Joan Luby. 2015. "Disruptive Behavior in Preschool Children: Distinguishing Normal Misbehavior from Markers of Current and Later Childhood Conduct Disorder." *Journal of Pediatrics* 166(3): 723–730.

Hoover, Sarah. 2006. *Report to the Colorado Division of Child Care for Supporting an Environmental Scan and Study of Current Status of Children with Social, Emotional, and Behavioral Concerns and the Providers Who Support Them*. Denver, CO: JFK Partners at the University of Colorado at Denver and Health Sciences Center. https://www.researchgate.net/publication/279947049_Report_to_the_Colorado_Division_of_Child_Care_Children_with_Social_Emotional_and_Behavioral_Concerns

Hoover, Sarah, et al. 2012. "Influence of Behavioral Concerns and Early Childhood Expulsions on the Development of Early Childhood Mental Health Consultation in Colorado." *Infant Mental Health Journal* 33(3): 246–255.

Howard, Gary. 2006. *We Can't Teach What We Don't Know: White Teachers, Multiracial Schools*. 2nd ed. New York, NY: Teachers College Press.

Huang, Yu-Xia, and Yue-Jia Luo. 2006. "Temporal Course of Emotional Negativity Bias: An ERP Study." *Neuroscience Letters* 398(1–2): 91–96.

Hutchings, Judy, et al. 2013. "A Randomized Controlled Trial of the Impact of a Teacher Classroom Management Program on the Classroom Behavior of Children with and without Behavior Problems." *Journal of School Psychology* 51(5): 571–585.

Individuals with Disabilities Education Act. 2004. 20 U.S.C. Ch. 33.

Irwin, Julia, Alice Carter, and Margaret Briggs-Gowan. 2002. "The Social-Emotional Development of 'Late-Talking' Toddlers." *Journal of the American Academy of Child and Adolescent Psychiatry* 41(11): 1324–1332.

Iwata, Brian, et al. 1994. "Toward a Functional Analysis of Self-Injury." *Journal of Applied Behavior Analysis* 27(2): 197-209.

Jay, Timothy. 2000. *Why We Curse: A Neuro-Psycho-Social Theory of Speech*. Philadelphia, PA: J. Benjamins.

Johns Hopkins Medicine. "Age-Appropriate Speech and Language Milestones." Johns Hopkins Medicine. https://www.hopkinsmedicine.org/healthlibrary/conditions/pediatrics/age-appropriate_speech_and_language_milestones_90,p02170

Joyce, Bruce, and Beverly Showers. 1982. "The Coaching of Teaching." *Educational Leadership* 40(1): 4–10.

Joyce, Bruce, and Beverly Showers. 2002. *Student Achievement through Staff Development.* 3rd ed. Alexandria, VA: Association for Supervision and Curriculum Development.

Judah, Gaby, Benjamin Gardner, and Robert Aunger. 2013. "Forming a Flossing Habit: An Exploratory Study of the Psychological Determinants of Habit Formation." *British Journal of Health Psychology* 18(2): 338–353.

Kahn, Joan, and Leonard Pearlin. 2006. "Financial Strain over the Life Course and Health among Older Adults." *Journal of Health and Social Behavior 47(1):* 17–31.

Kahn, Robert, et al. 1999. "The Scope of Unmet Maternal Health Needs in Pediatric Settings." *Pediatrics* 103(3): 576–581.

Kanfer, Frederick, and George Saslow. 1969. "Behavioral Diagnosis." In *Behavior Therapy: Appraisal and Status.* New York, NY: McGraw-Hill.

Kierkegaard, Søren. 1996. *Papers and Journals: A Selection.* New York, NY: Penguin Books.

Kingston, Lisa, and Margot Prior. 1995. "The Development of Patterns of Stable, Transient, and School-Age Onset Aggressive Behavior in Young Children." *Journal of the American Academy of Child and Adolescent Psychiatry* 34(3): 348–358.

Kisley, Michael, Stacey Wood, and Christina Burrows. 2007. "Looking at the Sunny Side of Life: Age-Related Change in an Event-Related Potential Measure of the Negativity Bias." *Psychological Science* 18(9): 838–843.

Kloo, Daniela, Josef Perner, and Thomas Giritzer. 2010. "Object-Based Set-Shifting in Preschoolers: Relations to Theory of Mind." In *Self and Social Regulation: Social Interaction and the Development of Social Understanding and Executive Functions.* New York, NY: Oxford University Press.

Kneebone, Elizabeth, Carey Nadeau, and Alan Berube. 2011. *The Re-Emergence of Concentrated Poverty: Metropolitan Trends in the 2000s.* Washington, DC: Brookings Institution. https://www.brookings.edu/wp-content/uploads/2016/06/1103_poverty_kneebone_nadeau_berube.pdf

Knost, L. R. 2013. *Whispers through Time: Communication through the Ages and Stages of Childhood.* Saint Cloud, FL: Little Hearts Books.

Kuhn, Cynthia, Stephen Butler, and Saul Schanberg. 1978. "Selective Depression of Serum Growth Hormone During Maternal Deprivation in Rat Pups." *Science* 201(4360): 1034–1036.

Kupersmidt, Janis, Donna Bryant, and Michael Willoughby. 2000. "Prevalence of Aggressive Behaviors among Preschoolers in Head Start and Community Child Care Programs." *Behavioral Disorders* 26(1): 42–52.

Lally, Phillippa, et al. 2010. "How Are Habits Formed: Modelling Habit Formation in the Real World." *European Journal of Social Psychology* 40(6): 998–1009.

Lamont, Jeffrey, et al. 2013. "Policy Statement: Out-of-School Suspension and Expulsion." *Pediatrics* 131(3): e1000–e1007. http://pediatrics.aappublications.org/content/pediatrics/131/3/e1000.full.pdf

La Paro, Karen, Robert Pianta, and Megan Stuhlman. 2004. "The Classroom Assessment Scoring System: Findings from the Prekindergarten Year." *Elementary School Journal* 104(5): 409–426.

Leidy, Melinda, Nancy Guerra, and Rosa Toro. 2010. "Positive Parenting, Family Cohesion, and Child Social Competence among Immigrant Latino Families." *Journal of Family Psychology* 24(3): 252–260.

Leslie, Alan, Joshua Knobe, and Adam Cohen. 2006. "Acting Intentionally and the Side-Effect Effect: Theory of Mind and Moral Judgment." *Psychological Science* 17(5): 421–427.

Loeber, Rolf, et al. 1989. "Optimal Informants on Childhood Disruptive Behaviors." *Development and Psychopathology* 1(4): 317–337.

Loeber, Rolf, et al. 1989. "Continuity and Desistance in Disruptive Boys' Early Fighting at School." *Development and Psychopathology* 1(1): 39–50.

Losen, Daniel, and Tia Martinez. 2013. *Out of School and Off Track: The Overuse of Suspensions in American Middle and High Schools*. Los Angeles, CA: UCLA Center for Civil Rights Remedies at The Civil Rights Project. https://files.eric.ed.gov/fulltext/ED541735.pdf

Losen, Daniel, and Russell Skiba. 2010. *Suspended Education: Urban Middle Schools in Crisis*. Montgomery, AL: Southern Poverty Law Center. https://www.civilrightsproject.ucla.edu/research/k-12-education/school-discipline/suspended-education-urban-middle-schools-in-crisis/Suspended-Education_FINAL-2.pdf

Mace, F. Charles, and Barbara West. 1986. "Analysis of Demand Conditions Associated with Reluctant Speech." *Journal of Behavior Therapy and Experimental Psychiatry* 17(4): 285–294.

Machalicek, Wendy, et al. 2007. "A Review of Interventions to Reduce Challenging Behavior in School Settings for Students with Autism Spectrum Disorders." *Research in Autism Spectrum Disorders* 1(3): 229–246.

Malik, Rasheed. 2017. "New Data Reveal 250 Preschoolers Are Suspended or Expelled Every Day." Center for American Progress. https://www.americanprogress.org/issues/early-childhood/news/2017/11/06/442280/new-data-reveal-250-preschoolers-suspended-expelled-every-day/

Marchant, Gregory, Sharon Paulson, and Barbara Rothlisberg. 2001. "Relations of Middle School Students' Perceptions of Family and School Contexts with Academic Achievement." *Psychology in the Schools* 38(6): 505–519.

McEwen, Bruce. 1998. "Protective and Damaging Effects of Stress Mediators." *New England Journal of Medicine* 338(3): 171–179.

McLaughlin, Colleen. 2003. "The Feeling of Finding Out: The Role of Emotions in Research." *Educational Action Research* 11(1): 65–78.

McLoyd, Vonnie. 1990. "The Impact of Economic Hardship on Black Families and Children: Psychological Distress, Parenting, and Socioemotional Development." *Child Development* 61(2): 311–346.

Mendez, Linda. 2003. "Predictors of Suspension and Negative School Outcomes: A Longitudinal Investigation." *New Directions for Youth Development* 2003(99): 17–33.

Mitchell, Mary, and Catherine Bradshaw. 2013. "Examining Classroom Influences on Student Perceptions of School Climate: The Role of Classroom Management and Exclusionary Discipline Strategies." *Journal of School Psychology* 51(5): 599–610.

Moffett, Lillie, Henrike Moll, and Lily FitzGibbon. 2018. "Future Planning in Preschool Children." *Developmental Psychology* 54(5): 866–874.

Mullen, Gayle, and Mary Tallent-Runnels. 2006. "Student Outcomes and Perceptions of Instructors' Demands and Support in Online and Traditional Classrooms." *The Internet and Higher Education* 9(4): 257–266.

Murphy, Mark. 2018. "Neuroscience Explains Why You Need to Write Down Your Goals If You Actually Want to Achieve Them." Forbes. https://www.forbes.com/sites/markmurphy/2018/04/15/neuroscience-explains-why-you-need-to-write-down-your-goals-if-you-actually-want-to-achieve-them/#6ee268be7905

Murray, Carol Garboden. 2018. *Simple Signing with Young Children: A Guide for Infant, Toddler, and Preschool Teachers.* Rev. ed. Lewisville, NC: Gryphon House.

National Center for Children in Poverty. 2018. "Poverty by the Numbers: By Race, White Children Make Up the Biggest Percentage of America's Poor." National Center for Children in Poverty. http://www.nccp.org/media/releases/release_34.html

National Scientific Council on the Developing Child. 2005. *Excessive Stress Disrupts the Architecture of the Developing Brain: Working Paper 3.* Cambridge, MA: Center on the Developing Child. https://developingchild.harvard.edu/wp-content/uploads/2005/05/Stress_Disrupts_Architecture_Developing_Brain-1.pdf

Nichols, Joe, William Ludwin, and Peter Iadicola. 1999. "A Darker Shade of Gray: A Year-End Analysis of Discipline and Suspension Data." *Equity and Excellence in Education* 32(1): 43–55.

Noltemeyer, Amity, and Caven Mcloughlin. 2010. "Patterns of Exclusionary Discipline by School Typology, Ethnicity, and Their Interaction." *Penn GSE Perspectives on Urban Education* 7(1): 27–40.

Odgers, Candice, et al. 2008. "Female and Male Antisocial Trajectories: From Childhood Origins to Adult Outcomes." *Development and Psychopathology* 20(2): 673–716.

Office of Head Start. 2017. "Head Start Programs." Administration for Children and Families, US Department of Health and Human Services, Office of Head Start. https://www.acf.hhs.gov/ohs/about/head-start

Okonofua, Jason, Gregory Walton, and Jennifer Eberhardt. 2016. "A Vicious Cycle: A Social-Psychological Account of Extreme Racial Disparities in School Discipline." *Perspectives on Psychological Science* 11(3): 381–398.

Paas, Fred, Alexander Renkl, and John Sweller. 2003. "Cognitive Load Theory and Instructional Design: Recent Developments." *Educational Psychologist* 38(1): 1–4.

Paley, Vivian. 1992. *You Can't Say You Can't Play.* Cambridge, MA: Harvard University Press.

Palmer, Parker. 2007. *The Courage to Teach: Exploring the Inner Landscape of a Teacher's Life.* 10th anniversary ed. San Francisco, CA: Jossey-Bass.

Pas, Elise, et al. 2015. "Profiles of Classroom Behavior in High Schools: Associations with Teacher Behavior Management Strategies and Classroom Composition." *Journal of School Psychology* 53(2): 137–148.

Patton, Stacey. 2017. "Stop Beating Black Children." *The New York Times,* March 10. https://www.nytimes.com/2017/03/10/opinion/sunday/stop-beating-black-children.html

PBS Parents. 2019. "Social and Emotional Growth." PBS Parents. http://www.pbs.org/parents/childdevelopmenttracker/eight/socialandemotionalgrowth.html

PBS Parents. 2018. "Your Six-Year-Old." PBS Parents. http://www.pbs.org/parents/childdevelopmenttracker/six/index.html

Pearson, Deborah, and David Lane. 1991. "Auditory Attention Switching: A Developmental Study." *Journal of Experimental Child Psychology* 51(2): 320–334.

Perner, Josef, Susan Leekam, and Heinz Wimmer. 1987. "Three-Year-Olds' Difficulty with False Belief: The Case for a Conceptual Deficit." *British Journal of Developmental Psychology* 5(2): 125–137.

Perry, Brea, and Edward Morris. 2014. "Suspending Progress: Collateral Consequences of Exclusionary Punishment in Public Schools." *American Sociological Review* 79(6): 1067–1087.

Perry, Bruce. 1997. "Incubated in Terror: Neurodevelopmental Factors in the 'Cycle of Violence.'" In *Children in a Violent Society.* New York, NY: Guilford Press.

Perry, Bruce. 2001. "The Neurodevelopmental Impact of Violence in Childhood." In *Textbook of Child and Adolescent Forensic Psychiatry.* Washington, DC: American Psychiatric Press.

Perry, Bruce. 2007. *Stress, Trauma, and Post-Traumatic Stress Disorders in Children: An Introduction.* Houston, TX: ChildTrauma Academy. https://childtrauma.org/wp-content/uploads/2013/11/PTSD_Caregivers.pdf

Perry, Bruce, and Maia Szalavitz. 2017. *The Boy Who Was Raised as a Dog, and Other Stories from a Child Psychiatrist's Notebook.* Rev. and updated ed. New York, NY: Basic Books.

Perry, Deborah, et al. 2011. "Challenging Behavior and Expulsion from Child Care: The Role of Mental Health Consultation." *Zero to Three* 32(2): 4–11.

Perry, Nicole, et al. 2015. "Maternal Punitive Reactions to Children's Negative Emotions and Young Adult Trait Anger: Effect of Gender and Emotional Closeness." *Marriage and Family Review* 51(3): 1–17.

Pexman, Penny, and Melanie Glenwright. 2007. "How Do Typically Developing Children Grasp the Meaning of Verbal Irony?" *Journal of Neurolinguistics* 20(2): 178–196.

Piaget, Jean. 1952. *The Origins of Intelligence in Children.* New York, NY: International Universities Press.

Pianta, Robert, Karen La Paro, and Bridget Hamre. 2008. *Pre-K–3 CLASS Manual.* Charlottesville, VA: Teachstone Training.

Qi, Cathy, and Ann Kaiser. 2003. "Behavior Problems of Preschool Children from Low-Income Families: Review of the Literature." *Topics in Early Childhood Special Education* 23(4): 188–216.

Raising Children Network (Australia) Ltd. 2017. "3–4 Years: Preschooler Development." Raisingchildren.net.au. https://raisingchildren.net.au/preschoolers/development/development-tracker/3-4-years

Ramey, David. 2015. "The Social Structure of Criminalized and Medicalized School Discipline." *Sociology of Education* 88(3): 181–201.

Rao, Malla, et al. 2004. "Long Term Cognitive Development in Children with Prolonged Crying." *Archives of Disease in Childhood* 89(11): 989–992.

Rausch, M. Karega, and Russell Skiba. 2004. "Unplanned Outcomes: Suspension and Expulsions in Indiana." *Indiana Youth Services Association Education Policy Briefs* 2(2): 1–8.

Reid, John. 1993. "Prevention of Conduct Disorder Before and After School Entry: Relating Interventions to Developmental Findings." *Development and Psychopathology* 5(1–2): 243–262.

Renk, Kimberly. 2008. "Disorders of Conduct in Young Children: Developmental Considerations, Diagnoses, and Other Characteristics." *Developmental Review* 28(3): 316–341.

Rhoades, Brittany, Mark Greenberg, and Celene Domitrovich. 2009. "The Contribution of Inhibitory Control to Preschoolers' Social-Emotional Competence." *Journal of Applied Developmental Psychology* 30(3): 310–320.

Rimm-Kaufman, Sara, et al. 2009. "The Contribution of Children's Self-Regulation and Classroom Quality to Children's Adaptive Behaviors in the Kindergarten Classroom." *Developmental Psychology* 45(4): 958–972.

Safer, Daniel. 1986. "Planning and Administration: Nonpromotion Correlates and Outcomes at Different Grade Levels." *Journal of Learning Disabilities* 19(8): 500–503.

Safer, Daniel, Ronald Reaton, and Frank Parker. 1981. "A Behavioral Program for Disruptive Junior High School Students: Results and Follow-Up." *Journal of Abnormal Child Psychology* 9(4): 483–494.

Schimke, Ann. 2015. "New Push to Quantify, Prevent Preschool Expulsions in Colorado." Chalkbeat. https://www.chalkbeat.org/posts/co/2015/02/19/new-push-to-quantify-prevent-preschool-expulsions-in-colorado/

Schore, Allan. 1996. "The Experience-Dependent Maturation of a Regulatory System in the Orbital Prefrontal Cortex and the Origin of Developmental Psychopathology." *Development and Psychopathology* 8(1): 59–87.

Scott, Terrance, Peter Alter, and Kathleen McQuillan. 2010. "Functional Behavior Assessment in Classroom Settings: Scaling Down to Scale Up." *Intervention in School and Clinic* 46(2): 87–94.

Simons, Ronald, et al. 1993. "Childhood Experience, Conceptions of Parenting, and Attitudes of Spouse as Determinants of Parental Behavior." *Journal of Marriage and Family* 55(1): 91–106.

Skinner, Burrhus Frederic. 1953. *Science and Human Behavior.* New York, NY: Macmillan.

Skiba, Russell, and Natasha Williams. 2014. *Are Black Kids Worse? Myths and Facts about Racial Differences in Behavior: A Summary of the Literature.* Bloomington, IN: The Equity Project at Indiana University, Center for Evaluation and Education Policy. http://www.indiana.edu/~atlantic/wp-content/uploads/2014/03/African-American-Differential-Behavior_031214.pdf

Smith, Adam. 1776. *An Inquiry into the Nature and Causes of the Wealth of Nations.* London, UK: W. Strahan and T. Cadell.

Smith, N. Kyle, et al. 2006. "Being Bad Isn't Always Good: Affective Context Moderates the Attention Bias toward Negative Information." *Journal of Personality and Social Psychology* 90(2): 210–220.

Solomon, C. Ruth, and Françoise Serres. 1999. "Effects of Parental Verbal Aggression on Children's Self-Esteem and School Marks." *Child Abuse and Neglect* 23(4): 339–351.

Spiers, Hugo, et al. 2017. "Anterior Temporal Lobe Tracks the Formation of Prejudice." *Journal of Cognitive Neuroscience* 29(3): 530–544.

Sprenger, Marilee. 2007. *Becoming a "Wiz" at Brain-Based Teaching: How to Make Every Year Your Best Year.* 2nd ed. Thousand Oaks, CA: Corwin Press.

Squires, Jane, and Robert Nickel. 2003. "Never Too Soon: Identifying Social-Emotional Problems in Infants and Toddlers." *Contemporary Pediatrics* 20(3): 117–125.

Sroufe, L. Alan. 1985. "Attachment Classification from the Perspective of Infant-Caregiver Relationships and Infant Temperament." *Child Development* 56(1): 1–14.

Sroufe, L. Alan, Nancy Fox, and Van Pancake. 1983. "Attachment and Dependency in Developmental Perspective." *Child Development* 54(6): 1615–1627.

State Capacity Building Center. 2018. *Building a Comprehensive State Policy Strategy to Prevent Expulsion from Early Learning Settings.* 2nd ed. Fairfax, VA: State Capacity Building Center. https://childcareta.acf.hhs.gov/sites/default/files/public/expulsion_tool_revised_june_2018.pdf

Stifter, Cynthia, and Tracy Spinrad. 2002. "The Effect of Excessive Crying on the Development of Emotion Regulation." *Infancy* 3(2): 133–152.

Stolier, Ryan, and Jonathan Freeman. 2016. "Neural Pattern Similarity Reveals the Inherent Intersection of Social Categories." *Nature Neuroscience* 19(6): 795–797.

Substance Abuse and Mental Health Services Administration. 2014. "Understanding the Impact of Trauma." In *Trauma-Informed Care in Behavioral Health Services.* Rockville, MD: US Department of Health and Human Services, Substance Abuse and Mental Health Services Administration.

Substance Abuse and Mental Health Services Administration. 2016. "Types of Trauma and Violence." US Department of Health and Human Services, Substance Abuse and Mental Health Services Administration. https://www.samhsa.gov/trauma-violence/types

Suddendorf, Thomas, Mark Nielsen, and Rebecca von Gehlen. 2011. "Children's Capacity to Remember a Novel Problem and to Secure a Future Solution." *Developmental Science* 14(1): 26–33.

Sutherland, Kevin, and Donald Oswald. 2005. "The Relationship between Teacher and Student Behavior in Classrooms for Students with Emotional and Behavioral Disorders: Transactional Processes." *Journal of Child and Family Studies* 14(1): 1–14.

Sylwester, Robert. 1998. "Art for the Brain's Sake." *Educational Leadership* 56(3): 31–35.

Sylwester, Robert. 2005. *How to Explain a Brain: An Educator's Handbook of Brain Terms and Cognitive Processes.* Thousand Oaks, CA: Corwin Press.

Talwar, Victoria, and Kang Lee. 2002. "Development of Lying to Conceal a Transgression: Children's Control of Expressive Behavior during Verbal Deception." *International Journal of Behavioral Development* 26(5): 436–444.

Talwar, Victoria, and Kang Lee. 2008. "Social and Cognitive Correlates of Children's Lying Behavior." *Child Development* 79(4): 866–881.

T. D. Jakes Ministries. 2015. "You don't have to get yourself out of trouble before you begin to change your life; you just have to get your mind out of trouble." Facebook. https://www.facebook.com/bishopjakes/posts/you-dont-have-to-get-yourself-out-of-trouble-before-you-begin-to-change-your-lif/10153567636943322/

Teaford, Patricia, et al., eds. 2010. *HELP 3–6 Assessment Manual.* 2nd ed. Menlo Park, CA: VORT Corporation.

Todd, Andrew, Kelsey Thiem, and Rebecca Neel. 2016. "Does Seeing Faces of Young Black Boys Facilitate the Identification of Threatening Stimuli?" *Psychological Science* 27(3): 384–393.

Tomoda, Akemi, et al. 2009. "Reduced Prefrontal Cortical Gray Matter Volume in Young Adults Exposed to Harsh Corporal Punishment." *NeuroImage* 47: T66–T71, supplement 2.

Touchette, Paul, Rebecca MacDonald, and Susan Langer. 1985. "A Scatter Plot for Identifying Stimulus Control of Problem Behavior." *Journal of Applied Behavior Analysis* 18(4): 343–351.

Tremblay, Richard. 2000. "The Development of Aggressive Behavior during Childhood: What Have We Learned in the Past Century?" *International Journal of Behavioral Development* 24(2): 129–141.

Tremblay, Richard. 2002a. "Development of Physical Aggression from Early Childhood to Adulthood." In *Encyclopedia on Early Childhood Development.* Montreal, QC: Centre of Excellence for Early Childhood Development. http://citeseerx.ist.psu.edu/viewdoc/download?doi=10.1.1.569.3682&rep=rep1&type=pdf

Tremblay, Richard. 2002b. "Prevention of Injury by Early Socialization of Aggressive Behavior." *Injury Prevention* 8(Suppl. IV): iv17–iv21.

Tremblay, Richard, et al. 1996. "Do Children in Canada Become More Aggressive as They Approach Adolescence?" In *Growing Up in Canada: National Longitudinal Survey of Children and Youth.* Ottawa, ON: Statistics Canada. http://publications.gc.ca/collections/collection_2016/statcan/CS89-550-1996-1-eng.pdf

Tremblay, Richard, Willard Hartup, and John Archer, eds. 2005. *Developmental Origins of Aggression.* New York, NY: Guilford Press.

Tremblay, Richard, et al. 1992. "Early Disruptive Behavior, Poor School Achievement, Delinquent Behavior, and Delinquent Personality: Longitudinal Analyses." *Journal of Consulting and Clinical Psychology* 60(1): 64–72.

Tremblay, Richard, et al. 1996. "From Childhood Physical Aggression to Adolescent Maladjustment: The Montreal Prevention Experiment." In *Preventing Childhood Disorders, Substance Abuse, and Delinquency.* Thousand Oaks, CA: SAGE Publications.

Tremblay, Richard, et al. 2004. "Physical Aggression during Early Childhood: Trajectories and Predictors." *Pediatrics* 114(1): e43–e50. http://pediatrics.aappublications.org/content/pediatrics/114/1/e43.full.pdf

Tversky, Amos, and Daniel Kahneman. 1983. "Extensional versus Intuitive Reasoning: The Conjunction Fallacy in Probability Judgment." *Psychological Review* 90(4): 293–315.

US Department of Education Office for Civil Rights. 2014a. *Data Snapshot: Early Childhood Education.* Washington, DC: Civil Rights Data Collection. https://www2.ed.gov/about/offices/list/ocr/docs/crdc-early-learning-snapshot.pdf

US Department of Education Office for Civil Rights. 2014b. *Data Snapshot: School Discipline.* Washington, DC: Civil Rights Data Collection. https://ocrdata.ed.gov/downloads/crdc-school-discipline-snapshot.pdf

US Department of Education Office for Civil Rights. 2018. *2015–16 Civil Rights Data Collection: School Climate and Safety.* Washington, DC: US Department of Education Office for Civil Rights. https://www2.ed.gov/about/offices/list/ocr/docs/school-climate-and-safety.pdf

US Department of Health and Human Services, and US Department of Education. 2014. *Policy Statement on Expulsion and Suspension Policies in Early Childhood Settings.* Washington, DC: US Department of Health and Human Services and US Department of Education. https://www2.ed.gov/policy/gen/guid/school-discipline/policy-statement-ece-expulsions-suspensions.pdf

Vásquez-Levy, Dorothy. 1993. "The Use of Practical Arguments in Clarifying and Changing Practical Reasoning and Classroom Practices: Two Cases." *Journal of Curriculum Studies* 25(2): 125–143.

Vissing, Yvonne, et al. 1991. "Verbal Aggression by Parents and Psychosocial Problems of Children." *Child Abuse and Neglect* 15(3): 223–238.

Vitiello, Virginia, et al. 2012. "Variation in Children's Classroom Engagement throughout a Day in Preschool: Relations to Classroom and Child Factors." *Early Childhood Research Quarterly* 27(2): 210–220.

Vlachou, Maria, et al. 2011. "Bully/Victim Problems among Preschool Children: A Review of Current Research Evidence." *Educational Psychology Review* 23(3): 329–358.

Volling, Brenda. 2012. "Family Transitions Following the Birth of a Sibling: An Empirical Review of Changes in the Firstborn's Adjustment." *Psychological Bulletin* 138(3): 497–528.

Volling, Brenda, et al. 2014. "Children's Responses to Mother-Infant and Father-Infant Interaction with a Baby Sibling: Jealousy or Joy?" *Journal of Family Psychology* 28(5): 634–644.

Wallace, William Ross. n.d. "The Hand That Rocks the Cradle Is the Hand That Rules the World." Poets' Corner. http://www.theotherpages.org/poems/index.html

Warshaw, Stephanie, et al. 2006. *Inside HELP 0–3 (Administration and Reference Manual).* Menlo Park, CA: VORT Corporation.

Webster-Stratton, Carolyn, and Mary Hammond. 1998. "Conduct Problems and Level of Social Competence in Head Start Children: Prevalence, Pervasiveness, and Associated Risk Factors." *Clinical Child and Family Psychology Review* 1(2): 101–124.

Wehby, Joseph, et al. 1993. "School Behavior of First-Grade Children Identified as At-Risk for Development of Conduct Problems." *Behavioral Disorders* 19(1): 67–78.

Wehlage, Gary, and Robert Rutter. 1986. "Dropping Out: How Much Do Schools Contribute to the Problem?" *Teachers College Record* 87(3): 374–392.

Welch, Ginger, Laura Wilhelm, and Heather Johnson. 2013. *The Neglected Child: How to Recognize, Respond, and Prevent.* Lewisville, NC: Gryphon House.

Westby, Carol, and Lee Robinson. 2014. "A Developmental Perspective for Promoting Theory of Mind." *Topics in Language Disorders* 34(4): 362–382.

Williford, Amanda, et al. 2013. "Children's Engagement within the Preschool Classroom and Their Development of Self-Regulation." *Early Education and Development* 24(2): 162–187.

Wolke, Dieter, Ayten Bilgin, and Muthanna Samara. 2017. "Systematic Review and Meta-Analysis: Fussing and Crying Durations and Prevalence of Colic in Infants." *The Journal of Pediatrics* 185: 55–61.e4.

Woodhouse, Kathleen. 2017. "Implicit Bias—Is It Really?" Forbes. https://www.forbes.com/sites/forbescoachescouncil/2017/12/19/implicit-bias-is-it-really/#2d4a6cfa59ce

Wu, Shi-Chang, et al. 1982. "Student Suspension: A Critical Reappraisal." *The Urban Review* 14(4): 245–303.

Yoshikawa, Hirokazu, and Edward Zigler. 2000. "Mental Health in Head Start: New Directions for the Twenty-First Century." *Early Education and Development* 11(3): 247–264.

Zaghlawan, Hasan, and Michaelene Ostrosky. 2011. "Circle Time: An Exploratory Study of Activities and Challenging Behavior in Head Start Classrooms." *Early Childhood Education Journal* 38(6): 439–448.

Zander, Benjamin. 2008. "The Transformative Power of Classical Music." TED video. https://www.ted.com/talks/benjamin_zander_on_music_and_passion#t-1227198

Zero to Three, and the Bezos Family Foundation. 2016. *Tuning In: Parents of Young Children Speak Up about What They Think, Know, and Need.* Washington, DC: Zero to Three. https://www.zerotothree.org/resources/1425-national-parent-survey-report

Zuckerman, June. 2007. "Classroom Management in Secondary Schools: A Study of Student Teachers' Successful Strategies." *American Secondary Education* 35(2): 4–16.

Index

PUSH PAST IT!

F

families/family members. *See also* home factors
    and addressing challenging behavior, 63–64
    behavior-review systems and, 113
    case studies on, 42–43, 57, 65
    commonly misinterpreted behaviors of, 58–60
    communication and, 60–62
    exercises on, 56, 57–58
    family-member behaviors, 58–60
    stress and aggression and, 93
    using PUSH PAST It for, 56–57
    when a family is falling apart, 64–65
    working with, 55
fight-or-flight mode, 84, 90
focus, 85, 103, 115
free play, 102, 137–138
friends
    bullying and exclusion and, 101, 131–132
    cognitive development and, 75
    language development and, 73
    social-emotional development and, 74, 78, 80
    verbal aggression and, 97, 98
functional assessment, 107

G

girls, aggression and, 13

H

home factors
    bullying and exclusion and, 101–102
    clinginess, crying, and tantrums and, 106
    lying and, 100
    not listening, noncompliance, defiance, and reluctance to participate and, 103
    physical aggression and, 93
    verbal aggression and, 98
hyperactivity, 69
hyperarousal, 84

I

implementation strategies
    5R cycle, 141–144
    behavior-review systems and, 114
    case study on, 116
    MATCH (modify, adjust, take into account, consider, hash out), 115
    records for, 117
    trying time, 141
    WERK it, 115
intentions
    bullying and exclusion and, 101
    cognitive development and, 71
    lying and, 100
    social-emotional and self-regulation development and, 76

K

keeping your cool, 118–119

L

labeling emotions, 106, 129, 135
labels, negative, 37
language development
    emotions and, 98
    hitting and, 80
    verbal aggression and, 97, 130
lesson planning, 106
lifestyle changes, 108
lying
    challenging behaviors and, 99
    environmental and home factors and, 100
    exercises on, 100
    social-emotional development and, 76

M

manipulation and cognitive development, 71
MATCH (modify, adjust, take into account, consider, hash out), 115
Meaning-Making Machine
    case studies on, 109–110